JOSEPHINE
BAKER
and the RAINBOW
TRIBE

JOSEPHINE
BAKER
and the RAINBOW
TRIBE

Matthew Pratt Guterl

The Belknap Press of
Harvard University Press
Cambridge, Massachusetts
London, England
2014

Library of Congress Cataloging-in-Publication Data
Guterl, Matthew Pratt.
    Josephine Baker and the Rainbow Tribe / Matthew Pratt Guterl.
      pages   cm
    Includes bibliographical references and index.
    ISBN 978-0-674-04755-6 (alk. paper)
    1. Baker, Josephine, 1906–1975—Family.   2. Dancers—France—Biography.
  3. African American entertainers—France—Biography.   I. Title.
  GV1785.B3G88   2014
  792.8092—dc23
  [B]   2013037831

For Robert and Maya and Sandi

Contents

JOSEPHINE
BAKER
and the RAINBOW
TRIBE

Prologue

She wore a skirt made of bananas.

In her former lover's 1927 portrait—the portrait that made the skirt iconic—she seems a slip of a thing, light on her feet, arms held aloft. Her back is to us and her face is turned away, but still a nipple winks at us, a dark spot on what is otherwise presented as a uniformly light brown body. Jubilantly coiled, she is all curves and bent limbs, without a single straight line. A banana skirt rings the very center of her body, with her upper torso and her arms being perfectly balanced by her legs. The bright, ripe bananas protrude outward, defying gravity. Erect and disorderly, they can be read as a marker of her exoticism and her primitivism, as if she were a jungle-bred native, wearing a strange copy of the ballerina's tutu. Or they can be seen as markers of her eroticism, a bold clutch of phalli strung like hunter's trophies around her slim, conquering waistline. This image, the centerpiece of Paul Colin's lush folio of black dance and song, is the most famous nude of the modern age. You can find it in every bookstall along the Seine and in every card shop in Paris, affixed to coffee mugs and aprons, T-shirts and note cards.[1]

Her early route to Paris—and to the banana skirt—is the stuff of legend. Born dirt poor in the crudely segregated city of St. Louis, she learned to dance by candlelight, reveling in the spotlight, in the dim glamour of her homemade stage. When the city of her birth was shattered by the race riots of 1917, she fled for Manhattan, where a far bigger stage and much brighter lights were waiting. Capitalizing on her good humor, her practiced athleticism, and her skillful stage-craft, she earned a job as the comedic end-of-the-line girl, sometimes in blackface, always in burlesque. And then, with barely a chance to leave a footprint, she was off to Paris, a part of the African American avant-garde's victory march through the smoldering ruins of post-war France. A blackened Horatio Alger fable, she was the poor girl who got rich not merely because of good fortune, honorable conduct, or clever pluck, but also through the troubling display of her naked, racially marked, lusted-over body. Coming to Paris in an unusually perverse moment in history, when whites hungered for undiluted "African" or "Negro" art as a panacea for the "overcivilization" that had so recently driven the world to war, she exploited this eagerness for something real, something not so refined and restrained, and transformed herself into an icon of race and sex. She became the capstone expression of centuries of racial obsession, but she also became something new and different: the world's first colored superstar.[2]

Before Josephine Baker was twenty years old, she was a totem of primeval sex. On the high-end stages of Paris, wearing that banana skirt or a ring of palm fronds, she arched and shimmied and twisted and smiled all at once, and the attending shock coursed not from her partial nudity—common in French nightclubs—but from her pitch-perfect expression of the dangerous, primitive ideal. Well-dressed older men, thoroughly middle-class and civilized in their everyday lives, would gasp, tightly gripping the armrests of their chairs, their hearts pounding with excitement, when the bright stage lights first settled on her dark, naked body. White women, if they were present,

were horrified, and greeted her with clenched teeth and a scandal-
ized sneer. The "wicked Josephine Baker," one writer archly described
her, was a "lubricious idol," the embodiment of "carnal splendor,"
"who drives males to despair."[3] Poet E. E. Cummings, a member of the
"Lost Generation" of writers drifting across Europe in the 1920s, remembered her as a "wand of golden flesh" to be loved, loathed, and
feared.[4] At the peak of this sexualized celebrity, she would stroll
down the Champs-Elysées with a cheetah on a leash, two exotic crea-
tures, objects of obsession and dread, spectacularly out of place amid
the neoclassical buildings that lined the grand boulevard.[5]

There is more to Josephine Baker than a banana skirt.

Thirty years after Colin's famous folio, Baker posed for a very different image. Nine children, sitting in the sunshine, posed together
as a family, along with Josephine. She was no longer a solitary figure
dancing on the stage, but instead part of an ensemble, a vision of
heterotopia on earth. The image is a collective color portrait of a
family that might have been taken anywhere were it not for the late
medieval castle in the background and the celebrity in the middle of
the group. All of the boys are wearing some version of the same outfit, including corduroy pants, plaid flannel shirts, and gray cardigans,
except for the youngest, who wears white; the only girl wears pink. "Jo
et Joséphine"—the husband and wife who crouch in the back of the
group—smile adoringly at the camera. In loud contrast to the girl
who once wore the banana skirt, Baker is dressed as a mature, de-
mure, fashionable mother, wearing a conservative blouse with a Peter
Pan collar, a light pink jacket, and a white headband. The colorful
balls suggest a family at play, and the prominently displayed juice
glasses gesture to health, vigor, and abundance.

Just as we recognize this assemblage as a single family, we are also
meant to acknowledge racial variety in tone and shade and type. The
uniform clothing on the children speaks to a common cause, but the
radically different physicality signals uncommon origins. While
they wear what amounts to a uniform—the typical schoolchild's

ensemble—their various tones and textures are yoked together in the service of some unstated creed. They seem like more than a family, like a symbol of something bigger. Their togetherness, their variegation, and their domestic idyll command attention and compel investigation; it is at once a question, a project, a problem, and a plot. We are meant to look, to see, and to wonder: what exactly is this? Most of all, we are meant to see Baker's maternal chic and to remember those dangling bananas, that complicated history of exoticism and excess. The groomed, manicured family image contains hidden material, hints of something older, something erased, something almost lost. The bananas are erased, but their erasure catches the eye.

In 1953, after a decade of planning and construction, Baker built a family from scratch. She set out, with great intent and determination, to adopt a cadre of what she imagined as racially diverse children from around the world, bringing them to southwest France in what was the start of an extraordinary experiment. Out of the French countryside, she created a vast theme-park-cum-circus—complete with hotels, a collective farm, rides, and, of course, singing and dancing—that would focus on the family of the future, which she vaingloriously named the "Rainbow Tribe." She trained the children to be racial exemplars, to represent specific continents, religions, and histories, to perform stereotypes, just as she had once done on the music hall stage. She dispatched them, as walking, talking, and sometimes costumed icons of racial typecasting, over the sprawling campus surrounding Les Milandes, her name for the fifteenth-century castle at the center of this enterprise, itself a symbol of the French past and the global future. And she used them, collectively, as a blunt instrument in her war against inequality, racism, and prejudice.

What seems like an innocent snapshot is, then, an advertisement swollen with the fantastic, a siren's call to an adoring public to visit, drawing them deep into rural France to spend money on a utopian vision, and to worship at the throne of Josephine, the mother of the world. And what looks like a clutch of children, innocently and hastily gathered up by Mother for a family portrait, is really an ensemble of commercial archetypes, sent out like the roving Disney characters one finds in that other, more famous post–WWII theme park. Like stock characters at a Hollywood studio, the children were originally marshaled out to that sunny landscape to advertise a juice drink—hence those full glasses—but Baker repurposed the vignette and put it on a postcard, to be sold, of course, at Les Milandes, within eyeshot of the Tribe. And then, once purchased, it was supposed to be circulated or dispersed, to travel far and wide, with every set of hands and eyes on it pausing to hold it, to look it over, to make sense of the startling image.

No one had ever seen a black woman adopt a white child before. No one had ever seen a black woman adopt twelve children. Or raise them in a castle. Or house them in a theme park. Or use them in advertisements. Or portray them as soldiers in a struggle for justice. This family did weird, powerful, and dangerous work. Its fabrication was, in its day, unsettling, as was its display. And it still is, if for different reasons. It kicks us off our foundations and propels us away from what seems solid and reassuring. It makes us laugh uncomfortably, and then asks us to stop and stand still, in wonderment and astonishment, awed at the impossibility of thinking and doing something quite like that.

The creation emerged at a very specific historical moment. Very few people remember Baker's role—long after her greatest fame—in the civil rights movement or the human rights campaigns of the tumultuous 1950s and 1960s. Most histories and biographies celebrate the innovations and provocations of the 1920s but shy away from a long, close look at the inscrutable creation that comes later, at what seems in most imaginings to be a trivial and naive outlier. As a consequence, very few remember that she had created a big, dazzling, strange family of twelve children, a metaphorical rainbow of colors and types, all raised in a castle in the midst of the Cold War. Almost no one understands what this family was supposed to mean or what sort of work it was meant to do in the age of protests and riots and war.

This book is an attempt to repair our memory, to reimagine Baker as a serious and determined, if wildly iconoclastic, thinker and activist in the age of modern revolutions. It aims to change what we remember about one of the most iconic personalities of the modern age. Its most important goal is to clarify, as never before, the meaning of the Rainbow Tribe. And it proposes that the mad display of the mixed-race adoptive family can help us to better understand the present, our mixed-up, hybrid, globe-trotting world. It can remind us, in the end, of the extraordinary power we give to celebrity, and of the costs of such power.

The meaning of the Rainbow Tribe is hidden in the subterranean continuities linking the young Josephine Baker of Paul Colin's imagination with the *maman* in the pretty pink suit. She kept a museum dedicated to her history on the grounds of Les Milandes but refused to let her children see it. She wore a dress—modern, perhaps Dior, and beautiful—decorated with an image of her younger self in that famous banana skirt. In the 1970s, doodling on a piece of paper while in a hotel in Copenhagen, Baker drew herself as young, naked, and triumphant, and then forwarded the sketch to her children. Clad in a banana skirt and a feathered headdress, a stick-figure Baker leads her twelve children, all wearing the same headdress and the same celebrated banana skirt, in a direction of her own choosing. In truth, though many of the children were in their late teens by that date, they are presented here as diminutive, as *les enfants tous ensembles,* miniature reflections of Baker's younger, dark-skinned, and supposedly primitive past. Baker positioned herself well above them, so that her family—drawn as small and racially homogeneous—must climb up to meet her ambitions. She is by far the largest figure and more boldly drawn, with finer details, and every child after her gets smaller, as if she lost interest with the drawing of each successive child, or as if every new arrival was somehow less important.[6] The family was the world's future, but it was shaped by her past.

The story unfolds slowly and with a purpose. The building up of the Rainbow Tribe took time, because the idea of it came to Baker gradually, like something brought, through much effort, to the murky surface of a drifting river. Our narrative thus begins not with the very first adoption, nor with the purchase of Les Milandes, her castle in the Dordogne. It starts about a decade before she first set out to claim a child, with the end of WWII. It continues into the late 1940s with her personal reinvention, and then into the early Cold War with her civil rights struggles at home and abroad. This is an indispensable prehistory, one that makes the political purpose of the great assemblage all the more clear. It lets us know where the idea came from. It helps us to understand how and why the children were adopted and in what sequence they were brought to Les Milandes. It clarifies the stakes for Josephine, the historic rationale behind the endless family photo ops, the strange cycles of public and private reinvention, and the need to be on tour and in the spotlight, even if it meant being away from her family.

As a historical subject, this postwar version of Josephine Baker is hard to track. Recognizable but relatively unknown or misunderstood, she appears—usually as a casual reference—across the widest spectrum of cultural and historical story lines. Peripatetic and unbounded, she defined herself by relentless movement, dislocation, and self-transformation, from her mother's migration from Charleston to St. Louis, to her own relocation from the Midwest to New York and her re-creation there, from New York to Paris, the Dordogne, and Monaco, with stops in Morocco, Tunisia, Brazil, Perón's Argentina, and "Uncle Fidel's" pool. She repeatedly resisted conventional racial and national markers, claiming an indigenous heritage, enthusing over mixture and hybridity, and fashioning an identity as a woman without a single country and a woman who was her own country, a slippery cosmopolitanism that has obscured her life. She was a playful and creative performer, sometimes a "plain ghetto girl" (as Ishmael Reed once called her), sometimes a vagabond, sometimes the quintessential cosmopolite, sometimes a French colonial, and sometimes the queen mother of her own peculiar nation-state.[7] Because we often frame our histories through the nation-state, this makes her life a challenging artifact, one that should remind us now—in an age we like to think is uniquely global and boundless—that personal expressions of racial and national complexity aren't new at all, and that the history of rights and revolution is bigger than one place.

Still, this is a story we know in our bones. Or so we think. *People* magazine tells us so, along with gossip websites and that pulpy tell-all magazine we read at the beach. Every ornamental costume or every pet chimpanzee gestures, we think, to Michael Jackson and his carnivalesque Neverland Ranch, his sequined gloves and starched epaulets. Each opportunistic adoption reminds us of the public image of Madonna, Mia Farrow, or Angelina Jolie and the celebrity creation of spotlighted big families apparently aimed, the press tells us, to make a point about racial diversity. The theme park along the Dordogne looks, from a distance, like Disney, or like every other smaller Adventureland or Six Flags in the world. The swimming pool in the shape of a J and the self-aggrandizing museum on-site echo the stylings of the megalomaniacal celebrity with money to burn and an immense ego to satisfy. This familiarity makes it easy to read Les Milandes as an early version of *MTV Cribs* or *Keeping Up with the' Kardashians*, because the language of the strange and the famous is readily available to us. But this same easy familiarity makes it harder to understand Les Milandes, not easier, because we rarely allow celebrity egocentrism to be serious or important. Our habit is to hear these stories and laugh, if sometimes with a touch of sadness, and then to dismiss them.

Set aside everything you think you know about Josephine Baker. Put the banana skirt out of your mind, at least for a little while. Don't think of her as an apolitical stage performer sitting in a cage dressed as a peacock or walking her cheetah on a leash. And put down what you remember about the civil rights movement. Imagine that Josephine Baker, nestled in the French countryside, is every once in a while at the very center of that movement. Prepare as well to be reintroduced to one of the most universally inventive, if strangely iconoclastic, theorists of antiracism, a woman who in private was mercurial and impulsive, demanding obedience from the small boys and girls she fashioned. And who, in public, was everything to everyone, often on purpose, but always doggedly and outrageously insistent that racism could never bind her, and that her creatively engineered Tribe was the solution to worldwide racial prejudice. In a grim, difficult moment, when it looked like the world had gone mad, Baker's construction of Les Milandes and her assemblage of the Rainbow Tribe were not mere trifles, not just clever attempts to reclaim the spotlight; they were also remarkable, unprecedented political acts, conceived after a lifetime of thoughtful experimentation by a superstar who could be held down by no rule and no social convention.

This is the story of one woman who earned her fame wearing a banana skirt. She used her race as a fetish to lure white audiences, got rich fast, and became a superstar. Late in life, that woman decided to change her image and change the world. She did something so offbeat, so unexpected, and so dramatic that it still resonates today: she built a vast family out of the dangerous material of race, defined it as a commodity assembled for the public, and used it to wage a quixotic war for the hearts and minds of the modern age. What catches us off guard is her bold clarity—her extraordinary lucidity—about the symbolic function of children, the instrumental deployment of her variegated children and family as agents meant to transform the political life of the nation and the world, and the stories of those caught up in the turbulent passage of her celebrity.[8]

1

Too Busy to Die

I want a baby more than anything else in the world!
—Josephine Baker (ca. 1943)

Josephine Baker was dead. Or so the rumor went.

It was 1942, in the midst of the terrible world war, when the news first broke in Harlem. Lingering in exile in Casablanca after the conquest of Paris, and "heart-broken before the Nazi terror," Baker, the story went, had taken "her last bow on the human stage, ill, disillusioned, and penniless." No cause of death was revealed, and there were few medical details of any kind. "Death came," the obituary continued melodramatically, emphasizing the performer's tragic fall from grace and fame, "as she lay between the tawdry sheets of a charity hospital," weighed down by having "lost everything," and unable to "return to America." The author, repeating a thinly sourced bit of gossip, concluded by metaphorically wrapping Baker in patriotism, enlisting her in the war effort, and attributing her death more generally to the hellish environment of Hitler's Europe. "So it was," the piece concluded, "that the mailed Nazi heel, which has crushed nations large and small, brought grief and pain to household after household, pierced the throat of the brown-skinned lark, whose caroling had caused many a lover of music to stand agape. After so many triumphs on stage, all of them staged against the odds, it was the

Nazis—and not Jim Crow—who had ruined and murdered Josephine Baker."[1]

The story of the Rainbow Tribe begins with the false report of the superstar's death and the very real illness that sat quietly behind it. It begins in North Africa, with a political awakening and a charismatic reinvention, all staged in the twilight of the old European empires and just before the dawn of the American Century. The Josephine Baker who emerged from this false death was not merely the sexy, comedic stage performer of yore but a new, much more serious icon, which was confusing to her various publics. Deeply politicized and physically damaged, she staged her first real comeback, returning from the grave. In doing so, she laid the groundwork for an alternative tradition of radicalism, one rooted not in appeals to the "rights" of the national citizen but in calls for a multiracial cosmopolitanism, a partial transgression of the nation state. Without the rumor of her death, without these tectonic shifts in world history, her story—and the story of the Tribe—would be different. She needed to die before she could be reborn.

As any consumer of contemporary popular culture can tell you, celebrity has a naturalized arc, in which the dizzying height of the climb marks the terrifying speed of the fall. Baker's incredible rise from rags to riches, noted in the rushed accounts of her death, only ensured the inevitability of her spectacularly fast demise. Recognizable for her conspicuous consumption and excessive display of jewelry, furs, men, and mansions, Baker couldn't just die poor but had to be penniless, in a poor city hospital, and buried without fanfare in a nearby cemetery. Adored for her laughing, joyful public persona and her physical vigor and health, she was doomed to be, in her last days, ill and disillusioned, struck down by a nameless lingering ailment, possessed of a broken body and shattered soul. An indomitable titan of pop culture, she couldn't have been brought to her end merely by some lowly virus or failed organ; no less a figure than Adolf Hitler himself had to raze her adopted homeland, conquering all of Europe just to crush her spirit and strip away her fortune. The news of this dramatic conclusion was so widely broadcast, so shocking, and so convincing that as late as 1964, Baker was still meeting people who believed that she had died during the war.[2]

Rumors of death and demise, even when false, are telling indicators of where a celebrity sits along that supposedly natural arc of fame. They mark age and decline, or the rise of newer, younger stars. For Baker, the news of her own death was a clear sign that something had to change, that the old ways were no longer working. Only thirty-six in 1942, she'd been marked, like too many other performers, as too old, too easily replaced, a relic of an older time. Her trip to the United States before the war, when she'd joined the Ziegfeld Follies in 1936, had been a failure by every measure, and especially by her own. In addition to her failures in the spotlight, she'd been poorly treated offstage. After a triumphant decade in France and a successful film career, back in the United States she'd been branded a moral reprobate, kept away from the finest hotels by Jim Crow, and generally treated like a social untouchable. That visit had been a reminder that she would always be just a "Negro" in the land of her birth. And then the war had come, and she'd gone underground, forced there by German aggression. Her supposed physical death in North Africa was merely a confirmation of the rapid decline of her fame. She was a curiosity of the interwar years, an antique needing replacement.

To come back from that strange forgetting—the rendering of an icon in the past tense, the death of celebrity—Baker would have to do something impossibly bold. She would need to embody something new, something modern, something defiant and heroic. It would take a little while before the general repairs that she undertook on her reputation could be welded into the conception of the Rainbow Tribe—before she settled on Les Milandes as the staging ground for her world's work and before she decided what, exactly, that work might be. The first steps to the Tribe, though, were taken in North Africa.

She was, we need to remember, also a woman who was ready to start a family. A simple, noble, plain aspiration, perhaps, but in her case, this desire to have a child was tangled up with her return from the threshold of death's door. We need to untangle the story here, to separate what is surely myth from what is likely fact. But a complete separation is simply impossible. There was, for Baker, a habit of shifting between the true and false, the real and the fairy tale, a habit that gets us lost a bit in the overlapping worlds.

Was she really dead? The *Baltimore Afro-American* wasn't so sure. Other contrary rumors soon emerged, restoring Baker as a mythic, outsized character, turning her into an urban legend of sorts. Within weeks of the initial report, the "Arab press" was insisting that Baker, once quite ill but now recovered, had "borrowed a page from Arabian Nights" and was now living in the Arab quarter in Casablanca. The songstress, the newspaper reported, was in "good health" and "living a simple and quiet life as a French subject." Of course, that "simple and quiet life"—a life she had never before experienced—was routinely abridged by her trademark wild, extravagant ways. "She thrills the natives," went the urban folklore passed along by the *Afro-American,* "by driving to the market behind a team of prancing Arabian ponies."[3] If Josephine Baker wasn't dead, the public would expect this sort of extravagance.

It took a little while for the fuller, carefully managed truth to come out. In early 1943, George Padmore—the global pan-Africanist provocateur, who was moonlighting as the London correspondent of the *Chicago Defender*—reported that Baker had been seen alive in Casablanca.[4] And a few months later, with many still mourning Baker's supposedly tragic death, Ollie Stewart, war correspondent for the *Baltimore Afro-American,* found her in Marrakesh. Interviewed in a richly Orientalist context—"flanked by pillows, as she reclined with her face lifted towards the nearby Atlas Peaks"—Stewart found Baker garrulous, chatty, and laughing, "much alive" and "vivacious as ever." She was the same, he implied, but also different, scarred by her experiences and prone to become "serious without warning." In quieter tones, she spoke for a long time about her fresh, clear-eyed understanding of the suffering that comes with war. "I have worked in canteens and fed women and children shaking from starvation," she confessed, in a pitch-perfect expression of noblesse oblige after disaster, and "after seeing what some people suffered I feel well off just having lost my house and property." "She admitted her illness," Stewart noted casually, as if it were no big deal, "but said she was practically well."[5]

Once recovered, she got back to work as a performer, entertaining the Allied troops in the area. Baker, as Langston Hughes put it in 1944, had "miraculously come alive again" and was newly renowned as "the reigning theatrical star of France-in-Exile." At night she sang "J'ai Deux Amours" alongside "La Marseillaise," bringing audiences to tears. During the day she worked for the Red Cross, raised money for the French underground, or met with wounded soldiers. Ranging widely across North Africa, hobnobbing with the pasha of Marrakesh or taking tea with officers of the British Army, she was a one-woman morale booster. "A glamorously beautiful American colored girl," Hughes summed up, "respected and loved by all the natives and all the whites of the region," she was also a "heartening and stimulating" reminder for the large numbers of African American troops serving abroad of what was possible in a truly equalitarian world, and a symbol of the war's true aim: the end of autocracy and the fostering of democracy.[6] And she routinely refused to make a big deal of her illness. "I was too busy to die," she said a few years later, when the war was over and she had returned to France.[7]

Hughes, celebrating the news that Baker was indeed alive, remarked, "True greatness is also goodness." Black Americans, he thought, should be thrilled to have Baker as an icon. Despite her great wealth and success in France, the chanteuse had refused to become "a snob, nor snotty, nor stuck-up." She had a vigilant connection to those who are "poor, and colored, and never get anywhere." She was "kind and generous." Even if she had married "up," he reminded his readers, she never stopped writing letters home. When Baker had come back to the United States during the Depression, Hughes recalled, she had been ridiculed for putting on airs—for "her French maid," for speaking in French, and for her "white dancing partners"—and many on both sides of the color line had been angered when she'd stayed at the Waldorf Astoria instead of some hotel in Harlem that catered to African Americans. "Strange paradox of race," the poet noted, "that when some of us succeed in breaking color bars, others of us get mad."[8] Hughes asked his audience to let Josephine find her own route to success, her own path to goodness and greatness, because what mattered most was that she was on the side of the angels, even when she was sleeping at an exclusive, usually all-white hotel, or being led around town by a team of prancing stallions.

The illness is an important part of our story. Remembering the war, Baker writes innocently and sensationally of North Africa as a great turning point on her journey to global motherhood. Brought to Casablanca for the climate and buoyed by the fresh air, she impetuously got an X-ray because she had heard good things about the medical establishment there and wanted to know just one thing: if she could have a child. "I want a baby more than anything else in the world!" she told the attending physician, who was more than happy to reassure her. The relatively new technology promised scientific certainty, a definitive answer to a question that had long haunted her. But after leaving Casablanca "on a pink cloud" and still waiting for the results of her test, she was brought back to earth by a terrible case of peritonitis. The fever struck her down, forcing her hospitalization. "Dear God," she thought to herself, "please let me have children." Unconscious and in dire medical need, rushed by truck over the long road from Marrakesh back to Casablanca, she woke days later, her body laced up with suture wire, her fever just barely abated. Over the months and weeks that followed, Baker lay in a hospital bed, slowly and imperfectly recovering, even as rumors of her death swirled globally.

Those rumors reached her months later in her hospital bed, while she was reading deeply in the history of the Middle Ages and imagining herself as a knight of the Crusades, sent far away to wage a just war. Her ex-lover, Maurice Chevalier, the literary gadfly and stage performer, had told the French press that he'd found Baker "dying and penniless" in Casablanca. "What nonsense!" Baker recalled thinking. Still, she had been ill for well over a year, and the circulation of the rumor meant that she needed to do something: "I *must* return to the stage soon," she thought, "and *prove* I wasn't dead."[9]

Her autobiography—the source of these recollections—is a troublesome document, simultaneously raising and eliding the connection between her illness, her desire to have a family, and her decision to adopt. It screws around with timelines. It changes details. Accepting the book on its own terms would lead us to believe that Baker's illness had nothing to do with pregnancy, that it was an innocent affliction, a consequence of a childlike desire to experiment with a new machine, the sort of uneven encounter between the primitive and the modern that one finds repeatedly in her Depression-era movies.

The fragments in the autobiography also suggest that the decision to adopt was without radical politics, at least at first. As her ex-husband Jo Bouillon continues the story, she was on a tour of the Americas sometime after the war when her epic quest to have a child came to an end. The tour had been a triumphant return to the stage, and she had already danced and sung her way from Argentina to Peru. "I think I'm pregnant, Jo!" she effused one day, bursting with excitement. Bouillon, worried about her health, tried to cancel the tour, but Baker, ever the self-sacrificing star, reminded him that "a contract's a contract" before adding that she felt "marvelous." ("She was obviously telling the truth," Bouillon adds editorially.) Skirting the rim of the Caribbean, reveling in the spotlight and the return to fame she craved, she and Jo planned the renovations of their medieval château in the Dordogne. Josephine wanted a big playroom, and a second child to come later, lest their firstborn become a "lonely, selfish little king." But she worried, Bouillon tells us, that she might not be able to have another, given how difficult it had been to get pregnant the first time.

There were so many needy children in the world, Bouillon mused. "Why not adopt?" she asked, only newly pregnant but also plotting her future quest for more. "Why not, *chérie*," the agreeable Bouillon responded, adding: "What we can't manufacture, we'll find ready made."

This exchange is worth a little time and thought. The peculiar distinction between "manufacture" and "ready made"—or between a child born of the womb and a child adopted—was meant, perhaps, to make light of a delicate subject. If Josephine Baker wanted a child, her reassuring husband wished to stress, she could always have one, even she didn't "produce" it herself, because, to continue the metaphor, the supply chain was global and the market was saturated. But that same humorous distinction grafts the language of commerce onto something that isn't, in the end, mechanically created, that doesn't emerge from a forge or a factory or a field. Written long after the events of that year, it reveals, unwittingly, a conception of children as commodities, of the family as a product line, of parenting as assemblage, where disruptions in the delivery of a product for the market result in the replacement of one supplier with another. This language of children one could either "manufacture" or find "ready made" was, then, an intimate shorthand, offered up in a moment of strain as an abbreviation of a much more complicated subject, and remembered sometime later in the midst of writing a memoir; but it was a revealing shorthand, too, because it captures something of Baker's entrepreneurial, commercial spirit. Bouillon's response to her question—"Why not adopt?"—relied on a tried and tested metaphor that he knew would be soothing, one that he knew she, a historical figment of the world marketplace, would intuitively understand and enthusiastically embrace.

The innocent dream of a fairy-tale prince and his adopted sibling, Bouillon tells us, ended in Mexico. There, a pregnant Josephine enjoyed a day of singing with small children who were members of a traveling French choir, Les Petits Chanteurs à la Croix de Bois. This welcome idyll—a reminder, perhaps, of her growing family—was succeeded a few hours later by a gory bullfight, which she detested. An ill wind followed close behind. "That night the pains began," Bouillon remembered, and by morning, "her hopes of motherhood had been destroyed, this time probably for good."[10]

The movement from a soft-hued concerto with children to a sporting slaughterhouse was a useful literary device in a story built for Hollywood. An aging superstar, forgotten and presumed dead, recovers from a serious illness and takes the stage. She is determined to let people know that she exists, that she still matters, and that her talents are unrivaled. More privately, though, after decades of performing a certain naiveté on stage, she has grown up and wants to have a child of her own. Shaken by a near-death experience—and specifically by her rumored death reported in the press—she embarks on a sprawling, global tour. She gets pregnant on the road and tries to reclaim her fans, satisfy the terms of a boilerplate contract, and keep her unborn child, too. Tragically, her body is too weak, too fragile, to satisfy all these desires. In a nighttime debacle, symbolically preceded by an angelic chorus of children and a gruesome bullfight, she loses the unborn infant—a child she has already anointed, in her mind, as a king. The tension between career and family, work and home, is the story of every woman. It generates enormous sympathy and sadness. It explains implicitly, without connecting the dots too directly or too boldly, her creation of the Rainbow Tribe, her willful construction of the ready-made family. She lost her unborn child and decided to adopt. It is that clean and simple.

This is a false plot, though, a linear narrative presented by a manifestly ambitious corporate author. It serves Baker, not us. Anthropologists distinguish between what they call official and unofficial transcripts to explain the gap between what the state tells us and what ordinary people tell us about any particular moment. Baker's autobiography is, we might say, a commercial transcript, following the well-established conventions of the Hollywood studio system and mainstream feminism. Stitched together posthumously by a team of writers, all yoked together in the service of her memory, it cannot be fully trusted, especially when it comes to the subject of her family. Sometimes truthful and often revealing, it is always—*always*—an advertisement.

In the wake of her death in 1975, Jo Bouillon, by then her estranged husband who was living in Argentina, hastily gathered together the unfinished, fugitive scraps of memoir he found in drawers and boxes and bags and arranged them thematically into the form of a larger volume—a fittingly heroic life, he thought, for the departed superstar, and a marketing match for a developing film idea. Others were working feverishly on competing tell-all memoirs, and Bouillon wanted his book to be first and to be authoritative, so that its sale might "[ensure] the survival of our Rainbow Family." There were gaps in the record, though. "Wherever there was information lacking," he confessed in the volume's introduction, "I turned to Josephine's friends, her sister Margaret, our children, and my own memory to fill the gap."[11] All of the adopted children participated, adding a vignette here or a string of paragraphs there. The full range of the contributions is marked, inevitably, by the still-fresh shock at the sudden death of an outsized parent, friend, or lover. But one truth is inescapable: Bouillon's restructuring and stage-management of Baker's written life—in a book that is presented as an autobiography but is really a carefully edited selection of memories, some of them hers and some belonging to others—was meant to make money, or to make it possible to make money in some other way; it was never meant to be full, robust, or honest.

Selling Josephine, though, was old business. A much-desired product since the 1920s, Baker was a skilled salesman of herself. The "autobiography" ultimately crafted by Bouillon was meant to confirm the public role Baker had scripted for herself since her rumored death during WWII. In this deeper, more profound revision of her public portrait, Baker was a willing participant, if not the chief writer. The banana skirts would have to go. So, too, would the prurient rumors of sex, nudity, and wildness. In their place, Josephine and Jo would offer up a sort of heterotopia, more closely aligned with the moral universe of the postwar era. Theirs might not have been the story of a typical housewife in the car-friendly suburbs, watching the kids play in the backyard through a big bay window and welcoming Father home from his day at the office, but it was, in its own way, as close to that idealized world as Josephine Baker could possibly get. Sex sells, Baker knew. But other things sell, too. Character was a durable good. The tragic loss of her pregnancy in Mexico would be the first pillar of her new identity, allowing women everywhere to identify with her.

The story line she offered to her public—a mysterious illness in North Africa, a noble sacrifice to fans and country, with consequences later on, after she'd gotten married to a good man and tried to start a family—was a lie. She was in a hospital, we know. Her biographers disagree on just about everything else. Lynn Haney, after locating a local nurse and interviewing her, suggests that Baker had a stillborn child years earlier—a result of her rich love life in Casablanca—but that a serious postpartum infection led to a hysterectomy, which led to peritonitis, and then septicemia.[12] While Phyllis Rose repeats Haney's plotline, she emphasizes not Baker's relentless love affairs in North Africa but her continued work on behalf of the Resistance, in which all those wonderful parties, it seems, were a front for intelligence gathering. It was during a return to Marrakesh after one such event, Rose proposes, that Baker stopped off in Casablanca to consult a doctor, innocently asking about X-ray technology, and unwittingly getting pricked with a dirty needle, which resulted in the infection.[13] Jean-Claude Baker, whose detective work was comprehensive, emphasizes that Baker was determinedly questing for the scientific means to get pregnant and had resorted to consulting practitioners of dubious reputation.[14] During one of those consultations an experimental procedure was used, with tragic results. If the exact sequence of events is unclear, the consequences for Baker were terrible and persistent. By the late 1940s, she privately complained that she'd been operated on so many times by so many different doctors that it would have been good to have a zipper installed; the pain, she confessed to friends, was almost too difficult to endure.[15] As a consequence of the tangled and ever-expanding web of medical issues, treatments, and surgeries, whatever chance she may have had for a child of her own was dashed long before that tour of Mexico.

This was never just about her public image. Her decision to not tell *this* story, and to instead offer up a canned, commodified fabrication, reminds us that for her, the personal stakes were very, very high. Parentage, broadly conceived, had been an ambition—and a tactic—for nearly all of her life. Married at thirteen in St. Louis, Baker had feigned pregnancy to please her husband, Willie Wells, going so far as to knit infant's clothing, an invocation of prospective paternity that quickly became a habit. She'd routinely told sexual partners that she wanted to have a child, routinely sought to have one, and just as routinely failed. Her desire to have a rich, healthy family—to have the sort of domestic life that only wealthy white women had—was a great and heavy motif, endlessly returning and repeating over her roughly twenty years in exile. But what Baker describes as a tragic, unforeseeable consequence of an unfortunate and unrelated illness is, her biographers assure us, directly linked to this great pursuit of parentage. "Her fantastic determination to have a child," Jean-Claude suggests, "had driven her to consult so many quacks, to try so many risky treatments, that finally the poor body had rebelled."[16] This theme of extraordinary desperation—brought out in her will to stay famous and in her desire to have children—repeats so often in her autobiography, and emerges so unpredictably, disrupting the flow of ordinary storytelling, that it acts like the proverbial Freudian slip. She tries too hard to make the story seem innocent, and it comes out false.

There is no doubt that she wanted to have a child. And there should be no doubt that she was crushed, whenever it happened and under whatever circumstances, to learn that she could never have one of her own "manufacture." But the subterfuge in the autobiography was as much stagecraft as psychology.

Baker hated to live alone as much as she hated to perform alone. She loved a supporting cast, and a child would have been a welcome addition. Her tactical interest in sequenced collection, assemblage, and orchestration, a prerequisite for any chorus girl or performer with a band behind her, was critical to her need for a child and, later, to her philosophies of parentage, adoption, and public display. Long before Les Milandes, she was a collector, pulling together an ensemble to accompany her performances, under the lights or on the street. Wherever she went, at each stage of her life, she was surrounded by band members, animals, children, and lovers. When she escaped to North Africa, she dispatched someone to her estate to fetch "her animals," leading to the rescue of one dog, three monkeys, and two mice, all of whom accompanied her as she left by boat from Marseille. Once on board, she opened their cages and laughed at the disorderly, cacophonous tumult.[17] In Marrakesh, she adopted another dog and dressed it up in a coat. When Baker rescues a cat from a well, feeds a stray dog, or fusses amusingly over someone else's children, one can't help thinking of the fairy-tale global family she would assemble after WWII. Other people's children and other people's animals—these, in the absence of her own children, were the animated bricks and mortar of her own peculiar domestic paradise.

These initial, unrealized dreams of having a child of her own might seem the two-dimensional wishes of a childless woman for a family life that she had never experienced herself. A prodigy of the Jim Crow South, with an elusive, missing father, she was raised by an extended family, a set of informal "aunts" and "uncles" and "cousins" all clinging together, grappling for food and shelter and warmth, just trying to survive one of the lowest, most awful moments in American race relations. She wanted a different life, for sure. Still, there was more going on here in this wish for a child and in the narrative of sacrifice she offered up after the war. There she was, recovering from illness, brushing up on her medieval history in a hospital bed, knowing that she could never give birth to a child, dreaming about the castle she owned in southern France, plotting a comeback, and imagining that any child of hers might well become royalty. This is the stuff of fairy tales—of Arabian Nights and Cinderella—emerging in her life at exactly the moment when such fantastic folk stories were gracing the Hollywood screen, when fairy tales were becoming central to the mythos of American culture. She was already storyboarding, thinking about lighting and scenery, thoughtfully assembling a new supporting ensemble for the next great performance.

The first casting decision of her new, fairy-tale life was her postwar marriage to the handsome man with the winning smile. As a prospective groom, Jo Bouillon, a respectable, modestly acclaimed bandleader with a tainted recent history in Vichy France, was a poor match for Baker in the eyes of some. Henry Hurford Janes, Baker's friend from North Africa, was simply stunned at their professional partnership, the first step toward marriage, and assumed there must be some financial motive. "There is a studied attempt," he wrote to Josephine in a moment of candor, "to give an impression that Josephine et Jo are a single act, equally dependent upon one another. But that is not true." Baker alone was the real star, a real heroine; Bouillon was nothing special. Pushing a little further, Janes noted how the emphasis on the collaboration between Bouillon and Baker displaced everything else. "Your splendid war service," he wrote in 1946, "pales into insignificance besides the glories of 'Josephine et Jo.' " " 'Jo sans Josephine' is not nearly the draw," he concluded, urging her to withdraw from future engagements with her new partner and return to the stage as just plain "Josephine."[18]

But Bouillon—scarred by Pétainisme and in need of restoration— was a pliant and accompanying sort, eager to play the role Baker wrote for him. He was also good-looking and had an amiable smile, adding the right kind of down-to-earth charm to her blinding super-stardom. And he wanted her to return to the stage. "Many people grouped her with the has-beens, the outmoded prewar stars," Bouil-lon later remembered, thinking back to when they'd met after the war. "Rumor had it that she was no longer in any condition to appear on stage—in short, that she was through." He set out to help her "demobilize" the army spy and return the superstar to the stage.[19] Where Janes felt that Baker was diminished by her partnership with a lesser performer, Bouillon suggested that she would have nothing without him. Two very different men, each vaingloriously imagining that they alone could help her.

A year later, in 1947, when Baker and Bouillon were married and their seemingly adorable pairing was featured in magazines and newspapers, Janes was forced to backtrack a little, revealing some-thing of the woman he knew well. He recalled, thinking of their earlier conversations, that his first opinion had been colored by circumstance: Bouillon had been "ill with feverish cold," and Baker had been "tired and over-worked." "In illness and adversity one finds one's true friends and if you have suffered it is only right you should obtain comfort now. You have always struck me as a very lonely person and in your new life please God this will never be again for loneliness is a terrible state of mind."[20] Janes's first instincts had been to see the marriage of "Jo et Jo" as a product rollout meant for public consumption, a con-trived sham intended for the press and for her fans. His second take on it, though, stressed her long-term loneliness.

Together, Baker and Bouillon purchased an old château along the Dordogne River. It had but one bathroom and no heat, and was set in a crumbling, decaying landscape. Josephine knew it well, having vacationed there before, and having used it during the war as a refuge, hiding Allied servicemen in its "secret nooks and crannies." "Les Milandes seemed the end of the world," she remembered, thinking back on the war; "how peaceful it was in this beautiful setting." The "setting," Jo Bouillon wrote, remembering the first time he'd seen it, "was magnificent, deep in the wonderfully harmonious countryside." "This is the real France," Josephine said to him. The towers of the château reminded her of the stories she'd read as a child. "It's so peaceful here, Jo," she continued, "so calm . . . like a beautiful dream, a paradise on earth. It would make a perfect center for people who wanted to get back to nature. And what a wonderful place for children." She immersed herself in medieval history, studying the physical details of the château, built by the de Caumont family in the fifteenth century to satisfy the desire of the lady of the manor, who detested the more Spartan confines at the massive garrison upriver at Castelnaud.

She bought the entire thing, whimsically, when Jo Bouillon wasn't looking, and presented it to him as if it were a gift. Her postwar tour, culminating in this new version of La Baker, had been a straightforward savings plan for the purchase and repair of Les Milandes: "Every performance," she lectured Jo Bouillon, "means a few more building stones, an acre or two!"[21] She did little things and she did big things. She shipped her favorite garden statuary down from her now-reclaimed mansion in the posh Paris suburb of Le Vésinet. She brought running water and electricity to the top of the hill where the château was located—an extraordinary feat for a private citizen. She decorated much of the interior of the castle in the classic English country style, with dark hardwoods, medieval tile, stained-glass windows, and white plaster walls. The kitchen was iconic French country, with green-and-white tile floors and hand-painted tiles on the wall. The bathrooms were bright, with jewel-toned tiles and splashy, expensive fixtures, all of it meant to look, as many have noted, like an Arpège perfume bottle.

Baker and Bouillon were married in the ancient chapel attached to the castle. In the official photograph marking their union they appear as a perfect couple. She, wearing white, is laughing, but also demurely covering her mouth, trying (and failing) to "suppress a giggle." Jo smiles happily, neatly and formally dressed. The two stand in front of the mayor of Castelnaud-Fayrac, who presides over some joke (the source of the giggle), wearing an ornate sash and black robes, holding a microphone in one hand and a script in the other. In the background, a small sea of happy, supportive faces joins in the levity. Baker, her hair done up, her arms covered, wearing a long wedding dress, is the picture of the innocent blushing bride. Lonely no longer, we are meant to believe.

Fairy tales require a suspension of disbelief, a willingness to forget earth-bound realities. They depend on fairy godmothers, on magic, on wishes that come true. But beyond France, in 1947—the year of her marriage to Bouillon—there was precious little magic in the air. "St. Louis Woman Takes Fourth Husband," *See* magazine reported, turning her into a serial consort. Labeling her a "dusky," "U.S. born," "ex-Harlem Negro," and noting that she had only once married "a member of her own race," the monthly seemed suspicious of her wedding to "a white orchestra leader."[22] The barely concealed worry was that Baker had become a proponent of miscegenation, her high-profile interracial marriage impacting the current, fragile state of black-white relations. A careful reader of her own press, and a curator of her public image, Baker would have recognized, merely by glancing at the headline, that she still had some work to do. Her enchanted postwar return to fame—to a full life, a castle, her adorable and handsome prince, her great wealth—would eventually need to confront Jim Crow.

Beneath the fairy-tale marriage, though, there were secrets to be kept, and important reasons to want to keep them. She was barren before the war ended. She hid the news about her illness from the public. She worked hard to rewrite her story, playing up a savvy, sympathetic angle, suggesting that she only learned much later that she couldn't have children of her own. It was easy to be sorry for a woman who had given up everything—including a child, the thing she most wanted—for her fans. The messier, more desperate truth wouldn't do the same work. She had bounced back with a new husband and a new, extraordinary domestic setting. The stage— literally—was set for the rollout of her fairy tale. All she needed to complete the comeback was a new image, sleek and modern, perfect for a postwar world addicted to machine-age aesthetics and global themes.

2

No More Bananas

She changes costumes 13 times a day.

—Life magazine (1951)

In a photo taken for *Paris Match* in 1951, a very different Josephine Baker appears. She is in a full-length gown, her shoulders bare. A long, layered ponytail cascades behind her. Her back is arched, her face in profile, her chin tilted up, her full body in a regal, balletic pose. She seems on the verge of a twirl or a jump. Here she is La Baker in full postwar costume, restored to greatness, an updated, mature edition of the young girl who earned her fame in *la danse sauvage*. To accentuate the revision, La Baker's skirt is decorated with images of a younger Josephine, a stereotyped caricature dancing in a banana skirt, her body a liquid, bending thing, in stark contrast to the machined, formal physique of 1951. The postwar version of Baker is the same but different, related but changed, altered and sobered by age, by experience, by her brush with death. In the modern age, the new and improved La Baker is simply a more relevant muse.

This image captures an artist and an activist in transition. Since her arrival in post–WWI France, Baker had been renowned for creating her own stories. In doing so, she relied on a very unique cosmopolitanism, a sense of herself as loosely bound, if at all, by the dominant conventions of either national or racial identity. She was, in so many ways, the whole of the colonial tropics in one body. "All of Baker's French stage and screen performances," writes scholar Jayna Brown, "were based in discourses of French colonial encounters in Southeast Asia and North Africa, their plotlines those of French romantic Orientalist fiction."[1] By the time WWII ended, she'd been working on that unusual cosmopolitanism for two decades, but the global conflict gave her new contexts, both personal and political, in which to reshape her professional image, opening up this cosmopolitan beyond the motifs of colonialism. By the early 1950s, Baker had a reputation as a national war hero, a well-earned reputation at odds with the sexualized, exotic, foreign public persona she'd established during the interwar years. She was more modest as well, confessing, "No one over forty should go nude." Stripping away the primitivism that had once seemed permanently attached to her naked physique, the *nouvelle* La Baker—an old nickname, capable of revision—now had a chic, modern, and decidedly continental aesthetic, singing in multiple languages, donning costumes that were global and multicultural, that strayed beyond French colonial history.

To be a serious champion of racial equality—a necessary precondition to her impending global motherhood—Baker needed to become a modern cosmopolitan. She went about this with all of the seriousness of a veteran stage performer. And the results—begun at the war's end and completed in time for a momentous American tour in 1951—were important, reminding us that her cosmopolitanism has a history, too. In this narrow window, before her ideas about the Rainbow Tribe and Les Milandes had been finalized, she substantially revised her public self.

Even before the war ended, long before she sang to rooftop audiences in dusty Marrakesh, Josephine Baker was questing for a new image, a sparkling and fresh corporate personality, one that would address all of her concerns, enabling her to champion the cause of the down-trodden and to simultaneously increase the power and cutting-edge feel of her brand.

Her war record did a lot of the early work, offering up a heroic iteration of Josephine Baker for public consumption. In her "official" postwar portrait, taken at the Harcourt studio in Paris, Baker is clad in a Free French uniform, with her cap rakishly tipped to one side, her arms crossed, her once incendiary bosom covered by blue wool and brass buttons, her gaze level, serious, stately. She is "Captain Josephine Baker," as Langston Hughes called her, a French heroine through and through, with the scars to prove it, and not a mere wandering child brought to the continent by the whims of fate, dancing on the stage for the enjoyment of white folks and embodying the primitive material they so desperately craved. She might, of course, still need a team of horses, or a shimmering dinner with the sultan, but she also had more important, more meaningful things to do. There were broken bodies that needed tending, soldiers who needed supporting, and, on a deeper level, a war against racism to be won. Here, she was the loyal subject from the colonies, serving France without complaint, but also, in a way, a modern revision of that old cliché.

Biographers celebrate her labors with the resistance and her military appointment—officially Captain Josephine Baker of the Women's Auxiliary of the French Air Force—because her actions in the war were, by any metric, genuinely heroic. In Paris she worked for the Red Cross, at veterans' shelters, and in benefit concerts for the war effort. At Christmas, she would send gifts to the front, along with autographed photos.[2] In southern France, she opened the estate where she vacationed—the one she would ultimately purchase for "Jo et Jo"—as a refugee camp of sorts. Pinning notes into her undergarments, she daringly used her celebrity as a shield, and assumed that German officers would never search her body. To some in the resistance, Phyllis Rose notes, she was an untrustworthy, modern-day Mata Hari, the seductive dancer and femme fatale accused of being a double agent during the Great War and executed by the French only a few years prior to the invasion of Poland. But to Jacques Abtey, the dashing young officer of the Deuxième Bureau, Baker was indispensable cover, and together they toured much of Europe and the Americas during the early 1940s, until it became too dangerous for her to move about Europe. At that point, heeding de Gaulle's call for resistance against Vichy appeasement, Baker went to North Africa, where she cheered on the troops and continued to troll for useful information.[3] None of this was without risk. And all of it was rooted in a sincere love of France and a genuine commitment to democracy and equality.

Baker tended to this newly earned reputation as a heroine carefully and constantly. Indeed, if much of what we know about Baker's wartime life as a spy reads like Hollywood folklore, this is partly because she always hoped it would be a movie. In the early 1940s, the *Milwaukee Sentinel*, in jest, traced Baker's misfortunes during the war to the singer's snide critique of Frau Göring's decrepit pet cheetah at a restaurant.[4] Abtey's memoirs of the war, published a few years after the war, lent firsthand authenticity to rumors and gossip. Later, Baker worked with screenwriter Stephen Papich on a memoir—published posthumously—that reads like the tales of Paul Bunyan, full of outsized, apocryphal events, each of which tests the mettle of our larger-than-life heroine. Hermann Göring, she told Papich, the Führer's designated head of the Luftwaffe, had sniffed out her espionage and tried to poison her at home. In a dramatic confrontation (told over several pages, and with a detailed accounting of her wardrobe in each scene), Göring had tried to force the chanteuse at gunpoint to consume some deadly soup. Relying on her wits, and plotting her escape by communicating in Spanish with her staff, Baker slipped the noose through a laundry chute. Baker's self-composed mythology—authenticated by Abtey and expanded by Papich's lavishly detailed memoir—gave her genuinely brave exploits as a spy the over-the-top feel of an Action Comics issue.

All around her, the war had awakened something dangerous and destabilizing. A cohort of African American soldiers, emboldened by their participation in the war, would return to the United States determined to continue the fight for democracy at home. White liberalism, which stuttered its way through the Great Depression, seemed eager to distance itself from the previously popular worldviews that had made the Holocaust possible. The colonies of Africa and Asia and the Caribbean, seeing that France, Britain, and Italy had been decimated by the war, began to request—or demand—autonomy and the right to self-governance, broadly conceived. Within only a few years of the war's end, the language of human rights would coalesce into the Universal Declaration of Human Rights, a strident commitment to the abstract ideals of equality and freedom. Viewed from the present, this all seems like a whisper of what was to come. Racism and colonialism proved to be surprisingly durable; the dismantling of them would be the bloody, soul-sapping, still-incomplete work of the generations to follow. But from the vantage point of 1945, it seemed like everything was on the threshold of revolution.

Baker's work in North Africa on behalf of this great global awakening was, of course, determinedly cosmopolitan. Langston Hughes recalled that Baker was perhaps the first to sing "La Marseillaise" after the "defeat of the Vichyites"—a performance he labels "both dangerous and brave." He also notes that her showstopper, "J'ai Deux Amours," had become "a kind of prayer," bringing tears to the eyes of her audiences. That song, her potent tribute to diaspora and dislocation, would be her signature piece forever, even in North Africa, even in front of African American soldiers or a mixed platoon of wounded veterans. "J'ai deux amours, mon pays et Paris" (I have two loves: my country and Paris), she would sing in the refrain, before the white-knuckled conclusion, in which a pronounced elongation of the vowels, creating a tremulous and powerful confusion between *et* and *est,* announced that something had changed, that "my country *is* Paris." The song was an explicit reminder that Baker was, all at once, French and American, black and colonial and an immigrant, an icon of movement and circulation. And that Paris, after all, belonged to the world. She had been singing that song for decades, and then, in the midst of a world war, it suddenly resonated differently, more powerfully, as a reminder that one could and perhaps should be a citizen of the world, not merely a flag-waving patriot.

This modern cosmopolitanism was troublesome. Even in her beloved France, few could safely navigate the widening gap between loyalty to country and commitment to global citizenship. To Baker France had always seemed hospitable, offering true celebrity to a foreign woman with dark skin, but as its empire abroad crumbled and its citizen-subjects from around the world came to Paris, the nation would be ever more interested in legislating unwavering fealty to France as a precondition for hospitality. Baker's extraordinary fame, coupled with her acquisition of French citizenship and her wartime service to the Resistance, insulated her from the worst of Gallic nativism. For many ordinary immigrants, though, a new home in postwar France came at the cost of abandoning everything about one's self that wasn't purely, definitively, perfectly "French." Of course, her commitment to *liberté, égalité, fraternité* still had to be squared with her celebrity, her glamour, and her abiding enthusiasm for champagne, caviar, and high living. Within France, she would lean heavily on her war record to insulate her from conservative abuse and to frame her adoring audience's responses.

Before the war—before her postwar reconstruction—Baker had a confusing public history. Her triumph on the stage in Paris marked the first of a series of crucial reinventions, for without careful management, she might have become a passing fad. "If she was to succeed in Europe in a permanent way," biographer Phyllis Rose writes, ticking off Baker's thought process, "she would have to transform herself into a European."[5] Her late-1920s "supposed marriage" to Pepito Abatino, an Italian "count," at the end of her dance-hall career was marked by his efforts and her eagerness to completely remake her physical presence, her mannerisms, and every aspect of her lifestyle to conform to this Francophone ideal without shedding her "Negro" past. "He was," as Barbara Chase-Riboud put it, "a kind of a Professor Higgins to Baker's Eliza Doolittle." Thrilled to be "royalty," Baker suggested that she would have to learn Italian, as she imagined becoming an opera singer.[6] More strategically, she learned to speak French and procured a formal country manor outside of Paris. At the end of their labors, she had become, as Chase-Riboud recalled, "an artiste, a performer who had no color, going from jazz to blues, from Parisian ballads to South American rhythms," with an "international and color-blind performing style."[7] She began her charity work with orphans and the poor during this period, and toured much of Europe, learning more than a little about the rising tide of anti-Semitism and racism. And as she settled into a life of more complicated performances, her official narrative focused on her assumption of the role of a French entertainer, celebrity, and soft-hearted ingénue.

These complicated performances relied on her well-known propensity to appropriate or mimic prevailing representations of the full range of French colonial peoples. This performance extended as well to an over-the-top assemblage of diverse representations, parts, styles, and genres, a technique of performance that is implicitly parodic, if not deeply subversive in unsettling ways. Baker's skill before the war, in short, lay not just in her limber limbs, arched back, and tawny color, but also in the unsubtle artistry of her jumbled-up exhibition of continental colonial culture. She wasn't a mere mimic, nor just a gifted dancer and singer. A comedic critic of empire, she stitched together the whole messy universe of colonialism into one vast backdrop, then offered herself up as an exemplar of everything outside of France, outside of the West, and outside of modern metropole. She became, in essence, a nascent expression of the Third World. Her comedy, or farce, lay in the bright, grotesque, bizarre display of so many aspects of colonialism on one body, breaching the expository walls that kept Indochina apart from Martinique and those apart from Algeria. To conceive of this technique, Baker needed only to think creatively about the familiar form of the music revue, itself the founding venue for her fame, which relied on the unsubtle orchestration of variation.

On the eve of the Great Depression, she released a remarkable series of films, each a perfect expression of some French colonial fantasy, and each also a platform for her unconventional celebrity. In *La sirène des tropiques,* her first, released in 1927, she played Papitou, an indigene with a vibrant personality who cannot, as luck would have it, keep her clothes on. Her habitual or partial nudity is naturalized throughout. Heated up and unable to cool down, she strips to bathe in a river. When she wakes after a fitful night's sleep and stands in her translucent shift, her naked body is silhouetted for the viewer by the moonlight. Her breasts are on routine display, whether she is slipping out of her loose-fitting top, lingering in an interior space, or frolicking in the bathtub. And for every man save one—the engineer who comes to survey her territory—she is a hotly desired object, a sexual element. By amplifying Papitou's supposedly native sexuality in a film where for many reasons she cannot have her man and where for true love's sake he cannot see her as an object of desire, the architects of this film, in grand and familiar fashion, stage colonialism as a potential romance fraught with dramatic physical complications. Race might be a part of the problem, but the bigger issue is simply that André loves someone else—someone *like* him, to be sure, but also someone he knew before he met Papitou.

The film uses Baker's breathtaking colonial pastiche with reckless abandon. Indeed, though the setting of the film is far removed from North Africa, the performance of Papitou's nudity is a part of what Malek Alloula names as the colonial "anthology of breasts," a tradition in Orientalist visual culture in which the bust of the "colonial harem" is displayed in one of three forms. The "'artistic' variant," he writes, "requires that between the breasts and the eyes there be interposed some gossamer fabric." The next form, which he describes as "roguish distraction," affords the breasts a mind of their own, as they

refuse to be bound by clothing and often take "advantage of an opening . . . to peek out and parade [a] nipple under the nose of the spec-
tator." Finally, there is simple "display," in which the colonial bust is
"at last freed from the garments designed only to be removed, [and]
offers itself either with arrogance or with submissive humility."[8] Baker's representation of Papitou conforms so closely to what Alloula
describes that she could almost serve as an object of all three variants
in the same postcard series.

She moves through the entire catalog of Near Eastern standards,
almost in sequence. Confirming the film's implicit Orientalism, there
is a scene near the end of the film where Baker, as Papitou—seated
like an odalisque on a divan, waiting for her colonial not-lover to
return—breaks the fourth wall and, like the women in so many Orientalist postcards from colonial culture, stares sadly, fleetingly, and
potently into the eyes of the viewer. In that moment, Baker acknowl-
edges her playful (and perhaps politically meaningful) appropriation
of an aesthetic of colonialism. She lets us know that she is in on it, that
she isn't unaware of the meaning of her performance. Watching *La si-
réne*, or studying Baker in these years, is like reading an unalphabet-
ized, cross-referenced, comprehensive encyclopedia of global colonial
culture. Baker's pioneering achievement—one that would endure, one
that she would repurpose after the war—was to embody the colony-
inside-and-outside-the-metropole as something frustratingly global
and surprisingly heterogeneous. Alloula suggests that the slight variations one finds in a sequence of representations—postcards of the sera-
glio, for instance—are a critically important feature of the colonial
order. "The repetition and tireless variation of the same pose," he offers, "constitute a sort of *enumeration*; the photographer thus proceeds
to a roll call of the inmates of an imaginary harem." "It is the nature of
pleasure," he concludes, "to scrutinize its object detail by detail, to take
possession of it in both a total and fragmented fashion."[9]

In these early performances, locating Josephine Baker on the
map of the world is a part of the thrill of discovery. Monte Puebla,

for instance, is the key to Baker's Papitou. Earlier, having decided to surreptitiously follow her secret love, André, back to France, Baker's Papitou must first take leave of her home in Monte Puebla. We have seen her home—shared with her father, Diego, an "old colonist"— before, as a reflection of every colony everywhere. It is a dense tangle of bamboo, beaded curtains, and mahogany, replete with mismatched furniture, dirt floors, and a hammock. Carefully making her way to the door, Papitou has dressed for transatlantic travel—at least as she imagines it, or as we believe she imagines it. Out of time and out of place, she is clad in turn-of-the-century Victoriana, wearing a trailing floor-length dress and a white hat. As always, she has her innumerable gold bracelets and her hoop earrings, additional markers of her confused colonial location, emphasizing the disorderly orderliness of the colonial body in the metropole.[10]

Like Papitou, Monte Puebla is a seemingly messy jumble of colonial stereotypes, a "repeating island" of French myths about the tropics.[11] The name of the place—along with the names of the people, such as Alvarez and Diego—suggests a former Spanish colony, now emancipated after the collapse of its former master. There are, to support this gesture, dozens of serapes in the film, draped over fence posts as geographic signposts for the viewer. Other details are confusing. Moccasins are the preferred footwear. There are also grass skirts and grass roofs on circular huts, suggesting a Polynesian influence. There are antelope skulls and animal pelts adorning every wall, inner roofline, and archway. Both day and night, the natives, who are marked by every conceivable physiognomy, dress like Mexican cartoons, complete with sombreros and festooned with layers of striped linen and cotton. Antiquated rifles hang from hooks and wall sconces, markers of temporal and geographic distance. In a room with half a dozen chairs, not a single piece of furniture matches—everything is from a different style, made with a different material, or in a different state of disrepair. At night, the local residents of Monte Puebla, strumming guitars and singing, dance the Charleston. To finish it off, Alvarez wears frontier buckskins and bandoliers throughout, as if to incorporate the settler motif of the American borderlands. In short, Monte Puebla is not just a stand-in for the French Antilles. The succession of Spanish place names and proper names suggests something in the Hispanophone world, which would make it a free republic and not a colony. Spanish colonies were—and are—signifiers of historical mixture and hybridity.

This colonial jumble revolves around Papitou, who is introduced as she descends from the jungle canopy. Her gold bangles and headscarf suggest North Africa or the West Indies, and they contrast with her flapper dress and her "white" hairstyle. She is the child of Diego, the hulking, enervated "old colonist" who seems content to drink himself into oblivion, but whose pale skin and location in the tropics— wherever these tropics might be—are themselves potential sources of his long-term racial decay. We know nothing of Papitou's mother, but that is a necessary elision, allowing Baker's character to drink deeply from the confusing well of racial representations without the threat of permanent association. It adds, implicitly, to the film's portrait of Diego as a settler who has been living for too long in the premodern, implicitly suggesting that his fathering of Papitou is a sign of his degeneration. Still, Papitou is clearly not like the other natives at Monte Pueblo, and many of her desirable qualities must, in the absence of her mother, come from Diego, and through him from Europe. Whatever we make of her—odalisque, indigene, colonial creole, African—we are surely supposed to conclude that her best features are drawn from everywhere. She is the very best of the colonial periphery, representing the most extraordinary parts of the global South in microcosm. Her embodiment of mixture is what makes her so unpredictable, so lively, and so amusing. She is sympathetically synthetic.[12]

This pastiche was a tactic. It enabled Baker to expand her racial repertoire, to have a stage persona that went beyond blackness. Though she had first arrived in Paris marked as a "black" expatriate, she had quickly assumed the representations of all of France's colonies and become, as Elizabeth Ezra puts it, "a floating signifier of cultural difference."[13] The tactic was a success, too. She'd been appointed "Queen of the Colonies" for the 1931 Exposition Coloniale Internationale, an honorific that reinforced her status as the woman who could be anything—anything with color—for France and, indeed, the world. By the mid-1930s, she had played to the crowds as if she were Indochinese, African, Caribbean, and Oriental. Her performance of "La Petite Tonkinoise" in the revue at the Casino de Paris featured, Phyllis Rose notes, "Madagascan drugs, Indian bells, and Algerian tambourines."[14] In her movie roles, she chose a trio of roles with dramatically different, if equally confused, racial origins. Papitou, child of the pale Diego, is impossible to place; Zouzou, a lost child of the French Antilles, sings nostalgically of Haiti from her perch in a giant birdcage; and Alwina, an Arab girl from the mixed-up Mediterranean, could not escape her past and her "primitive" roots, whatever they might be. "Mon père était blanc," she told her followers in her 1935 autobiography, "et tante Elvara—l'Indienne."[15] This is more misdirection; Elvira, Jean-Claude Baker tells us, was her grandmother, not her aunt, and Baker's father was not white.[16]

Seven years earlier, in the same year that she starred as Papitou, she told her public that her father was "Spanish," though the accompanying illustrations by Paul Colin feature blackness and excessively dark skin tones.[17] In the midst of WWII, Phyllis Rose tells us, she was pretending to be Jewish and "praying from a French-Hebrew prayer book," even as she wore a djellabah around Morocco.[18] In the US South, such confessions or rewritings—especially ones so clearly contrived for a celebrity reinvention—would have been an object of derision, if not public scrutiny and outrage. One drop of black blood, real or imagined, was all that it took to wash away ambiguity in America. But in France, Baker wisely surmised, there was the chance of more, even if that required her to appropriate ethnic costume and stereotype, to embody difference globally, in sequenced variety. The great question was, really, whether the machined production of diversity, with race drawn brightly if unconventionally, could unmake racism.

The Parisian Negrophilia of the 1920s and early 1930s had opened up different possibilities for Josephine Baker.[19] She was able to conceive of a bigger role for herself in French colonial culture by performing and then holding together a full range of imperial Others, including Papitou, the indigene from the Hispanophone Americas. In doing so, her original position as an African American expatriate was never lost or forgotten. Indeed, it was read, like an ancient palimpsest, through whichever role was in play, or in whatever performance she was presently engaged. But her double alienation—racially within the United States, and nationally from the United States—did not so much define her as it did allow her to manifest alienation across the colonial spectrum. And her somewhat facile expressions of fondness for her homeland—specifically, the oft-sung "J'ai Deux Amours"— lent her colonial performances a critically important doubled quality: they were expressions of love and alienation, echoing what audiences knew of the real. She was not yet French but no longer American, at once a creature of the colonies and of the metropole.

Her surprisingly playful relationship with the dreck of colonial culture is not, I think, a reflection of Baker's early disinterest in the progressive political world, broadly speaking. Nor is it a sign of her genuine commitment to *la mission civilisatrice*. Baker was, to sum it up glibly, troublesome in less obvious ways.[20] She would have been reminded every day that France provided her with opportunities for everything denied by the United States, opportunities beyond better cars, better apartments, better living, and access to the rich and the famous. And she wouldn't have had to look hard to understand what black life was like in the American South. She could remember the East St. Louis riot. She understood lynching. She had a world of migrants to *her* Paris with stories of their own. And she knew what it meant to live in a Jim Crow world. Just as important, in embodying this colonial pastiche she was able to claim individual artistic genius as few other African Americans had ever done before. She grew up in a world where the sorrow songs had no single author or performer and where the authors of folk tales were lost in the mists of time, but in this period of her life she found herself in a place where everyone could trace wonderful, much-beloved things specifically to her and where her qualities as a creative force were not so easily denied. It was not merely, then, that she was a fixture of advertisement, like Aunt Jemima or the Gold Dust Twins, but that her role in promoting products was unique, personal, and attributed to her and not simply to her darkness. In France, she was something else, something not easily named, something truly unique.

Baker's exceptionally clever use in the interwar years of the vast catalog of colonial representations, many of which *were* fairly demeaning and conceptually thin, was a fantasist's creation built out of these stereotypical small details and racist brushstrokes. No performer before or since has covered more geographical and temporal space in his or her work. No other performer has used such an untrustworthy palate. No other performer, just as certainly, has been known for the construction of such a dazzling pastiche, whatever its politics. Baker, to put it simply, boldly embodied colonial multitudes, celebrated the imperial majesty of France, and did both in ways that continue to shape, or perhaps haunt, our histories of black Paris.

At the war's end, however, it was clear that the age of European empires was ending and the American Century had begun. The continent was in ruins, its once splendid cityscapes reduced to dusty, charred piles of brick and mortar. Along with the scale of the war, news of the Holocaust called into question the nature of "civilization." The great empires of the nineteenth century had suffered cataclysmic damage. The United States, now a militarized global power strengthened by the war, would play an active role in repairing Europe, a restoration that came with strings attached. Formal empires, with their metropolitan market privileges and constrained circuits, were old news. Democracy in the American style, on a level economic playing field, where the stronger United States was certain to thrive, was the new order of things. Former colonies would be freed, given representative democracy, and modernized, ensuring their economic dependency on American goods, American technology, and American ideas. All this, in the end, to stave off the advance of the Soviet Union, the other great new power to emerge from WWII stronger and with new global ambitions. In the emerging Cold War between two superpowers, American culture, ideas, and values were weapons. Their circulation across Josephine Baker's Europe ensured that every conversation about race, rights, and revolution would have a New World character.

This American Century would complicate Baker's plans. Her cosmopolitan sensibilities, so deeply rooted in interwar Europe, were practically illegible across the Atlantic. In the American context, because of a long history dating back to slavery and eugenics, a single drop of black blood defined the "Negro" body. Over the first half of the twentieth century—as Baker fashioned her fabulous colonial pastiche—racial classification in the United States was streamlined, simplified, nationalized, and rendered monochromatically, making the new global hegemon a black-and-white place with significantly less ambiguity than Europe. What would have been the story of Baker's avatars—Papitou, Zouzou, or Alwina—if their adventures had been set in the United States? They would have ridden the Jim Crow car, drunk from the colored water fountain, or entered through the back door of the theater. They would have checked the "Negro" box on the census, learned to step aside if a white person was on the sidewalk, and been schooled to avert their eyes, to sit behind the line, to be racially deferent, polite, even obsequious. If they strayed from the informal rules and carefully worded laws of Jim Crow, the unfair diplomatic protocols that governed race relations, they would have ended up impoverished or watched by the local police, troubled by a dangerous reputation. They could serve champagne and caviar but they couldn't consume it. This racial order, an odd part of the US commitment to democracy and freedom, was about to become the new global order of things, exported alongside engineers and foodstuffs and development plans. Her old nemesis, Jim Crow, would find her in France.

And besides, the banana skirts, the nudity, and the stereotypical characters all seemed rooted in the deep past. Viewed from the perspective of 1951, Papitou seemed like a false image, a too honest projection of what white folks wanted to believe was true of the tropics, of the colonies, and of the people who came from either. Papitou belonged, Baker thought increasingly, in a museum. So, like the snap of a finger, that is exactly where she went. And Josephine, in that same instant, became modern, distancing herself from the past.

Was she now Captain Josephine or La Baker? Was she a hero of the nation or a fashionable citizen of the world? Was she best represented by the formal portrait of her in the Free French blues or the staged, balletic portrait of her, referencing her alluring past? Could she be both? Increasingly she was La Baker, with the elegant ponytail, the disorienting wardrobe changes, and the international style. Baker's political interests and personal goals demanded that she keep one foot in the nation and one foot in the world, and that both feet should be firmly planted in the modern age. And her audience, quite perceptibly, noticed the change. By March 1949, *Time,* transfixed by an image of Baker dressed from head to toe in an elaborate Latin American ensemble—complete, of course, with two birds perched atop a hat—lamented, "No bananas."[21]

If the bananas were gone, the pastiche remained. For Baker in this period, her frequent wardrobe changes and her global song list were elaborations of the argument that she was relevant or current; seen and heard together, they also stressed her great cosmopolitanism, her embodiment of an increasingly postcolonial world. She sang in Yiddish and Spanish, French and English. And she strayed far beyond the golden standards of the French cabaret age, choosing songs that she presumed represented the world's variety in all of its multihued, polyphonic complexity.

She changed her look, too. She mounted her hair into an elegant series of tresses and that long, regal ponytail. "Fashioned after an Egyptian inspiration," the result, as one newspaper described it, was "a striking three-tiered, four-foot hairdo which resembled an inverted ice cream cone ending in a long tassel," all of it "decorated with pearls and diamonds."[22] Wearing her haute couture dress imprinted with her past, a visual reminder that, like pre-Columbian adornments on an art deco skyscraper, Baker was a part of the contemporary moment, and not a relic. At a moment where design, architecture, fashion, and art all quested for the modern and looked to continental Europe for inspiration, there was La Baker, redesigned as a Hollywood-style icon for the machine age. Appearing in Los Angeles in 1951, Baker opened her performance in a long, elegant ball gown, deep magenta in color, with long gloves. Later, she invoked Carmen Miranda, the Brazilian songstress famous for her fruit cornucopia headdress. Wearing a patterned, ruffled dress, short in the front and long in the back, she appeared onstage with a large group of children, a common feature of her postwar performances. She had her hair wrapped up in a red scarf, with a white rooster and a white hen balanced on top. The *Afro-American,* tickled by the range of her costumes, noted that she traveled with no fewer than fourteen trunks of clothes.[23]

Noting that the old Baker was gone, another newspaper suggested that while "her fabled glory might not have been entirely what her first public anticipated, they quickly caught the mood."[24] Still another review—this time a response to her television debut in 1951—attended to the same details. "As a singer, her voice is thin and far from impressive," critic Jack Gould summarized, and "as a dancer her movements . . . were hardly demanding artistically, albeit subtly and suitably complementary to her lyrics. But Miss Baker as a performer is another matter. By sheer force of personality she establishes a mood which carries both herself and her song. In her work there are the hint of a Continental sense of naughtiness, an unflagging sense of rhythm, and thanks to a truly stunning wardrobe, an exciting aura of chic and sophistication.

Call it a lavish triumph of elemental femininity."[25] The atmosphere, for Baker, was worldly but not nostalgic, diverse but also forward-looking, as if she were representing the United Nations. If before the war every wardrobe change marked the arrival and departure of some antiquated French colonial dream, now in every trunk of clothes there lay some national tradition, modernized for the postwar world, ready for use by the most cosmopolitan woman on earth. Each facet of these performances—the songs, the costumes, or the spectacles on stage—was stripped of political meaning. All seemed playful and fun.

Indeed, whether "lugg[ing] around a huge fur coat," "wigg[ling] in a tight-fitting white gown fitted with sequins," or "dash[ing] around in an African costume of deep red accentuated with gold braid" or a "gold satin pantalooned dress of oriental fashion," Baker seemed enjoyably frivolous.[26] Each performance, though, required a lengthy summary, a forensic tabulation of the languages and cultures and peoples represented. Only when this mélange was held together, seen all together, was there the hint of a subversive point of view, chiefly the still fairly innocent notion that the grand, diverse landscape of song and sight was flat, that a Mexican ballad might be just as fun and interesting as a Jewish folk song or a mournful French torch song or that together the ensemble might be more interesting than any one of its parts—and that Baker alone was the single person capable of such a remarkable orchestration.

These updates to her public image were very important. They made it possible, in the end, for her to do bigger things: to push back against Jim Crow, to lobby for equality in the broadest sense, and to imagine herself as a part of the social and political vanguard yet again. They distanced her from the earlier, troublesome representation of colonial fantasy. They made Baker seem generally innocuous and charming, a tiny, enjoyable trifle, still sympathetically synthetic, even when she chose to speak up and push back, but no longer a mere imitative genius.

What matters, in the context of the story of the Rainbow Tribe, is not merely her heroism and her beatification as a member of the Resistance, her embodiment of diaspora and cosmopolitanism, or her clever penchant for self-reinvention, but also that she emerged from the war newly committed, as never before, to the service of rights and revolution, broadly conceived. It is important that she was fearful that her celebrity—her brand—had been permanently damaged, but it was just as important that she moved boldly and swiftly to challenge injustice and to speak of rights in the same sweepingly broad and abstract terms as the recently issued Universal Declaration of Human Rights. While she continued to represent a diverse ensemble, or to embody a nascent multiculturalism, she also refused to be a part of the colonial archive any longer. There would be no more bananas.

Anyone else who had tried this would have been branded a fool or a traitor. Most of Baker's African American contemporaries—Paul Robeson, James Baldwin, W. E. B. Du Bois, Langston Hughes—were increasingly speaking in terms that could be described as "global" or "cosmopolitan," yet all found the postwar environment newly constraining, difficult, and counterrevolutionary. All were marked as dangerous or suspect. But Baker broke away wildly from the emerging conventional wisdom that the nation was the center of everything, twirling her skirt at every step. Her reputation as a hero of the Resistance (and her friendship with and loyalty to de Gaulle) ensured that she was beyond reproach in France, no matter how strangely foreign she might sometimes seem. Her celebrity allowed her to travel anywhere with few disruptions and regulations and great freedom. Her commitment to a stunning, unrivaled cosmopolitanism allowed her to seem like a legitimate stakeholder in almost any context where race and rights were issues. As the Cold War loomed, her cultivated air of noblesse oblige, her love of high fashion, her penchant for glamour and excess, would make it incredibly difficult—but not impossible—to stamp her as a subversive, whatever her provocations. She had become the modern La Baker.

3

Citizen of the World

Colored folk don't have to incite incidents. They occur all the time.

—Josephine Baker (1951)

By 1951, even *Life* magazine—the conduit for the beloved American middlebrow—agreed: "La Baker Is back."[1] In a story that sprawled over several pages, the magazine celebrated the performer's return to Broadway, where she had been "singing love songs in five languages," switching out costumes frequently. The performance was a kaleidoscope of racial and ethnic stereotypes. Once, and briefly, she invoked the minstrel tradition to get a few laughs. "You make me so happy," she shouted out, her eyes crossed, her head turned to the sky, her hands grasping the sides of her golden pleated pantaloons. In another skit, this one saturated with Orientalist tones, she played the role of a "Tunisian vendor": she donned a fez and changed the socks of an audience member. She danced in a tightly wrapped gown, emblematic, she proposed, of the Brazilian native, who twirled and shook and sashayed along the nightscapes of Rio. And for "J'ai Deux Amours," her famous showstopper, her testament to a love of movement and diaspora and cosmopolitanism, she wore Dior and white fur. Every time the lights dimmed and the costumes changed, a different racial archetype appeared, but all were updated to match the modern sensibilities of the new and improved La Baker.

In the age of Jim Crow, it was the description of Baker's private life that was most powerful and, indeed, most threatening. "In addition to her apartment in Paris," *Life* reminded readers, winding down its summary of Baker's triumphant return, "she owns a 12th Century chateau with 50 rooms, where she sleeps on a bed used by Marie Antoinette." *Life* got the vintage of the chateau wrong, but the general details right. "She populated her estate," the essay continued, "with a swarm of dogs, monkeys, an aviary of tropical birds, and cages full of ducks, chickens, geese, pheasants, and turkeys." This "zoological chorus," Baker told *Life,* was comforting. "I love the quiet of the country," she joked. In New York, however, the glamorous La Baker had to settle for two rooms at the Park Sheraton Hotel, where she stayed with one of her pet cats and a monkey named Binkie, along with her chosen handmaiden, of course. One night in the hotel, while Baker was laid low with a cold, Binkie burned his hand on a hot water pipe. Ending with Baker the collector, not with a summary of the songs and dance numbers and costumes, *Life* wanted its readers to see the kaleidoscope not as a provocation but as proof of the performer's inner strangeness, or as evidence of her status as the incredibly tasteless standard-bearer for the nouveau riche. If Baker was trying to remake herself into a modern cosmopolitan, *Life* was looking for signs the revision wasn't complete, that beneath the polished veneer there was still a nouveau riche black girl.

The provocations were there for everyone with a discerning eye to note. In one of the magazine's most powerful photos, Baker sits in a leopard-skin robe in front of a round, gilded mirror while her attentive white French maid—as nameless and servile as the clichéd image of the black domestic—tends to her famous hair (or her "horse's tail," as she put it elsewhere).[2] In 1951, for the readership of *Life,* this was what revolution looked like: a black woman with a white maid in an opulent room, a strange reversal of the supposedly natural order of things.

For Baker, service to the cause of civil rights and racial equality went hand in glove with her new public life. The "new Jo," as the *Chi-*

cago Defender put it in a headline, "is a French maid on a mission."[3] In the midst of the war, she had been thought to be dead. Now she was alive, and not merely alive, it seemed, but also blessed with the perfect marriage, a storybook life in a castle, and an endless parade of ball gowns. Like Disney's Cinderella, she practically floated above a cartoon landscape of singing pets and adorable wildlife and warm-hearted French country folk. This new life hinted at the secret, persistent dreams of a poor girl scrambling to survive and then escape a desperate urban dystopia, who clung tenaciously and for all of her life to well-advertised fantasies of what it meant to be wealthy and famous. But the epic spectacle that was emerging wasn't merely a function of Baker's life. It was also a savvy response to market forces. Her rumored death had been outsized, so her comeback had to be twice as big. It needed to show off a new Baker, far more spectacular than the old. She was always, in the end, a product herself, in need of constant reinvention and updated marketing, depending on a constant revenue stream for everything—for the castles, the husband, the gowns, all of the distance that she put between herself and St. Louis. It was also a deeply felt, idiosyncratically imagined expression of her very particular politics, in which justice would always mean the right to be not just rich but also fabulously rich, whatever one's color. In 1951, bejeweled and costumed, spinning and singing, she would fight for this notion of justice in Jim Crow America.

The simple awning and the plain façade were deceiving. Once you were inside there were white tablecloths on every table, along with big silver champagne buckets. The rooms were filled with smoke, and at the center of every table there was an ashtray emblazoned with the name of the Stork Club so that any celebrity photographer who might snap a photo would also highlight the location. The rooms were dimly lit and windowless and the walls were covered with wood panels, with photos of the celebrities who ruled the roost. Sweeping curtains ran from floor to ceiling. Even the most intimate seating areas—the soft, circular booths with high-backed benches—were meant to be seen, defined so that they could be easily surveilled by the press, by fellow A-listers, or by those who managed to get into the place to seek a fleeting glimpse of fame personified. In Albert Dorne's classic mise-en-scène, composed for *Collier's* in the 1940s (and later repurposed as an illustration for the club's menu), there is a sea of smiling, famous-looking people, all of them looking, staring, gazing at the stars gathered up in what was not so much a private night-spot as it was a spectacularly public venue, a place to be seen, to attract attention.

The interior landscape was guarded by two well-known sentinels. At the front of the Cub Room, table no. 1 was occupied by Sherman Billingsley, the garrulous host and owner, who routinely played favorites, welcoming his guests and ensuring that they were well seated. And in the back, at table no. 50, there was Walter Winchell, the famed celebrity gossip columnist, whose chronicles of the rich and famous could be ruinous or open the door to opportunity. His fedora tilted, his gaze cynical, Winchell was the moral compass of the Stork Club, defining the ascent of the winners and the descent of the losers through an assessment of character and good patriotism. Like Billingsley, he rewarded his friends with good press and punished his enemies severely, labeling them political radicals or subversives. By the early 1950s, the venue—and the pairing that watched over the scene—was popular enough to have its own weekly television show, so that the dazzling material of Winchell's syndicated column could be broadcast for national consumption.

On the night of October 16, 1951, Josephine Baker and a handful of others ventured out to the Stork Club for dinner. Baker ordered a steak, and waited an hour—too long, she thought, given her prominence, and other tables were served faster. Baker's status as a celebrity seemed to have been trumped by her racial status as a black woman married to a white man. She left, her entourage swelled by the addition of Grace Kelly, a new acquaintance who was equally stunned. On the way out, Baker noted Winchell's watchful eye, and wondered why he, the self-appointed ethicist of the place, hadn't said or done more. The next day, in the midst of broadcasting her complaint about the club, she publicly blamed Winchell for passively supporting Jim Crow.

The ensuing scandal consumed everyone involved. By early November, the National Association for the Advancement of Colored People (NAACP) had arranged a picket line outside the nightclub, effectively turning any evening's admission to the club into a political statement. Baker had telegraphed President Harry Truman to alert him to "the undemocratic, discourteous treatment" she'd received at the hands of Billingsley—with a blind eye turned by Winchell—and to pray for an end to "the horrible discrimination disease that exists in this great land."[4] Winchell, in turn, had begun blasting Baker as a "Communist" and an "agitator," pushing for an FBI investigation into her activities, and using his column as an opportunity to challenge Baker's reputation. The affair was a bloody proving ground for Baker's political skills.

The story of the Stork Club actually begins much earlier. In February 1951, Baker returned to the United States for the first time since her ill-fated role in the Depression-era Ziegfeld Follies. Sustained by her renewed, postwar commitment to equality and justice, enthused by a successful stay in Havana and a tour of the Americas, she was eager to conquer the most sought-after entertainment market in the world.

Her timing was extraordinary. At the close of WWII, a real revolution in civil rights had seemed within reach. African Americans had served with great distinction in Europe, earning respect for their patriotism in the service and nearing a "Double V"—victory against tyranny abroad and racism at home. Spearheaded by A. Philip Randolph's March on Washington Movement, black activists had compelled the federal government to act—in minor though symbolically important ways—on behalf of their interests. President Roosevelt, cognizant of the demographic and electoral significance of a growing black electorate, was at the very least not hostile to African American concerns, and may well have been privately even more sympathetic. Compelled by Randolph's organizational skills, he issued Executive Order 8802 establishing the Fair Employment Practices Commission, ostensibly desegregating hiring practices in federal employment. His wife, the fabled Eleanor, was a more stalwart, open champion of a peaceful, equitable resolution of "the Negro question," speaking publicly before mixed audiences and serving as FDR's diplomatic liaison to the African American community, which was represented by the NAACP and the National Urban League. Behind closed doors, the Roosevelts relied on their "Black Cabinet" of unofficial advisors to steer them toward a new era in race relations. And in public, FDR's various vice presidents, Wendell Willkie and Harry Truman, were even more forthright spokesmen for "fairness" and "justice" for ordinary Americans, whether black or white.[5]

The Cold War redirected the emergent civil rights movement, opening up space for general and abstract commitments to equality and closing down consideration of structural or institutional impediments to fairness in housing, employment, wages, or a host of other bread-and-butter issues. The strongest commitments to civil rights for the mass of black Americans in this moment were rhetorical, color-blind, and devoid of any discussion of social and economic class. Pop culture celebrated Jackie Robinson's breaking of the color barrier in professional baseball as if it were the literal end to an uneven playing field, but few celebrated the integration of suburbs or the elimination of racial preference in hiring. The armed forces may have been desegregated in 1948, but the revolution by executive fiat of the *least* democratic unit of American life seemed largely symbolic. Color-blind admission to the University of Texas Law School had just been mandated by the Supreme Court, and the movement—run by lawyers and preachers and college men and women—was focused on access to lunch counters, to integrated schools, to clean travel and transportation hubs, all thoroughly middle-class interests, every one of them perfectly in lockstep with the Normal Rockwell–esque American dream. This was a concession to the new reality, a matter of strategy and tactics in which the NAACP and others saw an opening and tried to take advantage of it.

At the same time, embroiled in a conflict with the Soviet Union for world domination, and envisioning that conflict as a reflection of capitalism versus Communism, American political culture broadened its notion of radicalism and clamped down on internal dissent, subjecting protest leaders and internal critics to excessive surveillance, criminal prosecution, and other equally severe consequences. Jackie Robinson's 1949 testimony before the House Un-American Affairs Committee (HUAC), solicited as a representative response to African American activist Paul Robeson's supposed support of the Soviet Union, was a boilerplate expression of the moment. "We can win our fight without the Communists," he proposed, carefully navigating a difficult passage, "and we don't want their help." The dynamic tension between Robinson and Robeson was an invention of the political class, a modest, trifling difference of opinion crystallized into conflict by a culture in desperate search of a loyal opposition within an oppressed racial minority. As Robeson repeatedly said during his own 1956 interrogation before HUAC: "This is complete nonsense."[6] Nonsense indeed, but with terrible penalties. Late in life, Robinson confessed that his opposite in this forced melodrama, the actor and dramatist assailed by conjured charges of un-American activities, had "sacrificed himself, his career, and the wealth and comfort he once enjoyed" for a just cause, while the younger baseball star became the beloved cause célèbre of the new, color-blind Cold War order.[7]

The Cold War also globalized the context for the civil rights movement, turning what had once been an embarrassing domestic dispute between blacks and whites, largely relegated to the South, into a matter for the world to debate. The architects of postwar American political culture pitched their homeland as a beacon of liberty and freedom for oppressed peoples everywhere. In doing so, they opened themselves up to the charge of hypocrisy. The State Department marshaled exemplary African Americans to speak on behalf of the nation around the world, hoping to draw the emancipating colonies of the global South into the relation with the United States. And African American activists such as Robeson and their allies used the same international, "democratic" promotions of the United States, at great risk, to call attention to the irony of its domestic sanction of Jim Crow and the violent racism of the deepest South. What had once been a dirty little secret (one impoverished region's poor treatment of its black population) had suddenly become an international test of the American way.[8]

Baker's arrival on this deeply politicized scene began with a series of February 1951 performances at the Copa City Club in Miami, planned after her collaboration with José Ferrer, Katherine Dunham, and Ernest Hemingway on "the impact of Haitian culture and customs on outlanders" fell through.[9] Insisting that her audience should be desegregated, Baker and the club's owner, Ned Schuyler, agreed to an exception to the nightclub's standing Jim Crow rules, allowing for a color-blind admission. The exception wasn't durable, however. And the Copa wasn't the sort of place that blacks were clamoring to enter. As historian Mary Dudziak tells it, Baker had Schuyler "fly in African American and white celebrities from New York for her opening," a mixed bag racially but all of them a part of Manhattan's society pages.[10] The show lasted but thirty-five minutes, but it was improbably packed with smoothly executed costume changes, deftly negotiated shifts in language, and striking alterations of mood and tone. "She makes the lyrics sound international in essence," one reviewer remarked.[11] Beyond the entertainment value, though, something profound had happened. "At the command of one little brown girl," one columnist reported, "the walls of segregation came tumbling down."[12]

The success at the Copa—a beloved show in front of a desegregated audience—was a good sign. For a few incredible months afterward, Baker was a celebrity whirlwind, keeping pace with the movement, bridging her popular performances on stage with her activist piecework, and using her tour as an occasion for commentary on the national scope of Jim Crow. In New York in March, she'd scheduled a special interview session for the African American news corps, after learning that the Park Sheraton Hotel had limited access to white reporters only. Meeting with James Hicks of the *Afro-American,* she urged black entertainers to insist on equal pay.[13] In early April, she'd unexpectedly appeared at a courthouse in New Jersey where a sextet of young African American men—the "Trenton Six"—had been railroaded into confessions for a murder they didn't commit. Baker sat in the front row with the men's lawyers and made polite chitchat with "Mrs. Florence Adams, the only colored court attendant" present.[14] In mid-April, on the Chicago tarmac, she had intervened when paparazzi had asked her black club car attendant and a black porter to step out of the frame of a photo opportunity.[15] She'd famously refused to perform in her hometown, St. Louis, because she couldn't find a first-class hotel that would give her a room. A week later, from halfway across the country, she issued a telegram to plead once again for the Trenton Six. Calling for a "miracle," Baker asked the defendants' attorneys to remember that they needed to "fight as you have never fought before" for "the sake of colored people throughout the world."[16]

One day later, on April 22, she asked the nation to "pray for Willie McGee," a Mississippi man accused of the rape of a white woman and sentenced to death.[17] She knew McGee's case well, having planned to appear at a rally on his behalf sometime earlier but withdrawing at the last minute because she feared association with "Communists."[18] As the case drew to an unhappy close, Baker would pay for McGee's wife to fly from Detroit to Laurel, Mississippi, to see her husband once more before his execution.[19]

In all of this, she steered clear of any discussion of witch-hunts and blacklists, anything that might trouble her image as a creature of cosmopolitan consumer culture. Instead, story after story focused on her hair, her clothes, her servants, her adoring fans, and the wide-ranging performances. And, of course, her salary. "The exotic star," one paper reported excitedly, was drawing in tens of thousands of dollars every week.[20]

As a tribute to this litany of dramatic interventions, the New York branch of the NAACP named May 20 Josephine Baker Day. The singer, honored with a luncheon at the Hotel Theresa, a parade through Harlem, and a cocktail party in the Park Palace ballroom, was given three new outfits to wear by her favorite Parisian designers, Jean Dessès, Jacques Griffe, and Christian Dior.[21] The "blues Cinderella" rode in a cream-colored convertible at the head of a twenty-seven-car motorcade, all to the cheers of thousands of fans, standing curbside or leaning out of their windows to get a good look.[22]

The official recognition of the value of her work came by telegram. In May, Walter White, the legendary executive secretary of the NAACP, wired Josephine Baker to ask her, on behalf of the Atlanta branch, to attend a "reception in your honor" in late June, at the association's annual conference. The association had passed a resolution at its February meeting endorsing Baker's "stand against segregation in Florida," and White hoped to make a formal presentation of that resolution to the singer. "There will be no racial segregation at this affair," White assured the superstar, recognizing that she would be unwilling to appear were it otherwise.[23]

Privately, Baker wished to come to Atlanta as "a person and not an entertainer," so that her costumes might not distract from the more important matter at hand.[24] Publicly, though, she was delighted to be invited, indicating in a hasty telegram that she was eager to accept. White, at her request, set about including the stock phrase "no segregation at the auditorium" in his internal NAACP communiqués. Finally, C. L. Harper, the president of the local branch, hoping to sidestep any problems with public accommodations, suggested that "she will be housed in one of our best homes and Atlanta has many good homes." Writing to White, Harper wondered if Baker had a preference.

She did. Indeed, Baker's preference was telling, and it threatened to turn the event into a minor diplomatic incident. In a late May telegram to Secretary of State Dean Acheson, White wrote, "She insists as a matter of principle that we secure hotel accommodations without regard to race or color for herself and company." "Refusal of such accommodations," he continued, "to so distinguished and famous an artist will create as you know a most unfortunate international incident." He closed by asking for State Department assistance in getting the Atlanta Biltmore to accept Baker's reservations.[25] The Biltmore was, of course, the very best hotel in Atlanta, long reserved for white guests, and its imposing red brick edifice stood as an explicit acknowledgment that separate always meant unequal in the Deep South. In making this simple request for a "first class white hotel," Baker's approach to Jim Crow was class-conscious first and foremost, a nuance that few would accept.[26] Georgia law forbade white hotels from allowing black patrons to take a room, and few were eager to challenge the law.[27] As one of the hoteliers reportedly put it after a meeting to discuss Baker, "A nigger has never entered the front door of my hotel and never will."[28]

She may have been a unique talent, but in 1951 there simply was no "white" hotel in Atlanta with a room for Josephine Baker. Even the Georgian Terrace, owned by a French citizen, refused. "It is un-American and utterly stupid," White concluded in a letter to Baker at the end of May, "to deny you and your party rooms in a place of public accommodation like a hotel which even a white gangster would be permitted to use."[29] The city's mayor and chief of police all volunteered to buy tickets to any public performance by Baker, essentially committing themselves to appear in a racially mixed audience, despite the strict protocols governing race relations. The State Department phoned White to ask him what could be done.[30] White frantically appealed to diplomat and Nobel Peace Prize winner Ralph Bunche and former First Lady Eleanor Roosevelt to intervene for Baker, and he scrambled to assemble a press statement that might serve some political purpose.[31]

In a private telegram, Baker thanked White for understanding why she had refused the invitation. "The fact of being in a white hotel does not flatter me in the least," she wrote, "but it is a matter of being a Negro and not being able to go where you desire." For Baker, the refusal of the Biltmore, the Henry W. Grady, and the Georgian Terrace to confirm her reservation was reminiscent of "how our people are treated because of the color of their skins" and "humiliated by ignorant and cruel hearts only to hurt." "I keep thinking," she confessed, "of our colored men in far off Korea dying so the American flag can wave with pride while here in Atlanta or other southern states their families or friends don't dare go in hotel restaurants or public establishments through the front door."[32]

Smaller but familiar indignations surrounded the NAACP conference. In early July, during a one-day stop in Washington, DC, Baker was denied service at the lunch counter of a Hecht department store. Holding a press conference to discuss the slight, she expressed her disapproval of the use of blacks as political props on goodwill tours of Europe. "Europeans are not ignorant," she lectured. "They read and they visit America. They are quite familiar with the race situation in this country." She saved some scorn as well for black actors who accepted demeaning, stereotyped roles in order to make a living. "Honor comes first," said the woman who once danced wearing only a banana skirt in order to escape crushing poverty.[33]

Less than week after she was turned away from the Hecht lunch counter, a more telling story was broadcast nationally and internationally, matching the pattern she'd already set for herself. Traveling to the West Coast, Baker had been mobbed at the airport by fans, including one woman who was so thrilled to see the superstar that she "bulldozed through the crowd" and promptly "[upset] her high-salaried form," knocking it "kerplunk on the planeway."[34] After a wildly successful show in Los Angeles, the singer sat down at the high-end Biltmore Hotel for a meal with Bessie Buchanan, former star of *Shuffle Along*, recent co-chair of Harlem's Josephine Baker Day, and soon-to-be-elected assemblywoman in New York. At the table next to hers, a group of white patrons buzzed unhappily. Among them, Fred Harlan, a middle-aged traveling salesman from Texas, growled, "I won't stay in the same room with niggers." Baker, angry and offended—"mad as a hornet," as she put it—alerted the hotel detective, who called the police, who then arrested the man for public drunkenness. Following Harlan to jail, she later signed a citizen's complaint accusing him of "disturbing the peace" and issuing "insults directed not at me as a person, but at my race," insults she felt were "un democratic and un-American."[35]

The public drunkenness charge was dismissed, but Baker's civic-minded addition stuck. And so Harlan, in Los Angeles for the California Corset, Brassiere, and Lingerie Show, was fined $100 and had to be bailed out, the *Los Angeles Times* tells us, by his "blond wife," all because he'd ruined the atmosphere of Baker's repast. Appearing at the courthouse, Baker confessed that she'd filed her charges "in the interest of people everywhere," citing her long struggle against racism and, as proof of her commitment to equality, referencing her "three white husbands."[36] "Justice has been served," she announced outside the municipal courthouse, and "as far as the members of the minority races are concerned the hours he spent in prison will, I hope, make him understand that people are fighting for justice all over the world."[37]

As these encounters with Jim Crow escalated, the black press cheered her on.[38] "Instead of trying to get away from her former American Negro cousins," the *Kansas City Call* offered, "she has endeared herself to all true Americans by demanding for them the same privileges she has received in continental Europe." The *St. Louis American* congratulated her for "tolerat[ing] no form of Jim Crow." Isidore

Dollinger, a congressman from New York, read salutary comments into the *Congressional Record*.[39] Another Josephine Baker Day was planned, this time for Chicago under the auspices of the Chicago Urban League.[40]

Despite the accolades, the monotony of these encounters wore her down. By late July she had cancelled her US tour, blaming generally poor health and a bad case of laryngitis. And by mid-August she was gone, returning to France for a brief stopover, where she announced her intention to open up a hotel—the site of so many of her struggles—in the Dordogne.[41] She didn't stay in France for long, though. After a brief, restorative interlude in Europe—a return to her home turf after months in a hostile territory—Baker was back in Manhattan, venturing out to the Stork Club for that fateful dinner. And she was accompanied once again by the former showgirl and budding politician, Bessie Buchanan.

The long, slow buildup toward the Stork Club affair is a part of the story here. For much of 1951, Josephine Baker was determined to suffer not a single indignity and practiced a zero-tolerance policy when it came to segregation. She challenged even the smallest infractions—the sorts of routine, day-to-day features of Jim Crow that were rarely discussed and infrequently challenged, especially in the rural South, where even the rumor of a protest could cost someone his or her life. She'd been in the news routinely, had been feted in Harlem, celebrated in absentia in Atlanta, and received with genuine affection everywhere. So when she showed up at the Stork Club for dinner, it shouldn't have been surprising to anyone that she might get angry when it took an hour to deliver a steak dinner. At the same time, her entrance into the movement cut across the usual middle-class concerns of the NAACP and the National Urban League and strayed far from the issues that motivated the leftist and radical organizations. She was as interested in the humanity of Willie McGee as she was in having a set of rooms at a "white hotel" for herself and her attendants. There was no one else whose political work was so far-reaching, so attentive to disrupting the historic American attachment of race to class, blackness to poverty, and whiteness to aristocracy.

What happened that night in October fit this same pattern. But what was different about the incident at the Stork Club was the presence of Walter Winchell and her singling out of the veteran newsman for his nonchalant approval of segregation. She'd relied on the press as an ally for much of that year. Baker called out Winchell by name in a press conference the next day, suggesting that he had merely sat there and watched while she suffered her great humiliation. And she organized protests outside the Stork Club. Winchell, in turn, got mad, and then set out to get even. Using the bully pulpit of his newspaper column and his weekly radio address, Winchell returned fire. Baker's "campaigns against 'racial discrimination,'" he wrote dismissively, "are obvious publicity stunts."[42]

Ever vindictive, Winchell encouraged the FBI to investigate every conceivable rumor about Baker's possible affiliations with Communists. In submitting one letter in which someone claimed to have seen Baker in Leningrad in 1936—and wrote that "J.B. is just a highly colored copy and a poor one at that of Mata Hari"—Winchell asked, "Hoover, can we check this please?"[43] Fueled by the Cold War hysterics of the moment, another letter writer remembered that Baker had once tried to bring a Russian maid into the United States: "How do you like that? She won't even employ a Negro maid," as if that sort of thing was the gold standard of patriotism.[44] One southern correspondent, describing himself as a "nice Jew," informed the newsman that "I have tried several times to get a reservation at the Stork Club," without success, a reminder that Baker was already one of the very few allowed to enter the Cub Room.[45] "Since all Negroes can't afford Parisienne hospitality," concluded "a colored student," "we'll just have to stay here and improve our country."[46] Not content merely to forward these letters to the FBI without comment, Winchell spread the rumor that Baker was herself a racist, an anti-Semite who was envious of Jewish success, turning that into a talking point for the right wing.

"Josephine Baker, the breast-beater," he crowed, reading an earlier autobiography closely, "who cries to the Heavens against discrimination of herself, out-Goebbels Hitler."[47] Forwarding a set of memos to the McCarran Committee—a subcommittee of the Senate Judiciary Committee formed by Nevada's Pat McCarran to investigate the Communist threat—the FBI admitted that "there is no evidence that Miss Baker actually took part in these Communist activities," but the damage had been done in the public sphere, where Winchell's rumor-mongering prevailed, not in the back channels of Washington, where the FBI's circumspect memo might be found.[48] Reporter and longtime socialite Nora Holt, meeting with Baker in the midst of the Red-baiting, learned that the performer had been reading the press closely, and recognized that "the strain of the controversy could result in a complete breakdown for the average person."[49]

In Winchell's column, he singled out *Pittsburgh Courier* columnist George Schuyler's supportive missive as the "Letter of the Year." "One would think," Schuyler hypothesized archly, noting that Winchell had been just a guest at the club, that "you were the owner of that establishment and had personally ordered that the actress be insulted." A former protégé of H. L. Mencken, the African American satirist had always been a gifted writer. He appears to have taken considerable pleasure in rewriting the history of Baker's previous year in the United States, retelling it as if it were a chapter in the history of the Soviet Union, as if all the couture and high living were sponsored by "fellow-travellers and crypto-Communists." Her civil rights work was dismissed quickly as trivial and insignificant, part of an effort, he thought, to curry favor with her natural constituency. "She has been successful hornswoggling the colored brethren into accepting her as a group heroine and champion," but "we," he concluded, suggesting a change of heart within black America, "are dubious about buying this latest job of the once-glamorous Josephine."[50]

Over the Christmas holiday, Baker had been performing at the Apollo Theater and doing a brisk business, but the dustup with Winchell cost her dearly. In "smear[ing] her good name," Winchell, she claimed, had also "seriously impaired her earning capacity," leading Baker to file a quixotic $400,000 libel suit against Winchell, hoping to recoup her losses.[51] She announced, in a complementary offensive, an effort to compel the New York legislature to add some muscle to the state's civil rights law; Baker, attorney Arthur Garfield Hays reported, didn't want "personal differences or even 'personal discourtesies' to divert attention from what she considers to be the real issue—whether laws against discrimination are to be enforced a lot." And when Winchell charged that Baker had joined the war effort only when the outcome of the conflict seemed certain, she trotted out her distinguished war record in the Resistance, though it wasn't clear that Winchell's audience was listening.[52] At the end of 1951, S. W. Garlington of the *Amsterdam News* nominated her for "Woman of the Year." Her reputation had been tarnished, though, and soon she would leave the United States yet again, even more determined to use her fame to embarrass her birth country into fair and equal treatment.

Jim Crow was far more than a structural impediment to Baker's lifestyle. Though she was distanced from its worst material effects, it was still an affront to her soul, not to mention a challenge to her social position, her claim to be global and cosmopolitan, and her right to be human—to be, in some way, beyond blackness. After an absence from the United States of almost twenty years, the constant, daily, ground-level struggle for basic dignity that she saw there upon her return angered her. She was a citizen of the world, not a denizen of the Mississippi delta, and she was mad about the assumption of shared "Negro" status and just as steamed that places such as the delta still seemed unchanged.

Historians have given us penetrating readings of Josephine Baker as an African American expatriate, revealing her long-standing role in US-driven Cold War politics. Focusing on the early 1950s, they read her initial withdrawal into Old World domesticity as an unhappy consequence of repressive American foreign policy doctrines. For much of this period, Baker was followed by informants, had her speeches summarized for the FBI, and found it increasingly difficult to move about without some manner of harassment. The result of Baker's travel restrictions and surveillance, they suggest, was a breakdown of Baker's political potential, as the world's first black superstar was shunted off to Argentina and then sequestered away in France, losing her best chance to speak out against Jim Crow in the United States and the Americas. But there is another way to read this period. Baker had generated enormous sympathy during her tour of the United States, and she'd successfully managed to transition away from her tarnished past as a burlesque dancer. She had laid the groundwork for bigger things, not for a withdrawal from the storm's edge.

Winchell's reputation, like that of the nightclub, had been ruined by the tangle with Baker. His "long, torturous descent," biographer Neal Gabler writes, "actually began precisely at 11:15 p.m. on October 16, 1951, in the Cub Room of the Stork Club, when Josephine Baker entered."[53] Baker's complaint forced Winchell to be more aggressive, and it took away some of the luster from the nightclub (Mayor Vincent Impellitteri, for one, stopped showing up). That was also a fateful moment for the globe-trotting chanteuse. The scandal altered Baker's public image profoundly, branding her a dangerous radical, stripping away some of the innocent gaiety that had been attached to her name for so long. It didn't force her to directly confront Jim Crow, or to imagine herself in lockstep with the NAACP and other groups, all of them struggling to build upon very modest gains in civil rights and to break down white supremacy. She had been doing that for months. In a country where she was now doubly

alienated—black and French—she had spent half a year building co-
alitions with activists and using her star power to reorient the priorities of Cold War America.

The fight pushed her abroad once again, on an exploratory journey
of sorts, as she searched for a political practice that matched her
drives and desires. She wanted to enjoy the aristocratic perks of her
extraordinary fame. She hoped for a way out of Winchell's Cold War
frame-up. And so, perhaps inevitably, she drifted southward, through
the Caribbean, into Brazil, and then, finally, into Juan Perón's Argentina, where she found a new platform for her increasingly animated
critique of Jim Crow, and a new inspiration for her future: the idea of
a vast assemblage of children, displayed for political gain, and matched
to her unique view of the world.

4

Southern Muse

I think Mrs. Perón is my spiritual sister.

—Josephine Baker (1952)

When the *Afro-American* correspondent James Hicks rolled into Las Vegas, he wasn't sure what he'd find. Carved out of the desert, the city was a frontier backwater in 1952, but it was growing fast. If the real high rollers still preferred Havana, smaller cities where gambling was also legal, such as Galveston, Texas, had begun to lose ground to the modern oasis in the middle of nowhere. The once sleepy, loosely segregated Las Vegas, Hicks reported, had recently imported a stricter version of Jim Crow alongside a large body of black workers, brought to the arid West from Louisiana to work in a local magnesium plant. These captive workers, arriving by truck and railroad in the sprawling gambling mecca, lived in a vast shantytown in the Westside, which Hicks thought resembled the Hoovervilles of the Great Depression. "La Baker was there, too," he remembered. She was appearing at the Last Frontier hotel and was "the only colored person in town not in the Jim Crow area." Every other black person on the Strip, Hicks noted, was wearing a service uniform.[1]

"La Baker wooed 'em and wowed 'em," the review for *Variety* enthused, taking note of her "ultra-sophistication," "the Latin flavoring," and the vast portfolio of fashion, from deep green dresses with fur capes to a white ruffled outfit decorated with "brilliantly-hued bows." Appealing to the audience for laughter and applause, drawing them into conversation, she fit the mode of a revivalist preacher. But, singing in three languages and gliding across the stage, effortlessly changing tempos and styles, she was also "a parade of glamour personified."[2]

Offstage, she was just as busy. Even as she investigated whether she could have a gambling casino installed at her capacious estate in southern France, she continued her serious civil rights work, rejecting efforts by local hoteliers to send the African American members of her band off to the Westside and insisting that they should have rooms on the Strip.[3] Determined to show that her standard nondiscrimination clause was for real, she reserved a table for six directly in front of the stage for every night she performed and ordered the NAACP to fill it each night with a mixed group. When the hotel balked and began to claim that it had no open tables, she had white allies book the tables in advance, and then accepted the reservation herself. "When people see that Negroes know how to act," she argued, "and hotel officials find that their customers are not going to walk out, there will be no need for such discrimination." "Gaining admission to night clubs is not so important," she admitted, despite having fought for just that for most of the past year; "most important of all are job opportunities." "There is a lot to be done," she concluded, closing off one of the very first successful civil rights actions in Las Vegas, "all areas must be worked in—jobs first."[4]

Only a few weeks earlier, Baker had been in Mexico City, at the Rumba Casino, performing a review she called "Chez Elle." She'd hoped to go to Cuba, but the usurpation of power by General Fulgencio Batista, a steward of American interests, kept her away.[5] Happily stuck in the Distrito Federal, she attempted to launch her own personal version of the NAACP, which she named the World Anti-Racial Discrimination Association, with branches in five dissimilar locations: the United States, Cuba, Guatemala, El Salvador, and South Africa. The association's first effort was a partnership with the

Undernourished Children's Society, *Variety* reported. Also, a Far Eastern branch of Baker's organization was in the works, aimed at fighting discrimination in Asia against the mixed-race children resulting from liaisons between American servicemen and local women. Baker would preside as a spearhead for the group, *Variety* reported, until a more permanent leader might be found.[6]

The engagement at the Last Frontier was a follow-up to Mexico City. From Nevada, she was supposed to head to Ciro's in Hollywood, where she planned to debut a new wardrobe, then to the Tick Tock Club in Milwaukee, and then finally a return to New York. She planned to open a nightclub of her own, Chez Josephine Baker, in an "ultra smart East Side location." A new album was in the works. She was plotting a regular television series set at the nightclub, in imitation of the Stork Club's regular show featuring Winchell and Billingsley. And, not to be outdone, she was finishing off a screenplay for *The Josephine Baker Story*, set to be filmed, the press reported, in 1953.[7]

The fallout from Baker's confrontation with Winchell ruined these ambitious plans. There would be no film, no radio program, no nightclub, and no casino along the Dordogne. She had quickly become radioactive. So in the spring of 1952, still angered by her protracted tangles with Jim Crow, her future plans uncertain, Baker left for South America. She made her way slowly, inexorably southward, through Brazil and Uruguay, singing and dancing, laughing gaily at the tropical splendor all around her, and—with a reckless disregard for the conventions of the Cold War—laying waste to the reputation of the United States. Outside of the United States, she could speak the unvarnished truth.

In Brazil, which she called "the true racial democracy," she touted her earlier efforts to create two globally minded organizations, one (the World Anti–Racial Discrimination Association) an antidiscrimination effort and the other (the World Cultural Association) a group vaguely aimed at fostering brotherhood in the arts and sciences.[8] Speaking within the imposing art deco façade of the Biblioteca Mário de Andrade in São Paulo in July 1952, she began by invoking the popular belief that Brazil was a melting pot of races and peoples, a product of generations of mixture. "I rejoice," she began, gazing out into the audience and searching for clues of origins, "when I see in the faces of these people traces of their ancestral backgrounds, be they of the black race, white race, yellow or red." In a rapid-fire speech, she labeled Brazil "a symbol of democracy," "paradise on earth," and "a big family where all races have been molded into one Brazilian people."

She also provided an incisive, deeply informed diagnosis of the American condition. Pointedly referencing the famous Trenton Six case, the riot in Cicero, Illinois, that resulted from a single black family moving into a white neighborhood, and the Christmas bombing of NAACP leader Harry T. Moore's home that resulted in Moore's death, she told her audience that "the discrimination among people of the white and colored race in North America is worse than any human being could possibly imagine." She spoke of segregated housing, dilapidated and unequal facilities, the violence that accompanied desegregation, wage differentials, and the overlap of race and class. And she shared her thoughts about the impact of the Cold War. "When one talks of the equality of races or human beings," Baker said, speaking from experience, "one is immediately branded a liberal; anti-American; or a Communist," labeling the last of these terms a "leitmotif" of political discourse. "In the old days," she noted, "when a white man spoke of the equality of races, he was called a niggerlover. Today, the word has been changed to Communist." The overall impact of this constraint on expression, she concluded, was either silence or complicity. If they wanted to escape repression, black Americans and their allies needed to be quiet, lest they be branded as radicals. And they needed to sit silently and watch while a few African Americans (she mentioned lawyer Edith Sampson, a star of the pro-American

Round-the-World Town Meeting program, and conservative journalist George Schuyler) were dispatched "to foreign countries to tell the people that the colored man in North America is perfectly happy, and that he is better off than in any other part of the world." This last group—described as opportunistic liars engaged in diplomacy for Jim Crow—she named "the number one Uncle Toms of our time." Revolutionary sentiment, Baker believed, was most forcefully expressed by outsiders, dissidents, and exiles, by those who refused to be captives of the US State Department or tools of the Soviet Union.

Despite this point-by-point criticism of Cold War culture in the United States, Baker struggled to be understood roughly as nonaligned, as an advocate for a third way outside of the usual categories and doctrines. "Please," she implored, "do not believe for one second that I have a political affiliation or anything that resembles such; for I have not and do not wish to have any."[9]

By October of that year, as the Southern Hemisphere entered the warm season, she ended up in Juan Perón's Argentina. The self-described Paris of the Americas, Buenos Aires was both synthesis and hypothesis. It was an independent city, standing alone in Argentine politics, not the capital of some province but the personal fiefdom of the president. Its residents were known as *porteños,* which roughly means "people of the port," a proudly chosen sobriquet suggesting a civic identity rooted in comings and goings, in nearly constant change and exchange and mixture. The city's architecture, its most famous feature, cut sideways across modern custom and was impossible to categorize. Critics suggested that the architects of Buenos Aires merely aped European convention, but in the smaller details there were local distinctions that mattered, and differences of intensity and scale. The randomness of the place—so many different bold and perfect and astonishing expressions or extensions of so many different styles—was itself unique. The city's repeated cycles of political ambition corresponded to its clashing architectural styles, which were arranged not in a neat sequence radiating out from the ancient to the modern but jumbled and juxtaposed, the new pressed against the old, the baroque sutured to the modern, palm trees shadowing modernist facades. Even the local dialect—sounding more like Italian than Spanish, and accompanied by richly Mediterranean gestures—had a hybrid cadence. Beneath the Parisian veneer, Buenos Aires was the kind of mixed-up city Baker always loved, preaching the virtues of unexpected juxtaposition and rich, aesthetic diversity.

She had been to Buenos Aires several times before and was known there as a performer with considerable star power. In the 1920s, Baker's appearances in Argentina had caused riots, perhaps a consequence of her supposed marriage to a white man. (Local custom had also dictated that she wear considerably more clothing onstage than was typical for her.)[10] She had been featured in advertisements for the city's Bieckert brewery, which sold Cerveza Africana, a dark, thick lager. The traditional label on the bottle included a short-haired, dark-skinned woman, a smiling, contentedly domestic representative African, offering herself as a restorative elixir for general consumption. Surrounded by a golden frame, she stood as Argentina's answer to Aunt Jemima or Uncle Ben, assuring the buyer that the product in hand was meant to serve, and to serve happily. Baker's campaign for Bieckert was distinctly different. "Delicious and Refreshing Black Beer," confirms the ad in a modernist scrawl. At the center, enveloped in lush banana leaves, is Josephine, short hair slicked down and neatly parted, with her hoop earrings and nail polish perfectly in place. Her flirty smile and direct gaze, though, are aimed at a long, tall glass filled with black beer, its upper rim flaring outward. As she looks and smiles, she is caressing it sensually. If the original symbol of Cerveza Africana was a servile black woman, in this quite different image Baker was instantly recognizable as a celebrity—as *the* Josephine Baker—with an affect that was less servile than sexual, less satisfying than arousing. Delicious and refreshing, perhaps. But also tempting and risqué.

Arriving in late 1952, Baker found a country in mourning, still suffering the loss of Eva Perón. In June of that same year, Argentine voters had returned Juan Perón to power along with his beloved partner. In the victory parade, Evita, fading and seriously ill, had relied on a hastily constructed support stand, hidden under a fur coat, to enable her to wave to the adoring crowds. Women had voted for the first time in a national election and, in a richly symbolic move, Evita had been named "spiritual leader" for Argentina—*la jefa espiritual de la nación*. And then in late July she had passed away, a victim of rapidly progressing cervical cancer. In a series of carefully choreographed and sincere commemorations, Argentina wept, nourishing a new and durable myth of Evita as the patron saint of the lower classes and dispossessed children—the *descamisados,* as they were known—of the city and the countryside.

After the recently widowed Juan Perón attended her opening performance at the Opera Theatre, Baker was invited to the Casa Rosada, the executive mansion, for a private meeting. What followed was a ritualistic tour of Argentina. In early October she presented herself to Raúl Apold, subsecretary of information, and knelt to place a bouquet of flowers before an altar and a statue of "la presidenta" that had been set up in the lobby of the General Confederation of Labor's building. Access to Evita's sacred body—which was then being embalmed three floors above the lobby—was strictly forbidden, given government concerns about theft, which were driven by a widespread public faith in the body's miraculous healing power. As days turned to weeks, Baker collected information about the work of the Fundación Eva Perón. She visited a dormitory and paid public homage to "la señora." In her performances, she featured some of Perón's favorite designers—Dior, Fath, and others—and stressed her "nueva manera," her strengthening public image as a stylized Latin singer as comfortable in Spanish as in French and English. Within a few months she had informally taken over some of Evita's duties at the Foundation and was drawing support from Juan Perón for her antiracist association, which now aimed to stamp out racial prejudice in the New Argentina.[11] From that point, Baker and Juan were linked in a strange partnership, their attacks aimed at injustice very broadly defined, the two of them champions of a generic downtrodden class.

Perón needed a symbol and Baker needed a platform, and the two found common cause in attacking the United States as a false prophet of democracy. "The United States is not a free country," she said; "this is the naked truth about racial and religious discrimination."[12] She called for "love, understanding, and brotherhood," for "freedom of thought and respect for the thoughts of others," as if those things were entirely absent in North America. Drawing a contrast to the workings of Jim Crow, she romantically confessed that "if I loved someone, I wouldn't waste a second thinking about what race he was, or what color he had, or what religion he practiced."[13] If Baker was guilty of anything, it was largely a matter of speaking plainly and without nuance. The local headlines reflected her habit of speaking in simple, blunt terms, with broad brushstrokes, about the effect of racism on children ("Discrimination always annihilates the innocents") and on the quotidian experiences of everyday people ("People of color don't get hospitality at Yankee hotels").[14]

A hemispheric back-and-forth erupted. The Peronist press showered her with adoring headlines, calling her a "valiant paladin."[15] Perón's Ministry of Information provided a translation for her speeches, which were delivered in English, and that translator may well, as Mary Dudziak suggests, have creatively added emphasis. Still, it seems entirely plausible that Baker would say, as one press report suggests, that she felt "sorry for the people who live in the United States." "The United States," she continued, "is not a free country. I do not envy those who have to live there. I feel only compassion for those who live on its soil and admiration for those who struggle under such terrible circumstances."[16] African Americans, she claimed, were treated "like dogs."[17] When Baker's intemperate words earned her fuller local coverage in Argentina than the results of the 1952 American presidential election, the mainstream press in the United States cried foul.[18] A day later, and only a few weeks after singing to packed houses, rumors abounded that the State Department would bar her from reentry.[19] All of this, the Peronist press reported back in Argentina, was damning proof of racism and hypocrisy up north.[20]

The African American press, for the most part, steered clear of the mess. When one reader begged the *Amsterdam News* to report something—*anything*—so that the story wasn't simply dominated by the views of the white press, the editor of the *News* responded by noting that "the source of the current commentaries" was highly questionable.[21] Few wanted to repeat Baker's wide-ranging critique or to debate a set of Cold War talking points. Her figurative language—"not a free country," "treated like dogs"—resonated deeply in Harlem, but it was dangerous stuff, the sort of language that led to jail or worse.

After all, when black figures spoke out, their intemperate speech always led to punishment. As a consequence of Walter Winchell's unceasing character assaults and the negative coverage of her speeches in the American press, Baker began receiving death threats. "I fear no one," she responded, "and I have the courage to preach my beliefs."[22] Her exhortatory speech matched the emerging model of radical Cold War–era black American protest, in which an increasingly vocal group of African American activists and public figures tried to highlight the inconsistencies of its courtship of newly independent African, Asian, and Caribbean nations and its preservation of Jim Crow. As a consequence, many of these activists were silenced, challenged, and marginalized by federal, state, and local authorities, and by their supporters in the more conventional mainstream press. When Baker claimed that she'd seen "lynchings and electrocutions," she inadvertently opened herself up to the charge of fabrication, even though she'd seen a man killed on death row, had traveled the country as an active participant in the movement, and had read deeply in national news coverage of race relations.[23] She *had* seen such things, but they weren't described that way within the United States. A lynching, according to the grammar and syntax of that country, didn't happen in a courthouse, it happened outside of the law. And what Baker called an electrocution was, the same logic dictated, merely a form of criminal justice. In any case, as a French citizen since 1937, she was beyond the reach of American officials, but these provocations were so dangerously candid that the State Department nevertheless had her followed around in Buenos Aires and received regular reports of her speeches, workshops, and performances.

Black silence about radical speech and action, though, was a tacit admission of agreement. So every African American critique of Jim Crow hypocrisy required a "sane" response from someone else in Harlem. Thus did Congressman Adam Clayton Powell, whose civil rights work in the House mirrored much of what Baker had done offstage while on tour, quickly label the performer a foreigner. "The fight for equality of colored people is a tough one," he said in a statement after the State Department verified Baker's words, but "Miss Baker has not shared in this fight through the years at all. We do not need anyone to lie about the situation." Her words in Argentina, he continued, were a poor repayment for the hospitality she had so recently enjoyed. On her recent tour, Powell noted, she'd been well supported by her fans, "even though she had gotten to the place in her public career when she was no longer a great drawing card." Calling her a "manufactured Joan of Arc," Powell challenged her public relations claim that "she was the first and only one to fight for desegregation," providing a list of other notable African American artists who had done so, including his wife, the talented musician Hazel Scott.[24]

Of course, Powell's public shaming of Baker wouldn't change anything: within the decade, his wife, whom he touted as the real thing next to the false La Baker (and who, ironically, was a participant in Harlem's "Josephine Baker Day") would also flee to Paris.[25]

In Buenos Aires, this dispute made for great public relations. "In Argentina," one local headline read, attributing the phrase to Baker, "there wasn't just talk of democracy, there was also the practice of it."[26] Still, for Josephine Baker—French scold and American critic—Argentina wasn't without racial context. For a long time prior to Baker's visit, the country had reveled in its reputation as a *crisol de razas,* a white nation without any substantial black population. Baker was a racially marked subject of analysis, an object of great curiosity, in an Argentina that valued Evita's light skin and bottle-blond hair. The local advertisements for *"la 'vedette' de color"*—meaning, roughly, a star performer of great renown and charisma—featured Baker as a slender, elegant figure in a long evening gown with white gloves, Baker with hands held aloft in a graceful pose, and an actual photo of La Baker in her Latin American phase. They stand in sharp contrast to Argentina's version of Aunt Jemima, the squat, darker, kerchiefed, open-mouthed mammy figure who announced a big sale at Harrods. But they are also distinct from Evita's transformation into the Madonna. Reviews of Baker's various performances emphasized joy, sadness, and the unpredictability of "la Opera Josefina." Baker had, one reviewer opined, "el decorado sintético," a cosmopolitan nostalgia and synthetic aesthetic, infused with sensibilities of faraway port cites, distant trading posts, isolated tropical islands, and the ramshackle cabins of the Mississippi delta.[27] Baker called Argentina the true democracy in the hemisphere, but her skin tone and manner were analyzed regularly for racial content.

She surely stood out. Legend has it, looking around the Argentine landscape, that she asked Minister Ramón Carillo, who was biracial, "Where are the Negroes?" To which Carillo glibly replied: "There are only two, you and I."[28] Still, despite this rumored absence, blackness loomed large in the Argentine mind, an imagined reference point for any one person's whiteness. Black bodies were present in advertisements, just as they were in the United States and France. Black dolls were common, and haunting portraits of young children holding black dolls can today be found in any open-air market, stuffed into shoeboxes amid collections of old postcards and lost personal photos. In speech and in culture, blackness was regularly invoked in the negative, as a personal slander or to denigrate a class, workers, or, when it was used against the Peronistas, the working-class supporters of a political movement.[29] That Baker was understood as black—but not just, or merely, or typically, black—would have given her a distinctive political resonance, especially in the age of Perón.

As she moved through Buenos Aires, the spectacle of Evita—a woman with a scandalous past—lingered in her mind. "I think Mrs. Perón is my spiritual sister," she mused in one speech to her new Argentine public, "in the same way that I think you are. We are all brothers, we are children of God." "I respect and admire what she did for her people," she concluded, "and if I had the possibility of doing so, I would go around the world helping the poor in the same way she did here, in your country."[30]

Like Baker, Evita was globally famous. Her "Rainbow Tour" of Europe in 1947 was an unqualified success and culminated in a five-day stay in Paris, including a dinner with French president Vincent Auriol and a shopping trip with Madame Bidault, wife of another hero of the Resistance. The New Argentina was a strange amalgam of social justice populism and authoritarian fascism, and Evita was its public face. Europe and the United States were fascinated. "With her attractive appearance and evident charisma," Victoria Allison writes, "Evita was a spectacle; she proved that politics and Christian Dior could co-exist in (and on) the same body. . . . [H]er glamorous image became a commodity: it sold the . . . tabloids, photo-journal magazines, and gossip columns that made her story easily accessible to a mass audience."[31] While in Europe, Evita stressed that the rainbow—later to be the designated childlike symbol of Baker's fairy-tale family—was a variegated bridge joining two places, a symbol of multiculturalism. "I come as a rainbow between our two countries," she offered to the Spanish press.[32] *Time* called her an "Argentine rainbow" and a "Cinderella"; "shimmering with a new change of clothes at every appearance," the magazine purred, "coruscating with glittering jewels, shapely, brown-eyed Eva [is] unbeatable."[33] Through her own efforts and those of others, she was transformed into a dazzling, streaking metaphor both for cross-national connection and for harmonious cross-class collaboration. As such, she cut across the darkened, post–WWII European sky at precisely the moment when Josephine Baker was planning her soon-to-fail tour of the United States, struggling to stay relevant, to keep her flagging career afloat, and combating rumors that she had died during the war.

Baker's "infatuation with Eva Perón seems inevitable," writes one of her biographers, Phyllis Rose. "Both Josephine and Evita did things on a large scale with no thought to accounting; to both, it seemed mean-spirited to question where the money to fund their charities was coming from. Both were actresses, both had come from terrible poverty, both loved the poor with the sincerity of identification, and possibly, with their ditsy charities and mad display, spoke better to the fantasy life of those they aimed at helping than more efficient but imaginatively arid government programs."[34] Perón and Baker each had overcome hardscrabble beginnings, adored fine clothes, and appreciated the trappings of privilege, the symbolism of motherhood, and the orchestrations of celebrity. And, as Rose concludes, "Evita, with her luxury hotels for working women, her luxury resorts, where poor people were housed for a while before being shunted back to poverty, thought in terms that Josephine . . . could understand."[35]

Neither was able to have children. And Evita, anticipating Baker, turned that to her advantage. Her "real children," she argued in her autobiography, "were those she protected—the poor, the old, and the helpless of Argentina."[36] Seated behind the desk in her office, Evita, often dressed in haute couture, would receive lepers, the syphilitic, union leaders, mothers with children, and exiles from around the world. With patience, deep pockets, and a good measure of stagecraft, she offered herself up to the lowest citizens of her country and became "the ideal mother."

The agency responsible for this public image was the Fundación María Eva Duarte de Perón, a vast enterprise headquartered just a few blocks from the Casa Rosada. Funded by lottery taxes and large donations—some of them the result of arm-twisting—the Fundación played an outsized role in Argentinian society, building hospitals and schools and cities. Through it, Evita became the charismatic face of a very unique form of socialism in which spectacular, if largely symbolic, examples of wealth redistribution by the state were re-imagined as charitable work by a foundation. She received members of the public regularly, bestowing patronage and good fortune, giving funds, troubleshooting local problems, and even laying her hands on the sick to heal them. In return, she expected obedience and re-spect, if not adulation, and from her much beloved working poor, she typically received all of those things. In the wake of her death, she was beatified, rendered in print with a symbolic golden halo in front of children kneeling in prayer.[37]

This motherhood by state was a key feature of one of Evita's most popular creations: the Ciudad de los Niños, or the Ciudad Infantil. A miniature city built for poor children just outside of Buenos Aires, a fantasy sleep-away camp for the destitute, it featured tiny gas sta-tions and libraries and town halls, and offered an idealized approxi-mation of civic life in a community where every noble occupation was supposed to be respectably working-class and where the truly rich were villainized. Coming to the Ciudad was an escapist fantasy, like willingly entering a delusory photo op, allowing a child to be seduced by the promise of opportunity and to become a part of the vast promotional machine of Peronismo.

"In the New Argentina," Juan Perón once said, "the only privi-leged ones are the children." This was one of the "twenty truths of Justicialism"—the official name of Perón's political philosophy—and it is likely that Baker heard it over and over again during her six months in that country. One can imagine Josephine, isolated by the Cold War, considering her next move in Buenos Aires, so reminiscent of Paris, surrounded by mammoth, hagiographic billboards featuring her "sister" Evita, noting the broad social impact of Perón's efforts to establish orphanages and shelters for unwed mothers, to be the mother of this New Argentina.[38] She was "fascinated by the legend of Eva," Rose writes, largely because it seemed to mirror her own rags-to-riches story, and because of a parallel fascination with jewelry, fine clothing, and art.[39] But this identification with Evita was not merely about the trivialities of high fashion and biographical parallels: it was also rooted in a cagey recognition that Evita's political work offered Baker, now a savvy warrior in a human rights campaign, a model for new engagement with the politics of inequality.

It is impossible to know whether Baker began to feel the subtler sting of racism in Buenos Aires or whether she simply began to see past the glittering spectacle of Evita and to acknowledge the less-than-perfect record of the Peronistas in matters of social justice. "She was growing tired of playing understudy to the memory of Evita," her son writes, "and tired of the general, who spent his leisure chasing thirteen-year-old girls."[40] Lynn Haney, another biographer, suggests that Baker strayed from the prescribed tour and found the dark, subterranean world of the truly poor and disadvantaged in Juan Perón's Argentina.[41] Or perhaps, having figured out what she wanted to do, she was ready to get down to the business of actually doing it. In any case, something hastened her exit.

It is interesting to think of Baker in Buenos Aires, surrounded by flower-draped memorials to the recently departed patron saint of the *descamisados,* kneeling in front of Evita, stepping in to manage the maternalist state apparatus developed by the Peróns, and plotting her forthcoming domestic assemblage. And it is fascinating to see the world's first African American superstar find, in Evita's Fundación and in the Ciudad de los Niños, a model for her colorful family of refugees. It is intriguing to note how Baker, once back in France, began to sound like Evita, to talk about children as political symbols, as wards of the state, and to imagine the supervision and display of children as political acts. Here, ready for our interrogation but hidden from plain sight, are the Latin American roots of Josephine Baker's Les Milandes.

Her autobiography is, once again, especially unhelpful. But for a single, brief fragment written in 1953, there is no mention therein of Justicialism, Evita, the Ciudad de los Niños, or the half year spent in that other Paris. Neither she nor Jo Bouillon writes of the nighttime performances at the majestic opera houses of Buenos Aires, nor do either of them comment on her quite public agitation in São Paulo, Rio, and Buenos Aires against Jim Crow America. Despite her creation of a new global antiracist organization and the controversy that enveloped her and derailed her dreams of a television show, a movie, and a nightclub, there is nothing to find. The story of her life reads as if the scoring accusations of racial terror she offered in Brazil and Argentina never happened. Instead, there is a simple elision, a sliding step—a dancer's move turned into prose—from the wintertime Winchell affair in late 1952 to the springtime arrival in Les Milandes nearly a year and a half later. We are supposed to watch her jump and ignore the ground she sails over.

Elsewhere in the autobiography she is even more deceptive. In a fragment written many years later, Baker suggests that when Ned Schuyler, the owner of the Copa City club in Miami, had first approached her about coming to the United States for a tour, she immediately told him of her plans to adopt a family from around the world, a multicolored tribe of orphans. But there is nothing to confirm this. Not a single press release, newspaper story, or piece of private correspondence exists to suggest that this was so.

The simple truth is this: before Argentina, Baker was planning a life onstage, in film, on the radio, and on television, but afterward she was rapidly orchestrating an ensemble of children. Something had changed.

The reason for this omission—the burial of her time in Argentina, and the emphatic emphasis on other moments and places—is important, too. In 1952, Argentina seemed to Baker like an oasis in a rapidly dividing world. It was free of the Cold War polarities that had hamstrung her in New York. Juan Perón seemed like a sincere social democrat, committed to the same set of ideals, to the principles of universal brotherhood and racial equality. He also appeared committed to the memory of Evita, with whom Baker felt some close kinship. By the time Baker died, Perón's legacy had been soiled and the man himself had been revealed as a ruthless, autocratic despot. Her beloved Buenos Aires had become a war zone. And Evita's body—in front of which Baker had so religiously knelt—had been stolen away by the Argentine military.

Leaving while Perón was near the height of his global reputation, Baker found her return to the Dordogne difficult. She stopped in Havana, the wellspring of such good fortune, including her invitation to the Copa City in 1951. But she found herself harassed by the police and stonewalled out of her hotels of choice. Though she appeared at the local radio station, she was prevented from performing there, and had to settle for an old movie house. Her bad luck got worse fast. She tried to meet with President Batista but was passed off to someone else. She went onstage to perform and was arrested soon afterward. Charged as a Communist, she was photographed and fingerprinted, and the story made the international newspapers the next day.[42]

Soon afterward, she was headed back to Europe. And then, like a woman on a mission, she began to build something.

Historians have struggled to make sense of what came next for Baker. Many who study the civil rights movement dismiss her as unserious and uncommitted, simply shifting their focus to the traditionally heroic narratives of legal triumphs, marches, voter registration drives, and federal legislation. Baker's "ultimate embrace of domesticity as the locus of her politics in the late 1950s," Dudziak suggests, was a rushed retreat from formal activism and entertainment, and a direct consequence of her blacklisting. Just as "American women were forced out of the factory and into the maternity wards," she continues, so was "Baker blacklisted out of the international entertainment circuit" and contained "within French borders."[43] The very few scholars to scrutinize Baker in this moment, then, seem to have written her off, imagining that she was ruined by the Winchell affair, her political options limited to the fanciful and the strange. Baker, Dudziak admits, "was an international star who lived in a castle, who wore Dior gowns in concert, and whose most radical political idea seems to have been a hope that the world might someday live in racial harmony."[44]

We would do well to rethink what radicalism means if our current formulations cannot comfortably contain both black civil and human rights efforts and Baker's statist orchestration of the multiracial family as equally important provocations. When we measure Baker against the well-documented goals of the civil rights movement, she slips out of our timeline—out of what we might call "civil rights time." This doesn't help us understand anything, except of course those things that are conventional, standard, easy to see and describe. Forget what you know about periods, then. Let your landscapes get big. If nothing about what Baker did next makes sense, it is because we have grown used to telling one kind of story about one kind of struggle with one kind of outcome. The villain is always at the top of the social ladder. The little guy is always the hero. And the struggle is always over a fair deal, a level playing field, access to the basic necessities of life and citizenship. Whatever its political goals, Les Milandes was deeply and self-consciously rooted in a very antidemocratic history. It is not easy to knit Baker's celebration of the Benetton future into the flow of civil rights time. Imagine Josephine Baker as an example of the history of human rights, of the history of motherhood, and of the powerful history of celebrity. Imagine that the point of writing and reading new international stories isn't merely to reproduce the periods established within national histories as globally relevant but to provide as well new eras to match the new mappings of time and space and change. Imagine the girl with the castle as the heroine.

The question for Baker, in the context of the 1950s and 1960s, wasn't whether Jim Crow could be toppled but whether a better world for everyone everywhere was possible. The latter was bigger and more abstract, but it was every bit as central to the moment. And, discordantly, she wondered whether her fame and her skills could serve a humanitarian social purpose and still allow for limousines, castles, and jet-setting. These were questions that Evita had already answered in the affirmative. Baker's consideration of those answers, coming after her half year in Argentina, brought her to Les Milandes and to the Rainbow Tribe and forced her away from the heroic, small-bore self-sacrificial tactics and strategies of the civil rights movement. She had, her friend Donald Wyatt recalls, a "stake in the system."[45] But that didn't mean that she was going to take a bus with John Lewis from Alabama to Mississippi. She defined the system differently. Her formal civil rights efforts were constrained and awkward—fighting for equal treatment at the exclusive Stork Club, pushing to have pricey tickets in Las Vegas made available to black clientele. Symbolic gestures and, but for their immediate historical backdrop, no more and no less radical than Oprah Winfrey's desire to shop at Hermès at any hour of the day or to open a $40 million leadership academy in South Africa. When one close friend was told by an American official that Baker might be a Communist, the friend was "stunned": "I had never heard anything so ridiculous. She owned a castle!"[46] What, Baker, wondered, was the point of equality of opportunity for everyone without first class for some?

In the only piece of her autobiography from this moment, written just a few months after her return to France and after the announcement of her intention to build a family from the debris of war and poverty, Baker reminds us of the bigger stakes. Reaching London in the early summer, in time for the coronation of the young Queen

Elizabeth, she found herself routinely visiting Hyde Park, famed for its soapbox orators, where a few speakers—"men of color"—were gathered in a lonely protest against apartheid in South Africa. Intrigued, she went to Parliament to hear a daylong debate on "the South African Question." New legislation was sweeping across South Africa as the apartheid state emerged and refined its vast segregation of white, black, brown, and yellow: the Prohibition of Mixed Marriages Act of 1949, the Immorality Amendment Act of 1950, the Bantu Education Act of 1953, the Reservation of Separate Amenities Act of 1953. It was enough to cripple anyone's positive outlook. Baker, though, was inspired by the speakers in Hyde Park. If, she mused, "colored people, who covered three quarters of the globe, could band together, couldn't it bring about the extinction of the white race?" Divining the future, and echoing her speech in São Paulo at the Biblioteca Mário de Andrade, she thought that soon "people will mingle more quickly and easily until racial purity gradually disappears. But I'd like to see this happen through love and not hate."[47]

"I am very tired after four years of fighting," she added, dating the start of her revolutionary work to the creation of the new La Baker. Her globe-trotting work on behalf of justice and equality had come as the world tilted in the other direction, as the forces of massive resistance and racism rose up. Still, she was confident. "I'm convinced that I can realize my dream because I believe in the dignity of man. Jo and I plan to adopt four little children: red, yellow, white, and black. Four little children raised in the country, in my beautiful Dordogne. They will serve as an example of true Democracy, and be living proof that if people are left in peace, nature takes care of the rest."[48]

5

Ambitious Assemblages

I want you to find me a little baby, a purebred Japanese.

—Josephine Baker (1953)

In early 1953, *Le Monde* reported that Baker was on the verge of becoming "the mother of a family of all colors." "Joséphine Baker," the headline read, "adopte une famille panachée." Speaking to the press corps from Monte Carlo, Baker described her new family of adopted children, drawn to France from around the world, but especially from the global South—from Southeast Asia, from North and West Africa, from Latin America. Describing Baker as "an ardent proselyte of the antiracial struggle," the paper emphasized the political function of the family, noting that the children would be "raised like brothers," though each would also "maintain the language, the dress, the customs and the religion of his/her country." "I will make every effort so that each shows the utmost respect for the opinions and beliefs of the other," Baker claimed, and "through the example of these children developing according to their nature, I want to show people of color that not all whites are cruel and mean. I will prove that human beings can respect each other if given the chance."[1]

Une famille panachée. A mixed, colorful, impressive, exciting family. Not merely a diverse family, but also a showbiz family, meant for the stage and the spotlight, not for the private realm of the domestic.

A family conceived by a cagey, theatrically inclined superstar with a refined political platform, considerable experience in protest work, and a unique, international perspective.

By the end of that year, Baker had settled some of the children into her restored château in Castelnaud-Fayrac. The eager partnership of her husband, the pliant and accompanying bandleader Jo Bouillon, made it easier for her to adopt.[2] There, amid the crumbling medievalism and nationalist tourism of the Dordogne region, "Jo et Jo" would raise a family in which each child was presumed to be a representative of some perfect racial type. "She wanted all races, all religions," a family friend once recalled, "and she would give them the religion she wanted on the spot."[3] All of the children, in the end, would be racial exemplars, stereotypes brought to life and on proud display in Baker's well-intentioned "Village of the World." Bound together by her, this diverse group would be as brightly colored as a rainbow and, at the start, completely subservient to her wishes. In the first few years of the creation, the press would struggle to describe the Tribe, on one hand celebrating it as a fantastic family of all colors with Baker as mother and on the other describing it as "an interracial experiment" managed by the human rights activist Baker as a distant caretaker.[4]

Her appearance at the press conference wasn't impulsive. Her conviction that this was absolutely the right thing to do wasn't merely about capriciously satisfying a personal whim or questing for the spotlight. It was also about changing the beat of the conversations about race, rights, and revolution. She had spent almost a year in the United States, fighting a just war against Jim Crow. Badly framed by Cold War rhetoric, blackballed, adrift in the circum-Caribbean, and even arrested in Cuba, she'd headed to the deeper Americas, where she'd studied the nexus of statecraft, motherhood, and leadership. Her decision to adopt a multitude of children, representing a variety of races and religions, was, then, a logical extension of her life after WWII, not a great break or a radical departure. It flowed from many factors—her civil rights work, her knack for reinvention, her interest in ensemble, her sojourn in the New Argentina. When we know all this, it makes *sense*.

The specific form of the family—apostolic in scale, variegated in skin tone, global in orientation—required a careful construction. This would be a theatrical revue in miniature. So let us take some time to explore how and why she broke ground on this family, this assemblage meant to reveal to a watchful public a certain amount of meaningful flamboyance, style, and color. To understand what is unique about Baker's Rainbow Tribe—and what isn't—we need to survey the remarkable moment when the zeitgeist of the postwar era encouraged new social and cultural formations that were strikingly multiracial and multinational, sensational phenomena meant to dazzle the eye and provoke a new politics.

Writing to her friend Miki Sawada in May 1953, Baker spelled out her plans for a visit to Japan in July. After addressing some logistics of the upcoming trip, she got to the heart of the matter: she wanted Sawada to prepare for her arrival by finding her a son. "I want you," she said, with great specificity, "to find me a little baby, a purebred Japanese, a little boy of two years I can adopt." "Because," she continued, "I will adopt five small boys of two years each," including a "dark-skinned black" from South Africa ("un noir de race noire"), "an Indian from Peru, a Nordic, and an Israelite." "These small children will be like brothers, live together as a symbol of democracy." There was more, of course. She asked for a copy of "his papers," wished that he have a typically Japanese name, and also asked for "a little Japanese wardrobe," because she "want[ed] that little child to live in his national costume and not to forget his ancestors in my homeland."[5]

There is nothing impetuous about the request, though it grates on the modern ear. Her emphasis on purity of type—drawing on conventional classifications of the five principal races of mankind—seems clear-eyed and strategic. Her desire for all boys, who would be "brothers," matched her emphasis on fraternity and removed any chance that her assemblage might be seen, as the children aged, as an endorsement of interracial romance. Her need for a two-year-old child and not a newborn hints at a desire to have a child more gregarious, more photo-ready, with a revealing personality, a child ready to do public relations work, in a way. And her desire for papers and a "little Japanese wardrobe" and a Japanese name suggests that she wanted the work to commence immediately. Tellingly, she didn't ask Sawada to find her a happy child or a child with an ebullient personality, just as she didn't ask for a healthy child or for a child with a dramatic life story. In this first request, her emphasis is entirely on race, costuming, and performance.

Baker's burgeoning ensemble is a challenging artifact to locate in the histories of adoption, the family, and childhood, and much of the difficulty flows from the performer herself. While most histories have stressed the shifting conceptions of "nature," "kin," and "fit," none features celebrity enough—as a concept or in the form of a specific person—to include the Rainbow Tribe, and none makes allowances for a family headed—symbolically, politically—by a black woman, famous beyond measure, who spent a lifetime blurring the meaning of these same concepts *before* she decided to have a family. And while we have good and well-written chronicles of the transnationally adopted family as a policy problem or as a consequence of uneven foreign relations, these works are less useful in this case because of Baker's own acute and enduring cosmopolitanism—her shifting movements within and between nations, her appropriation of different racial and colonial identities for herself, and her often overlapping citizenship and rights-based claims. In these adoptions, she does not represent France or the West so much as she represents her own, very unique social position. She represents her own celebrity. As a wealthy woman with a disdain for rules and as a black woman in an age of extraordinary racial controls, Baker's assemblage often slipped loose of the larger, global story of the increasing regulation and oversight of adoption by nongovernmental organizations and governmental agencies, in which the rights of birth parents and the rights of children were increasingly safeguarded.

Miki Sawada was a longtime friend and supporter, having met Baker before the war through her husband, Renzo Sawada, later to be a diplomat assigned to the United Nations. The granddaughter of Baron Iwasaki, the paterfamilias of Mitsubishi, she became involved in the care and adoption of war orphans—chiefly mixed-race orphans, assumed to be outcasts in Japan because of their impure birth—after a fabled encounter in which she was wrongly accused of abandoning such a child. In that apocryphal story, as she sat down on a train, the body of a dead child wrapped up in newspaper and stored in the luggage rack above her dropped into her lap. "I feel the weight of that dead baby," she later recalled, "on my knees forever."[6] She proved her innocence, the story goes, but was shaken enough by the symbolism of that small, mortal body to subsequently found an orphanage, and to use her considerable connections to benefit the children produced, literally, as a by-product of the American occupation and then cast aside as junk. In 1948 she founded the Elizabeth Saunders Home, named after an Englishwoman who had served as a longtime governess in her family before becoming, once the family's fortunes suffered a reversal after the war, a personal patron to Sawada. After appealing for a restoration of sorts, Sawada established the home in an old family property and turned it into a node in the same network that eventually included novelist, Asia expert, Nobel Prize winner, and adoptive parent Pearl Buck, whose Welcome House adoption agency was founded only a year later.

Beyond her family connections, Sawada's orphanage benefited from a remarkable sea change in the way many people in the United States and in Europe thought about adoptions. Before the war, or- phanages, often run by the Catholic Church or the state, emphasized racial consanguinity, placing white children in white homes. That emphasis was a partial consequence of an increase in regulation in the twentieth century, as professional agencies with a social scientific interest replaced the loose, informal, local exchanges of the Gilded Age. Slowly this concern about finding the "right" home for any specific child, with racial "fit" being one of several categories used in this assessment, was replaced by a desire simply to find a loving environment.[7] The Elizabeth Saunders Home, which aimed to place mixed, illegitimate children halfway around the world in white, middle class, Christian families, was at the cutting edge of this revolution.

Because she emphasized the protection of "GI babies"—mixed-race progeny with white or black American fathers—Sawada surely raised an eyebrow at Baker's request for a "pure" Japanese type, but she continued to send Baker pictures of children, a part of her quest to find homes for all children under her care. "Every day," Baker wrote to Sawada in December, acknowledging the power of their story, "I look at the photographs of the children."[8] Only a few weeks later, serving as an "international delegate to the world rally against racism" organized by Bernard Lecache's Ligue internationale contre le racisme et l'antisémitisme, she described her motivations for years of struggle in a lecture, "Why I Fight Against Racism."

Baker had many plans for her stay in Tokyo in the late spring of 1954. She hoped to create a rich, media-friendly environment for her dramatic receipt of the child. With an eye on Sawada's orphanage—and her own fledgling anti-racist group, the World Cultural Association—Baker encouraged organizers to "sell my name in any commercial enterprise," to "take advantage of my visit to Japan to get the most for our organizations." She lobbied for time on radio and television. Finally, she asked them to arrange for public lectures on racial and religious discrimination. Her trip would not be a simple domestic excursion, aimed at the adoption of a child. The events that took place were to be public and revenue-generating—"des spectacles payant"—with all proceeds donated to the Elizabeth Saunders Home, a generous donation meant to commemorate the start of a new chapter in her life and in the struggle against racism.[9]

Onstage, she was as dynamic as ever. In late April she gave twice-daily performances at the whitewashed Imperial Theater in Tokyo, all for the benefit of the orphanage. As usual, there were costume changes and sumptuous gowns, along with an ever-changing song list, including not merely "chansons de Paris" but also a selection of Latin American music. She dressed, in one spectacular number, as a geisha. Wearing Sawada's daughter's kimono, which was decorated with flower blossoms, leaves, and arched stems, and with her hair bound up with flowers, she held a ceremonial fan in one hand behind her, illuminating the curtain and reminding the audience of her official international location, was the outline of the Eiffel Tower.[10]

This cool, tactical approach to the assemblage of the Rainbow Tribe runs deep underground, far below the sentimental surface exposed in Baker's autobiography. In her deceptive, challenging, fragmentary memoir—the source of many of our troubles—Baker announces the completion of interior renovations at Les Milandes with an innocent, saccharine tone, as if she were a normal housewife readying the house for a new family, a familiar, unsurprising act. "Little beds, little chairs," she lists, archiving the obvious changes, "little dressers, an array of small dishes, a stock of baby things acquired during my tours." Beyond the list making and general preparations, though, she seems nervous about the process of selection. "How would I recognize him?" she asks, giving voice to a universal concern. "How would I know that he was 'the one'?" "I could feel my heart thumping," she recalls, suddenly an everywoman, childless but standing on the threshold of meeting her first infant several thousand miles from home.[11]

Just a short while later, she was in Sawada's orphanage, surrounded by "children with straight black hair and dancing, slanting eyes." Drawn to one small child who was "as supple as a little fish," she asked for his backstory and was told that he was Korean and had been "found beneath an open umbrella that sheltered him from the elements." Named Akio, the child was wearing a small red bag, carrying a decorative plaque "engraved with the precepts of Buddhism." "You won't regret it," Miki told her, endorsing the selection. "He's a sweet loving child." Then, turning to leave, Baker spied "a grave-face baby sitting by a tree." "He was tiny, much smaller than Akio," she remembered, "with solemn eyes." Impulsively, struck by something in the child's gaze, she made the decision to adopt another: "I'll take him too." Named Teruya, he was, she remembers, part Japanese and of the Shinto religion, a complement to the half-Korean, Buddhist Akio. (Once she was back in France, however, she would change this second child's name to Janot, which she found easier to say.)[12] Back in France, as she presented the pair to Jo Bouillon at the Souillac rail station, she was asked by her husband, "Which one is it?" "Both," she answered. "You were right to order a double helping," Bouillon replied, again equating the children with commodities. After taking a moment to catch his breath, he continued, "This way we'll be twice as happy."[13]

Jean-Claude Baker, the biographer, restaurateur, and unofficially adopted "son," tells this story differently. This Jean-Claude (there are two) met Baker long after her initial adoptions when he was fourteen, becoming a chargé d'affaires and sympathetic attendant to the older performer, eventually earning the sobriquet of "son." Akio, he told me over lunch one day, was not the "half-breed" who typified Sawada's orphanage, "not the son of a girl raped or abused, or in love with a white American." His birth mother, fearful of having the infant exposed to the pouring rain, dropped him off at a tobacco shop, asking the proprietors to take care of him until she could return. Not sure what to do, the proprietors turned him over to the Elizabeth Saunders Home, where "fate" (as Baker saw it) intervened.[14] Similar rumors of unwitting theft—a consequence of her wealth and status—haunt her entire assemblage, inflecting it with a troubling, aristocratic air, as if her celebrity elevated her above the concerns of ordinary people and allowed her to pluck any desirable child from any location without checking the provenance, and without regard for normal procedure. Few of the regulatory agencies that exist today to ensure the ethics of international adoption were working back then, and Baker, a superstar, may not have felt bound to them anyway.

She had gone to get one, and returned with two. The gap between the clear-eyed private correspondence requiring a "pure" Japanese baby complete with costume and a more public, "commercial" transcript emphasizing the big-hearted, impulsive embrace of a second child as she was literally walking out the door exposes Baker's complicated inner workings. In private, she approached the entire affair with all the skill of a mechanic, manipulating the specific features she wanted, oiling the press machine that would generate coverage, and keeping her eye squarely on the creation of a new front in the war against racism. In public, though, she displayed a heartbreaking emotional drive to expand the original plan by bringing back a second Asian child to the Dordogne, even though the original conception had called for a quartet or a quintet, each representing a clearly marked color or geopolitical region. Just when she seemed like a cold-blooded realist, plotting to surround herself with racially symbolic child soldiers, she revealed herself to be a passionate idealist, tempted to "take them all," and trying to bridge the distance between her high-stakes political interests and her sentimental, madcap soul.[15] She needed variety, so she produced it. She took two and, despite what she wrote in her brief memoir, simply assigned both boys different national and religious identities.[16] Here and in the day-to-day practice of Les Milandes, she would always struggle to balance her instinct for realpolitik with her unscripted, unrehearsed sentimentality.

The scattered handful of photographs left behind of her eventful two-week stay in Japan shed some fractured light on what actually transpired, but, like a sample of family snapshots, they tell us far more about mood than about the day-to-day happenings: Josephine, holding candy in her hand, chasing Janot while a photographer tries to capture them both. Akio, sitting on Sawada's lap, while Josephine leans in and touches his shoulder, talking to him. Baker, now with two children in her lap, each wearing a robe, sitting before a group of photographers. Baker and Sawada, each holding a child, sitting in the Shinto shrine at the home. Another picture of the same moment, now taken from behind, showing the Shinto priests performing a ritual for the adoption. A group of women, one holding a child, talk while Baker, a small smile on her face, listens. Baker in geisha costume and makeup, animatedly talking to someone. And Baker in profile, seemingly unaware of the camera, her face serious, tired, businesslike, her shoulders slumped. The snapshots capture a woman still at the crest of a movement, righteously railing against racism in public, changing tactics to create a family, "a political experiment," that would continue her good work.

It wouldn't do to just have two children, and certainly not two who were so similar. The creation of *une famille panachée* required diversity that could be easily seen or understood. This was no time for subtlety or nuance. What Baker needed were representative types, human metaphors who could be displayed together for visual contrast, and whose play together could make a bigger point about common humanity and the roots of racism. "She wanted a doll!" Jean-Claude Baker summed it up.[17]

The acquisition of Akio and Janot marked the beginning of a great assemblage. Soon Jarry would join them from Finland, and then Luis from Colombia. In late 1955 the younger Jean-Claude (originally Phillippe) and Moïse arrived. In 1956, Marianne and Brahim, both from Algeria, arrived. Then Koffi came from Côte d'Ivoire and Mara from Venezuela. Poor Noël, found in a trash heap on Christmas Eve, was brought to Les Milandes in 1959. And the last was little Stellina, the diasporic child of a Moroccan émigré to Paris, arriving in 1964. All twelve children, in the end, would be racial exemplars, or stereotypes brought to life. "Akio," Bouillon later said, summarizing the children once they were adults or nearing adulthood, was a typical

Korean, "almond-eyed, sensitive, serious." Jarry, from Finland, was possessed of "Nordic fairness and stamina." Jean-Claude (or Phillippe), "our blond Frenchman," was "blessed with innate equilibrium." Mara, "a full blooded Indian," wanted only to become a doctor "because they are lacking in his native Venezuela." Janot, "the Japanese," was a lover of plants, flowers, and gardening. Brahim, "the son of an Arab," and Marianne, the granddaughter of a *pied noir* and named after the icon of the French Revolution, captured the two sides at war in Algeria. "Dusky Koffi from Abidjan" was suffused with "purity of spirit." Luis, the Colombian, was already married with children by that time, a fecund Latin through and through. Moïse, the Jew, had been instinctively drawn to the business world and was working in hotel management.[18] Within just a few years, a dozen strangers had been brought to Les Milandes, their races and religions—and even their names—redesigned to meet the political needs of the project, their individual identities yoked to conceptions of "family" and "brotherhood" that were as capacious as they were capricious.

In many countries there were few rules to govern international adoptions and certainly no precedent for a black woman adopting across racial lines, so Baker's luck in this ambitious assemblage was contingent on each and every national context. In Japan, she was adopting racially mixed war orphans, a nongovernmental agency had already been set up to facilitate the process, and the state was more than happy to celebrate their departure. Still, she needed to be respectful of the agency's rituals of possession. Her adoptions in France were comparatively easy, for despite the presence of the color line, she was merely a wealthy Frenchwoman adopting an abandoned orphan or otherwise unwanted child.

Everywhere she went, every show she gave, every hospital she visited in between shows, there was the chance of some new addition. Every orphan had a story. In some cases, local law or custom prevented her from adopting. In others, expediency determined a quick grab. As a consequence, the pattern of the adoptions seems at first glance whimsical, as if she compulsively grabbed whatever child was nearby and ran for the airport. And surely there was some compulsion involved, some deeper need to be surrounded by a supportive ensemble. We make a mistake, though, if we read this only as a demonstration of sentiment, as a soft expression of the age before second-wave feminism, when a woman's supposed need to be surrounded by children was a naturalized explanation for just about everything. She made choices, saying "yes" only to a few, for reasons that she felt were rational and politically useful.

Sometimes, too, things didn't work out the way she intended. Her original plans had included a Jewish child, and she labored to procure one, but these plans got scrambled.[19] On tour in Tel Aviv, she approached the office of the welfare minister, Haim Moshe Shapira, about the chance that she might be able to get an Israeli orphan. Hoping for an eight-month old, Baker "promised to bring the child up with a traditional Jewish religious education" before explaining that there would be six other adopted children in the family, each "to be instructed in their respective religions and languages."[20] The adoption, she hoped, would allow her to "educate [the child] in the spirit of peace and brotherhood between peoples." Shapira's spokesman noted that "Miss Baker's humanitarian impulse is appreciated," but then went on to say, "We cannot sanction taking a child away from Israel when great efforts are being made to bring children to Israel." Jewish families from around the world had been offering to adopt Israeli orphans, and they had been turned down, too.[21]

"Josephine was right," Jo Bouillon admitted, "a little Israeli was essential to our Rainbow Tribe." Her return from Israel empty-handed "astonished" him. Usually, her willfulness ensured success. "I explained to the authorities," Baker told him, "that in order for our Rainbow Tribe to have true symbolic value, our children must be raised together." Such explanations did little to change the official Israeli position on out-of-country adoptions, however. Bouillon and Baker ultimately adopted a French orphan she found through Legal Aid—"a dark skinned baby,"

Jo Bouillon recounts, "with a stubborn set to his chin"—assigned him a Jewish identity, and named him Moïse.[22]

She searched as well for a "little red-skinned brother." On tour in the United States, she set out between performances to find a Native American child to complement the existing members of the Tribe. For his part, Jo set about preparing the Tribe for a new addition, for what he imagined would be a "seventh and final son." Bouillon was the day-to-day manager of Les Milandes whenever Baker toured, and it fell to him to pay the bills and preside over the Tribe. But Baker's quest ended in a jail cell, when—for reasons entirely unrelated to her pursuit of another boy—she was charged with smuggling, a consequence of a business relation gone bad and a dispute over her expensive wardrobe, and Bouillon had to rely on friends to bail her out. "We'll find our little Indian eventually," she purred.

In the wake of such failures—or after adopting two children from Japan instead of one—the rationale for the Rainbow Tribe might change a little, and her predictions for the future of the full ensemble might be different, but the basic principle would always remain the same: a racially, religiously, and culturally diverse family, all living together in a castle, the family headed by none other than La Baker, the world's most amazing cosmopolitan.

Jean-Claude Baker points to her African American heritage as the wellspring of this amorphous "family." Margaret Wallace —Josephine's sister—might agree; she pointed to the complex interweaving of "half" relations into a whole family as the "seed" for the Rainbow Tribe.[23] African American history includes a great variety of domestic styles, from traditional two-parent households to expansive, informal arrangements. In the latter case, instances of adoption—nephews and nieces living with uncles and cousins—are not uncommon. Generations of sociologists have described the black family as "broken" or "destroyed" by slavery, simply because it could sometimes be organized differently, but such pejorative descriptions fail to capture the more general commitment to togetherness in the face of powerful, centrifugal structural forces. Baker's childhood in St. Louis featured an absent father, a larger-than-life grandmother, and the ubiquitous Mama Carrie. "Elvira," Jean-Claude recalls, "was born with a price tag on her shoulder, as a child born into slavery . . . the first five years of her life." "Josephine," he adds, cleverly playing with words, "was raised by her adoptive grandmother, the slave."[24] Viewed from this perspective, the Rainbow Tribe seems like an expression of the African American family, which had a history rooted in response to the worst of slavery and racism. Long before the Rainbow Tribe, for instance, Josephine Baker was informally adopting other men and women as "brothers" and "sisters," just as she was herself informally and briefly "adopted" by her grandmother, and just as she would later informally "adopt" Jean-Claude. Half-sisters and half-brothers became "brothers" and "sisters," but so too did friends and lovers. She gave these terms enormous elasticity. For Jean-Claude, this history, along with the presence of Mama Carrie and Josephine's sister Margaret and brother Richard, gave Les Milandes a distinctly African American texture, making the Tribe fit a particular historical tradition, at least when viewed from a certain angle.

Biographer Phyllis Rose, though, notes that Josephine's ensemble was a "rebuke" to the world from which she came. "If Carrie had sent her children out," Rose writes, "her daughter would take children in. If [Josephine and her siblings] had been poor and deprived, these children would be pampered. Where the Martins had been strictly disciplined, these children would never be punished. If there had been differences in skin color that distinguished Josephine from her sisters and brothers no matter what Carrie said, her own children would be so different in color that difference would be the norm."[25] Baker also broke some families even as she remade others. Mama Carrie, brought to Les Milandes after her daughter's visit to St. Louis in 1952, was airlifted away from the world she knew with the same measure of subtlety that would shape Baker's appropriation of the children. Josephine stole her mother, who had been married for years, and left Carrie's husband behind, thinking him much too young for her. And, with a growing brood of children in need of supervision and general attention, she brought Carrie to France out of sheer necessity. Long after Carrie's death, Jean-Claude Baker came into possession of her Bible and found inside a small portrait of the woman's husband, left to twist in the wind in St. Louis. Such presumptive power, wielded with little regard for the feelings of those around her, is an indication of the intoxicating effect of celebrity and an extraordinary political will.[26]

There are other historical traditions in play here, too, other ways of building a family. Within this same midcentury moment, and with just as much drama, a number of other large, symbolically potent families created through adoption had appeared—big, racially diverse families, brought together from the four corners of the earth, trotted out in the public eye, and infused with a political purpose. These internationalist, multiracial families may not have been headed by an expatriate African American superstar, but in many other ways they were quite similar. "We are dying to see the children," Essie Robeson wrote to Josephine, "and we think it is all a marvelous human experiment." "You may be interested to hear," she continued, "that Pearl Buck the novelist is doing something similar on a smaller scale out at her home in Perkasie, Pennsylvania, U.S.A." Buck's assemblage wasn't a precedent for the Rainbow Tribe so much as it was a parallel formation, reminding us that in the postwar era, the spirit of universalism and internationalism was infectious. Baker, for her part, took out a blue pen and carefully circled "Pearl Buck, the novelist," and "Perkasie, Pennsylvania, U.S.A."[27]

In general, these families were American, headed by white parents, and usually relied on a woman to serve as their chief spokesperson. Many of these families were religious, infused with a missionary zeal, and eager to receive the precious exports from places such as Sawada's home. Collateral creations of the Cold War, they addressed the fears and anxieties of an age notable for both, and addressed (if obliquely) strained international relations and warfare on the periphery. Would all of Asia fall to Communism? Where would Africa turn? Could Latin America be kept safe? In soft, highly metaphorical tones, mixed-up families of mixed-up children, many of them brought from the literal war zones of the Cold War, answered these questions positively. Presenting diversity yoked to a common cause, they stressed that everyone, really, could be brought into the Western system. These "U.N. families" were profiled in major magazines, featured in popular autobiographies, and sanctified for their generous, inclusive spirit.

In 1951, for example, *Life* celebrated the "One-Family U.N." of Helen and Carl Doss, a California couple with nine adopted children.[28] Their adoptions focused, as *Life* put it, on "unadoptable" children of "mixed racial parentage," many of them the product of wartime liaisons in the Far East. Stressing the "unwanted" quality of the children, and wagging a finger at the shameful racism of Asia, the public celebration of the Doss family allowed for a celebration of American openness. Much of the press reads today like sanctimonious, patriotic propaganda. A big Christian, American family like that of Helen and Carl Doss was intended as a humanitarian venture, a matter of "rescue," a soft extension of the U.N.'s mission to preserve peace and the dignity of humankind. But *Life* emphasized classic American scenes—including the reciting of the Pledge of Allegiance at school, the reading of prayers in church, and the imposition of fatherly discipline at home—which lent the entire story a deeper political purpose. When Carl invoked "standard Doss discipline," forcing antagonists in some recent conflict to "sit together until willing to kiss and make up," the children may have been representing the various nations of the world brought together in the United Nations, but the parent was a classic American archetype, looming over this diverse and fractious caucus.[29]

Despite the emphasis on absorbing American culture and values, the Doss family—later written about in *The Family Nobody Wanted,*

Helen's 1954 bestseller—was not color-blind.[30] If anything, it was hyperaware of racial difference. In her chronicle of the family's creation, Helen routinely stressed the importance of skin tone, eye shape, and body type. Helen and Carl accented behaviors, mannerisms, and habits that hinted at racial content. Likewise, the photographers at *Life* looked for opportunities to show differing complexions jumbled up together, different bodies working in harmony within a single unit. In order to demonstrate racial inclusion, in other words, such families needed to document racial diversity, needed to show and emphasize difference. In this fashion, these big adopted families helped to create a visual template for today's multiculturalism.

These delicate ensembles also required removal to the rural countryside to heighten the contrast between the past and the future. Miki Sawada, the heroic architect of the Elizabeth Saunders Home and the source of Baker's first two children, understood the looming threat posed by cities. In 1965, years after she sent Josephine home with Akio and Janot, she uprooted those of her "GI babies" who had not yet been adopted and moved them far from everything she knew. Deciding that Japanese society would never welcome them—they were too large, too different-looking, a reminder of a terrible past, and an indicator of an unwanted future—she worried that they would suffer in adulthood as a consequence. Just as imaginative as her friend Josephine, she decided to buy a large parcel of land in Brazil, that rumored great racial melting pot, where mixture might, she thought, be an advantage. She settled them near Belem on a tributary of the Amazon, where she built a dormitory and established a farm for poultry, horse breeding, and tropical fish cultivation. A sizable population of Japanese-Brazilians was nearby—a legacy of the early twentieth century, when an immigration treaty was signed—and Sawada found them to be "of pioneer stock, much more open minded" and "willing to accept my children as neighbors, and as members of their families later through marriage."[31] What the walls of the orphanage could not protect, dense foliage and a national commitment to celebrate miscegenation might.

In a similar vein, the Reverend Jim Jones—once a door-to-door salesman of exotic monkeys, and then a radical religious preacher who urged racial integration as salvation and established the People's Temple—adopted a handful of children of different races in the early 1950s. Like Baker, he used a familiar, happy metaphor, naming his group the "Rainbow Family," but his gospel was increasingly socialist and utopian. Extending his conceptions of "adoption" and "family" to include the members of his church, Jones drew them deeper and deeper into his delusional, charismatic embrace. They traveled by bus from Indianapolis to northern California, where they opened an agricultural commune and immersed themselves in Bay Area radical politics. At once a family, a religious community, and a political movement, Jones's "rainbow" vanguard aggressively agitated for an end to poverty and racial discrimination, for a better world here on earth. Then, to avoid what Jones saw as a looming nuclear apocalypse, they expatriated to the jungles of northwest Guyana, in South America, and carved a multiracial utopia out of the rain forest. The utopia was false, we now know, especially when Jones himself was present, and the colony infamously committed mass suicide in 1978. Still, with its emphasis on racial diversity and political change, the nuclear unit at the heart of the People's Temple shares a lot with Baker's contemporaneous creation.

There is a striking parallel here: two families, each multiracial and international, both of them formed at roughly the same time, imagined as a critique of racism, and requiring sequestration from the harsh realism of the present. In Baker's case, this meant that Les Milandes couldn't be established in Paris. It had to be created in the distant, premodern landscape of the Dordogne, only recently illumi nated by electricity and given running water. Families such as the Rainbow Tribe needed protection from urban spaces, from which all manner of deleterious and riotous forces emanated.

Soon after adopting Akio and Janot, Josephine found herself on a lecture tour in Scandinavia and hoping for a third child. Once the work of building the Tribe had started, it needed to be concluded quickly, so that the point of it all would be clear. She'd settled on Helsinki, Finland, because adoptions were said to be relatively simple there. The state made it easy, she recalled later, for families to place unwanted children into public orphanages without the shameful taint of abandonment. Given Baker's interest in finding a white counterpart for her growing family, Scandinavia—with its clichéd reputation for pale skin, blond hair, and blue eyes—was a logical site. Baker wrote in her autobiography that she began to have the same excited sensations she had had previously. "I wanted to choose from the heart," she said, pausing to reflect on her motives, but when confronted with so many different types—"serious or merry, blond or brunette, delicate or plump"—she found herself looking for details: "What was I looking for? What kind of sign?" Miraculously, a "tow-headed, chubby, pink-and-white baby boy kicked back his covers and held his arms out to me." She had good timing, too, she wrote, because it seemed that the boy was only days away from being turned out of the orphanage.

Another child had been saved or salvaged. Baker renamed him Jarry and had him baptized a Protestant, then brought him back to Les Milandes, where he met his "slant-eyed brothers" and "dark-skinned relatives," who'd arrived from St. Louis to be a part of the great experiment.[32] Though Baker had great plans to educate the children in their native tongues, it proved difficult to keep up Jarry's Finnish, and when he was reunited with his Finnish-speaking birth mother many years later, they needed to speak through a translator.

Baker's autobiography—that confounding commercial transcript—haunts this story line, however. A sincere but often dishonest document, it gives the story of Jarry's adoption a veneer of truth, of heartfelt accuracy. His story, though, was messier than Baker knew. One-year-old Jarry had been placed in the orphanage as a temporary matter, a consequence of an infant sister at home who was very ill. Baker had been guided to the orphanage by a wealthy friend and driven there by Jarry's birth father, an ambitious chauffeur in the midst of a marital dispute with his wife. "My father arranged everything," Jarry says. He tricked his wife into signing release papers for the boy to be adopted. He presented the infant to Josephine as an ideal type. He pocketed the cash for the transaction. He made sure that young Jarry was in just the right place at just the right time, ready to kick off those covers and hold out those arms. "I leaned over the blue-eyed Finn," she remembered, "certain that he was the one." But other forces, scheming for their own ends, had already determined the outcome of that stroll through the orphanage. Hoodwinked to make her "choice," she had unwittingly stolen away a child.

An aging superstar has lost the limelight. She decides, quite suddenly, to adopt a dozen children from around the world. Her serial adoptions come quickly and seem desperate; the family is displayed garishly, publicly, as if to grab attention. If you focus only on her aging—and if you assume, as you shouldn't, but as every *E! True Hollywood Story* instructs, that all aging superstars are desperate to cling to youth and fame—you might guess that the adoptions were compensatory, or even irrational. The story of her family, though, is far more complicated and more ambiguous than what we, as consumers of mass entertainment, have been trained to expect of celebrities as they lose the oxygen of our attention. We expect the spectacle of drugs and alcohol and tabloid excess. We expect the supposed madness of Michael Jackson's Neverland. We are conditioned to want what is prurient, wacky, and off-putting.

The central performance under close scrutiny here is Baker's late-in-life assembly, choreography, and display of a large multiracial adopted family, drawn from around the world, a collection of children she called the "Rainbow Tribe," and which she enacted within an antique château, one of many in the Dordogne region. The creation of the family—which has usually been seen as an ego-driven failure—immediately followed the six months she spent in an Argentina that was still reeling from Evita's recent death. In its details and in its general purpose, the construction of the Rainbow Tribe should be seen as Baker's unusual translation of Evita's social and political work, and not as the last, worst desperate effort of a silver screen has-been. She'd been thinking about building a casino at Les Milandes, or a hotel, or having her own talk show, or making a movie, but then, returning from Buenos Aires, she decided to do something very different with the place. She thought that she might be able to consolidate the best of these ideas, advancing her varied interests and changing the world for the better.

Josephine Baker's Rainbow Tribe tells us something about the history of the family in an age of democratic change and utopian dreams. It focuses our attention on the interior dynamics of families that were constructed to make a political point, featuring children who were significant primarily because of the power of their display. Instead of looking at vast public arenas and policy disputes, it asks us to consider the obliteration of the divide between public and private, and to ponder an intimate domestic imaginary where routine practice carried extraordinary weight, where a family dinner was a media spectacle, and where each little act performed together was a global miracle.

Paul Colin's rendition of the famous banana skirt. (Kharbine-Tapabor/The Art Archive at Art Resource, NY. © 2013 Artists Rights Society [ARS], New York/ADAGP, Paris)

Heterotopia at Les Milandes, from a postcard, ca. 1958. (Author's collection)

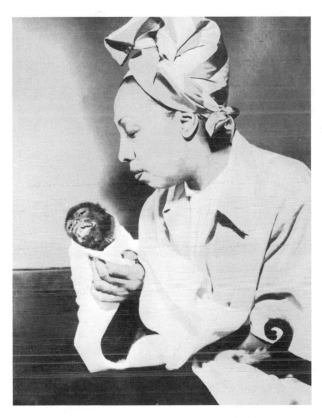

Josephine and one of her many pet monkeys. (AFP/Getty Images)

La Baker, newly reinvented. (Michael Ochs Archives/Getty Images)

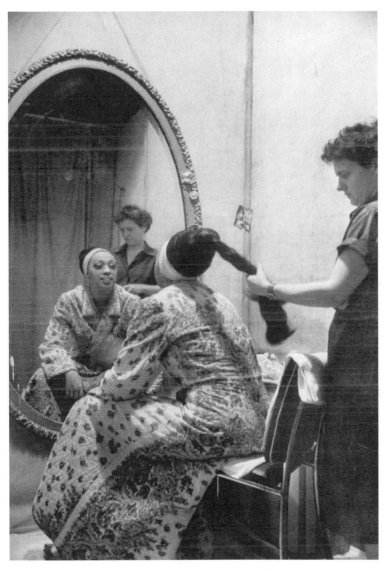

Having her "horse-tail" tended, or, revolution Baker style. (Alfred Eisenstaedt/Time & Life Pictures/Getty Images)

La Baker strikes a balletic pose onstage, wearing a dress emblazoned with her past. The dress is both a reminder of where she'd come from and a declaration of where she was headed. (Willy Rizzo/*Paris Match* Archive/Getty Images)

Josephine, at the Los Angeles County Municipal Court, after pressing charges against a potty-mouthed traveling salesman. (*Los Angeles Times* Photo Archive, University of California, Los Angeles)

Josephine, holding Akio and Janot, at Miki Sawada's compound. (Prints and Photographs Division, Schomburg Center for Research in Black Culture, New York Public Library, Astor, Lenox and Tilden Foundations)

In a geisha costume, during her stay in Japan, with the Eiffel Tower in the background, a reminder of her singular capacity to cross all manner of racial and national boundaries. (Prints and Photographs Division, Schomburg Center for Research in Black Culture, New York Public Library, Astor, Lenox and Tilden Foundations)

Baker with Marianne, Koffi, and Brahim at the Hotel Forresta in Sweden in 1957, a representation of abundance and excess. (AP Photo)

"Jo et Jo" and the children, on a Christmas postcard. The children, all dressed in white, look like presents arranged under the tree, ready for the world to open. (Prints and Photographs Division, Schomburg Center for Research in Black Culture, New York Public Library, Astor, Lenox and Tilden Foundations)

Mocking Jim Crow, Baker and Jarry and a black doll, on the cover of *Nå*, August 30, 1958. Bjørn Fjørtoft, photographer. (Josephine Baker Papers, Manuscripts and Rare Books Library, Emory University/The National Archives of Norway)

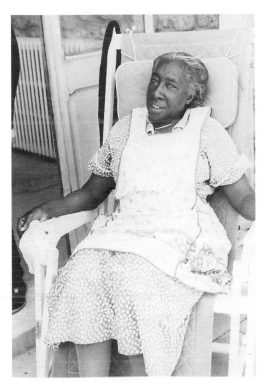

Mama Carrie. (Courtesy of the Spiers Foundation, Paris)

Les Milandes from above, empty and waiting for visitors. You can see the swimming pool in the shape of a J in the background. The Village du Monde would have been off to the right of the château. Postcard, ca. 1955. (Author's collection)

A road sign directing visitors to Les Milandes. (Reporters Associés/Gamma-Rapho/ Getty Images)

Jo et Jo and family, with the tower of the château in the background. (Maurice Zaleweski/Gamma-Rapho/Getty Images)

The Tribe out in the courtyard at play. (Reporters Associés/Gamma-Rapho/Getty Images)

Bringing the children to meet their fans, and introducing the product to its consumer base. (Georges Menager, *Paris Match* Archive/Getty Images)

 le merveilleux linge éponge en

An advertisement, featuring the Tribe, for bath towels. (From the Josephine Baker Collection, Schomburg Center for Research in Black Culture, New York Public Library, Astor, Lenox and Tilden Foundations)

Young Luis at school—a universal image, as resonant in France as in the United States. (Courtesy of the Jean-Claude Baker Foundation)

With Jo Bouillon gone, Josephine was left with eleven (later twelve) children at Les Milandes. (Keystone-France/Gamma-Keystone/Getty Images)

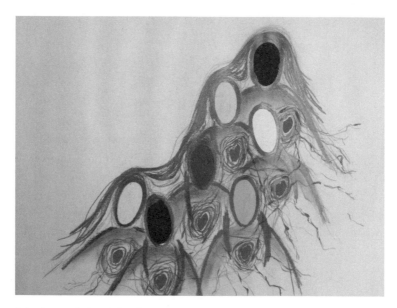

Baker's commissioned visualization of the Rainbow Tribe in the abstract. Note that all of the faces are gone, replaced by blank skin tones. (Josephine Baker Papers, Manuscripts and Rare Books Library, Emory University)

Josephine Baker, speaking at the March on Washington. (Library of Congress)

In her Free French uniform, lecturing her adopted children. (Georges Menager, Paris Match Archive/Getty Images)

With Les Milandes in crisis, the children were used to mobilize public support. (Patrice Habans/*Paris Match* Archive/Getty Images)

Baker, evicted from Les Milandes. (AFP/Getty Images)

The Tribe, gathered around the dinner table at Roquebrune. (Jack Garofalo, *Paris Match* Archive/Getty Images)

On the beach, in exile, after Les Milandes. (Henry Hurford Janes Papers, Yale University)

Jean-Claude Baker the elder. (Courtesy of the Jean-Claude Baker Foundation)

The crumbling entrance sign at Les Milandes, photographed in 2007. (Author photo)

6

French Disney

She has literally changed a wilderness into a paradise.

—Chicago Defender (1956)

The language of "show business" is infectious, easy to use and hard to control. It helps to explain something that seems unnatural—not the family itself, but its perversion into a public property by a woman who often seemed far more mercenary than maternal. The various landscapes of Les Milandes were like the carefully constructed scenic backdrops from a Hollywood movie set or the rides of a theme park. Like the rides at Disney World and Disneyland, they established mood and sentiment for whatever performance Baker wanted to script, whether it was a late-night song-and-dance routine with the children gazing with admiration or a Sunday morning family promenade with everyone dressed in white. Most of all, though, they allowed for the photographing of the group in contexts that served an explicit political end, that could circulate in the news as a counter to the ever larger number of stories about police beatings, riots, wars, and racial conflicts.

The colorful spectacle of Les Milandes was meant to be seen. That is, it was built for the eye, with sight lines that were supposed to capture our attention, draw us in, and leave us speechless. Big, symbolic adoptive families such as Baker's were meant to be seen, too, so that the eye could take in the juxtaposition of skin tones and hair textures and facial features, and gauge the future from those measurements. Never before, though, had anyone created an entire staging ground for the display of this sort of family, a staging ground that highlighted those same features and made it easy for anyone to see race and nation. Les Milandes wasn't merely a home, then; it was an engineered landscape or built environment, like a music hall stage, only much, much bigger. Every part worked in the service of the story, which was meant to be experienced in person.

To understand what it must have been like to visit Les Milandes— to see the mixed-race family as Baker wanted visitors to see it—go to Disneyland's "It's a Small World" exhibit. There, one descends to a subterranean stream and boards a small dinghy. If you are with children, as are the great bulk of the visitors, the first few moments are taken up with the usual details: seating assignments, safety, and photographs to capture the anticipation and realization of something magical. The music—the famous jingle that shares its name with the ride—can be heard in the distance, its chirpy cadence reduced to a gentle throbbing by dark curtains. The ride starts with a lurch. And as the dinghy moves forward along a route that covers the seven seas, passengers are pulled first into darkness, and then into a brightly colored, cosmopolitan journey around the world.

Emerging out of the same utopian sensibility as Les Milandes (and perhaps even partly inspired by Baker), "It's a Small World" opened at the 1964 World's Fair within eyeshot of the massive steel Unisphere, a symbol of a better, emerging world united by a commitment to progress and collective advancement. The exhibit, one contemporary account suggested, was the keystone to a rich corporate partnership. Ostensibly linked to UNICEF (like Baker), "It's a Small World" generated donations small and large from patrons at the fair; appearing in the Pepsi-Cola Pavilion, it called attention to the soft drink company's public service efforts; and the entire affair, of course, solicited family travel to the Disney resort. Despite charging a small admission fee—65 cents for children under twelve, and 95 cents for everyone else—the "It's a Small World" exhibit and the Pepsi-Cola Pavilion were popular enough to challenge the attendance figures generated by larger, free pavilions.[1]

Most accounts of the World's Fair took note of the exhibit, if only because the feel-good, sight-specific qualities of this children's tour of the world corresponded closely to the global multiculturalism of the larger affair. Along the route traced by the dinghy, animated dolls, each dressed in racially and culturally specific clothing, and surrounded by regionally distinctive landscapes, sang and danced to the ride's ubiquitous theme song. A row of French dolls, dressed like showgirls at the Moulin Rouge, danced the can-can. "Perched high on a camel," one newspaper noted in a photo spread, "a little Arab boy rides out of the desert." In another scene, a gaggle of Mexican children sit still, wearing straw hats under an enormous, smiling sun. Racial difference is a critical, enduring feature of the exhibit. Even today, the children of the African continent are silenced: they alone do not sing. As they enter the waters along the "dark continent," those in the dinghy hear only the steady beat of tribal drums, pulsating in tropical harmony with the distant, futuristic world of Disney.

A doe-eyed geopolitical metaphor, "It's a Small World" concludes with all of the children of the world now sharing a home, their once multihued racial costumes now reconceived as uniformly white, singing and dancing together. The song is louder here, the chorus thicker with the sounds of more voices, creating a sense of deep synchronicity. For many visitors, the focus was on the political meaning of that synchronicity, and specifically on the social function of a racialized world brought together onstage. It felt good, many thought, to challenge racism, but also to confirm race. Indeed, despite the pronounced utopian textures, "It's a Small World" is (and was) so racially aware, so saturated with difference, that a troupe of blind children, brought to the Pepsi-Cola pavilion in the early days of the World's Fair, left convinced that they could "distinguish some of the colors" along the trip.[2] Joining soundscapes to sightscapes, Walt Disney, American genius, had found a way to let even the blind see race.

Baker's Les Milandes worked the same way. It created a distance between the Rainbow Tribe and the tourists who ventured southward to watch them play. It established viewpoints and lines of sight for visitors to see what was presented as a private play. It brought color, race, and region into high, Technicolor relief. It was a beguiling sensory experience, eclipsing the rest of the world. It asked spectators to question the role of race in civil society even as it assured them that race was a central truth, a very real thing, easily seen and marked on the body and in costume. It provoked feelings of unease, and feelings of wonder and rapture.

Most of all, it required faith in utopian alternatives to an increasingly harsh reality. At a moment when the world was increasingly attentive to the violence of Jim Crow and when black activists were struggling, literally, just to get a seat on the bus, there was Josephine Baker, living in a castle—"a historic building," the *Defender* reminded its readers in a profile that appeared while the Montgomery bus boycott was ongoing, "that once housed royalty, among them Napoleon Bonaparte." At a time when swimming pools were strictly segregated and amusement parks were racially policed, there was Josephine Baker, building a desegregated playground for her multicolored family. And in the midst of race riots that were erupting every time a black family bought a single-family home, no matter how modest, in a "white neighborhood," no matter how depressed, there she was again, presiding over a complex so vast, so feudal, so epically grand, that the *Defender*'s photographer needed to take a picture from a window of her castle to capture even a single corner of it. Cleverly, the photographer made sure to capture the small group of white tourists looking over the same vista, each having paid admission.

The challenge, in thinking about it today, is to allow for these feelings of unease and wonder to coexist, to encourage a reading of Les

Milandes that makes us squirm *and* challenges us to revisit our assumptions about history, about the place of such a thing in the story of democracy and racial difference. Baker's provocation was upfront, lucid, and direct.

In the late summer of 1957, a woman named Violet purchased a postcard from a shop in La Roque-Gageac, a small, picture-perfect French town set into the cliffside along the Dordogne River. "I am having a very nice time here," she wrote. "Also getting fat with all the wonderful food." Then as now, this region of the Dordogne was bound by its medieval past to be a wellspring of French identity. In one stretch, a half dozen castles loom over the gentle river valley, their histories pockmarked with French or English possessions, destructions, and resurrections. It is impossible to tour the valley and not place yourself in the flow of national time and space.

On the cover of Violet's postcard, sent to friends in the UNESCO press division, was a portrait of the region's newest attraction: the "Village du Monde" created by Josephine Baker at Les Milandes. Even now, the image is extraordinary. At the center stands a late fifteenth-century château, perfectly preserved, surrounded by well-manicured, classically French gardens, mischievously decorated with magnolia trees and other hallmarks of the American South. Standing in front of the château, waving up at the helicopter from which the photo was taken, we can see "Jo et Jo." Baker is wearing a light-colored dress, while Jo Bouillon is in a dark suit. The shadows trailing behind them suggest a photo taken in midmorning. Alongside the château there is an old chapel. Between the château and the river, one can see the rest of the estate: tennis courts, a modernist music hall, a brasserie, and an outdoor "Cuban theater," with its striped screens and umbrellas. For children, one can easily make out the pedal-cart racetrack, the water slides and swings, and the day care center. Smaller details are harder to see, but the richness of the image implies such things. Les

Milandes does not seem cluttered at all. Despite the premodern castle at the center, it seems brilliantly clean, thoughtfully designed, and streamlined in typical midcentury fashion, like a social machine doing work. But it also seems empty. No one is sitting by the pool, shaped like a J in Josephine's honor. The park is open, beckoning, hungry for visitors.

Adopting the children and orchestrating them on paper was only a part of her plan. A big family needs an outsized home. Once assembled, the Rainbow Tribe had to be staged in a venue suited to spectacle and display. Fortunately, a specific site had already been cleared and renovated for such a staging. Josephine Baker had been vacationing in the historic Dordogne since the 1930s. In 1947 she purchased an old castle with dozens of rooms, one of many such places in a region renowned for its role in the Hundred Years' War. The château was a minor historic site, built as a romantic refuge from the front lines in the fifteenth century.

From Baker's standpoint, Les Milandes had the virtue of a great location. The Dordogne was a pastoral idyll, full of tiny towns, rolling fields, drifting rivers, and great valleys, far from Paris and removed as well from the smaller cities to the east, such as Périgueux and Bergerac. As a consequence, Les Milandes was well knit into the regional tourist network that connected the nearby fortress towns of Sarlat, Domme, Beynac, and Castelnaud, and other nearby landmarks of the defining conflict between England and France. Then as now, the Dordogne was a sort of hardscrabble summer tourist destination, full of chances to camp, picnic, and canoe, and famous for its medieval past. "It was really the countryside," Jarry Baker recalled. "A lot of tourists during the summer, not only in Les Milandes." In one brief stretch, a half dozen castles loom over the gentle river valley, their histories pockmarked with possessions, destructions, and resurrections by the French or the English. It is impossible to tour the valley and not place yourself in the flow of national time and space. "All those little castles and little towns," Jarry mused. Drawn together

against this profoundly medieval backdrop, staged within the riverside Les Milandes compound—"un hameau," Jarry calls it, a hamlet—
and offered up in play as an example for the world, the Rainbow Tribe
was a vision of a future in which all politics were routed through the
family.[3]

She had already commenced her repair of the château's interior.
Outside, she built up the grounds, installed parking lots, established
facilities for guests, and set up an advertising campaign. She installed
games and rides for children. She inscribed the entire place with her
personality and her celebrity. And, then, her labors complete and her
home now ready for its chief exhibit, she settled herself into her fairy-
tale castle, the stone-and-timber embodiment of France's thoroughly
antidemocratic past, and set about choreographing a revolution.

The result was an enclosed, self-contained theme park, a vision of
an alternate world in which magic and fantasy were real and thematically organized around a positive vision of the racial future. If
advertisements are fairy tales for a capitalist world, visions of lush
excess and overflowing cornucopias, then Les Milandes was a pro-
motion for a lavish imaging of multiculturalism that could be, in a
word, bought.[4] It worked like Disney World brought to life with living dolls instead of costumed performers, producing an eerie sensation in visitors. This staging forced them to see the landscape of Les
Milandes through Baker's eyes and to see the children as a symbolic
ensemble, right out of central casting. It also encouraged them to
bow down before Josephine.

Les Milandes, a busy summer tourist site, was an unusual addition
to the ruined castles and medieval towns of the Dordogne region, an
exotic commodity for French tourists who hope to escape the heat of
Paris in July and August and to rediscover their "Frenchness" in the
crucible of the Hundred Years' War. If you drifted downriver from
La Roque-Gageac or drove from nearby Sarlat or Domme, you would
see the castle up on a hill from miles away. Along the way, you might
pass the ruins of the imposing medieval fortress in Castelnaud, so

stern and so forbidding that Les Milandes was constructed as a romantic retreat for one noblewoman, an escape from the garrison lifestyle in the fifteenth century. You might, in fact, pass any number of castles and fortifications, or catch a glimpse of them off in the distance around this bend or that turn. Maybe you'd been staying in nearby Sarlat, renowned for its medieval architecture. Or maybe you'd been camping, soaking up the feudal ambiance of the blood-soaked battlegrounds of the Hundred Years' War. If you came by car from any direction, you might have passed through fields of walnut trees, newly planted in perfect, straight lines. You would pull your canoe out of the water at the jazz club at the bottom of the hill, a brick-and-stucco affair, or park your car in the lot right next door. Either way, almost as soon as you got there, you would probably hear the birds, some of them roaming free and others penned up in the ornate cages that decorated the park. You would hear the clatter of silverware and china from the club. You might hear the squeals of other people's children—not the ones you came to see, of course—playing at the on-site day care or enjoying one of the pedal cars or the eighteen-hole miniature golf course. Maybe there was a greyhound race that day. If you came at night, you might hear Josephine's voice booming from the club, resounding across the river valley for miles.

At some point you would ascend to the château. If you walked along the path from the parking lot, you'd end up at the cluster of buildings that encircled the castle at the very top of the hill. Walking up the narrow, stone-lined street, you would come to the Village du Monde, the public area carved into the hamlet, the center of which was Josephine Square. Halfway up the wall, you'd see a small carving of the Madonna, with Josephine's face, cradling two children. You'd find a deluxe motel with a full bar, and a small post office. You would pass the bakery and another café; peering to the right, you might get a glimpse of the beautiful Dordogne valley. Behind the motel, you knew there was a wax museum dedicated to Baker's life. At some point, as you wandered through this tiny piazza, you would notice that tiny stones had been pressed into the concrete everywhere, sometimes in the shape of a heart, and sometimes with little signature notes—"Jo et Jo," or "Notre Bar." You would begin to feel like you were in someone else's universe, like you'd been given access to something deeply, magically private.

This experience of climbing the hill and acknowledging the greatness of La Baker mimics the experience at the nearby pilgrimage site of Rocamadour. There, visitors to the retreat wind their way up from the bottom of a cliff, overlooking a tributary of the Dordogne, to the small clutch of chapels, shrines, and hermitages that have sprung up in the roughly thousand years since it became a wellspring of the miraculous. Along the way, following massive stone walkways, their route traces the stations of the cross. Rocamadour's well-trod pathways imagined spiritualism as a ritualistic ascent, and as a private, contemplative affair at the end, while in Les Milandes you rise out of the forested valley into the bright, clear sunshine of Josephine Baker's public life. Stopping for breath at the so-called Jorama—that wax museum in the Village du Monde—you walk through the stations of her life, pausing at each diorama, preparing yourself for the sight of her greatest achievement.

Ostensibly a wax museum dedicated to Josephine Baker's life, the Jorama was also a coercive experience, aimed at convincing the viewer that Baker's life had logically prepared her for Les Milandes. Mimicking the "stations of the cross," as critic Bennetta Jules-Rosette puts it, it included a sweeping narrative of vignettes, from her childhood in St. Louis to her audience with Pope Pius XII. A nearby case, Jo Bouillon notes, displayed her precious "war mementos," from flags and a bomber jacket to an autographed photo of de Gaulle. In one such tableau, Baker, wearing a long fur shawl, kneels before the Pope, who is dressed in simple white. In another, Baker wears one of her famous gowns, this one white, with a massive hoop skirt, silver and rhinestone details, and a vast fur cowl. Giant rabbit's feet dangle from her waist. In still one more, Baker leads a small group of her children up a hill—"nearby Mt. José," Jo Bouillon assures us—toward a cross, all of them holding hands, "a symbol," E. A. Wiggins helpfully telegraphed for the readers of the *Chicago Defender,* "of Light and Love."[5] In every corner there was a framed photo, a snippet of poetry, a small statue of Baker, or some trinket gathered up from somewhere, all of it meant, Wiggins continued, to embody "Josephine's creed and philosophy regarding the human race—and her initiative to create, if not a world, a small patch of it where human beings can be EQUAL and LOVE the dominating factor."

Rounding the corner at the top of the cobbled street, you would circle a weathered chapel, reputed to be much older, to get to the imposing gates that marked the entrance to the "private" residence. Outside of the immense doorway to the chapel, topped off with a cross, you might stop to read a big, arresting, gilded sign that welcomed you to Les Milandes, "village of the world," "capital of brotherhood," and "chapel of the Milandes." At the center of the sign, her eyes half closed, her lips parted, was a six-foot-tall image of La Baker's alluring face, accompanied by her signature with a sharp, twisted *J.* Framing the sign, you would see smaller portraits of the Rainbow Tribe, the golden faces of the castle's tiny inhabitants, each in costume. An arrow helpfully directed visitors to enter the chapel, where another small shop awaited.

Outside, you might start to notice a commercial logo, repeating on every sign: a stylized silhouette of the château, full of towers and archways. Two windows are illuminated, suggesting warmth and welcome. A logo, you might realize, suggests incorporation and the branding of a product or a corporate identity. You wouldn't have time to think for long. Maybe that logo made you wonder, though, what was for sale. And maybe it reminded you of the Disney castle.

The residence wasn't yet open, so outside the chapel you would cling to the gates along with everyone else, curious about the lifestyle of the famous residents—La Baker, of course, but also the children. You might see more birds, peacocks or parakeets. And monkeys and cats and dogs, of course. At some point before the gates opened, La Baker herself might come out, bringing a ball or some such toy, and encourage the children of the Rainbow Tribe to play in front of you. She isn't wearing what you would expect—she has no ball gown or banana skirt, just a head wrap and a simple housedress.

Or maybe the gates were already open. In that case, you would enter the garden and walk over to a low stone wall decorated with grimacing gargoyles and look down upon a lower terrace, where the children would play all day, like animals in a zoo. Watching the kids laugh together, run together, work together, and cry together, you admit that you have never seen anything like this before. You are amazed and uneasy all at once.

The entire point of visiting Les Milandes was to see the children. To see them, that is, as racial exemplars, as color-coded, costumed symbols of a diverse future. They seemed like the outsized cartoon characters at a Disney theme park, swirling and circulating, performing scripted and rehearsed roles for a public they would never truly meet, escorted around the park by their parents. In a world where representations of diversity were strained and violent, where peaceful, even jubilant encounters were few and far between, where fire hoses and machine guns, lynchings and bombings were the order of the day, the children were reminders of the way things ought to be. They were also reflections of their mother's extraordinary power: if her speeches and activist work couldn't make a difference, couldn't change the way people interacted, she would show people how to get along by building a parallel universe in the south of France, teaching a corps of children to get along, and making them perform in front of an audience. "We were living in that castle by ourselves, all together, never really moving through the world," Jarry remembered, "and then suddenly everything is open and everyone is on top of my mother and talking to me."

Visitors came by the hundreds and the thousands, though not—Baker was disappointed to learn—in numbers high enough to ensure the long-term profitability of Les Milandes. Three hundred thousand came in 1953, but the haste of construction and the lack of supervisory oversight meant that overcharging by contractors was rampant, work was shoddy or incomplete, and something always needed to be redone. Baker never had financial breathing room.[6]

Whatever the numbers, the power of the place was overwhelming for many. The Fowlers—three children and their parents, from Montreal—stayed at Les Milandes for the summer of 1958, an unusually long time for guests. But they had been through the Dordogne in the previous fall and had stopped at Les Milandes, where they were enchanted by Baker's vision. Planning a longer return trip took months, but Josephine was ready with a quick response to any question. Renting them the "Deux Amours," a family-sized residence, she prepared for their visit even as she traveled across Europe. Still, it was also clear that the Fowlers were concerned going in that not everything would be up and running, because much of the site was still under construction. Would the pool be open? Would the restaurant? And the *parc des attractions?* Could the baker and the butcher be instructed to prepare for guests? Could dishes and silverware and linens be bought in Sarlat or Souillac? Finally, "am I right in assuming that you and your children will also be spending your summer at Les Milandes, and shall we find you in residence when we arrive on July 1?"[7]

"The Milandes has become a beehive," Baker responded skillfully, as if all the preparations were merely for the Fowlers. "Everyone is running in and out of 'Le Pavillon des Deux Amours,'" she continued, breathlessly, "painters, cleaners, etc." With a reassuring tone, she let Shelia know that she'd reserved rooms at Le Tournoli, the motel in the Village du Monde, for a few friends of the Fowlers, but warned her that there was no bath in the rooms, only a simple wash basin. The entertainment calendar at Le Tournoli would be full. "You will be able to dance by moonshine, and candle-light." As for food, Baker said, "my sister will make special cakes for you." "Jo and I and our babies," she closed, "are hoping with all our hearts that you will become our neighbors, what a beautiful dream that would be!"[8]

All of Shelia's worries were for naught. The family stayed at the Deux Amours, everything was open, and by all accounts, the summer was a once-in-a-lifetime event. Staying at Les Milandes, Shelia wrote to Josephine, was "the achievement of a dream . . . more than a happy family summer in a beautiful district of France." "You have something quite remarkable in your village of Les Milandes," she continued. Shelia shared as well her grief at the news of Mama Carrie's passing.[9] But it was the children, in a brief poem sent to the Tribe as a token of their affection, who put into words the feelings of the Fowler clan. "Down in Southern France before Provence," the poem began:

> The Dordorgne swifts its lovely banks
> Set with a thousand wonders to be found,
> Lying in the midst of "Le Village du Monde."
> Wonderful with the Rainbow children running by, and the use,
> Of the park and the architecture of the old village,
> Wonderful for the beautiful castle gardens,
> And the weird magic of the Chateau Clair de Lune.

Signed by Bruce Fowler, a lad only a few years older than Akio, the poem closed with a small note, scribbled at the bottom, extending his love to the Tribe, all of them thanked by name.[10]

In this surreal universe, full of "weird magic," Josephine was both a princess and a fairy godmother. Looking back now on the royalist fantasy of Les Milandes, everyone talks about the modern dressing room installed at the top of the tallest tower. Old women lean back in their chairs and, with a gleam in their eyes, speak of the dresses, all from the finest designers, arranged perfectly, always on display for anyone who might enter the sacristy. The dressing room, in some real sense, was a twist on the classic fairy-tale narrative, in which the removed spire is often a place of isolation and intrigue. Every good princess gets locked up in a tower at some point, and the escape is usually a pivotal moment, a source of personal revolution and change. As the lady of Les Milandes, Baker would not be locked away in some spare chamber like a prisoner; instead, she would be surrounded by colorful fabric and ringed by glittering baubles, as if she were in some aristocratic cyclorama meant to obscure a life begun in bone-chilling poverty in St. Louis, or to mask her Cold War challenge to state-supported racism. Of course, in the 1950 Disney film Cinderella is lifted out of her forced poverty and unhappy oppression not through a progressive alliance with social equals—with the various anthropomorphized mice, birds, and farm animals who conspire to create her glamorous dress while she slaves away as a house servant, an effort that fails to get her to the ball—but by a fairy godmother with a magic wand who creates an extraordinary illusion and releases the young woman's beauty without touching the social fabric at all. At the end of the movie, Cinderella is a princess, and her comrades have joined her in the palace for the good life, but this transformation isn't a consequence of bootstrapping and hard work. A very different princess, Josephine Baker was the embodiment of self-help, willing her way across the ocean and winning her castle on her terms. There was no fairy godmother for her. Instead, there were mirrors and mannequins and rows and rows of shelves and closets bursting with jewels and fine fabrics.

You would have seen the tower from the river, peeking through the tall pines on the hillside. Its outline was at the center of that commercial logo. It loomed over you when you shelled out five francs to watch the children get cleaned up, fed, or spanked.

Of course, you had expectations of what you might see at the château. Maybe before you came there you'd have read something about the place. Perhaps it was a newspaper editorial. Or a glossy spread in a picture magazine. Or maybe you'd seen a postcard. Or perhaps, driving through the Dordogne, you'd seen a billboard advertising

Les Milandes. The first such billboards had portrayed the children like zoo animals and had been received so negatively that Baker replaced them with clean and bright signs, white under the spotlights, all with her name in capital letters at the very center.

Or perhaps you'd seen photographs, striking black-and-white images that masqueraded as family snapshots but were really public relations photos taken by the French press and used as magazine covers, postcards, or stock images. Carefully staged photographs emphasized the normalcy of everyday life at Les Milandes—three children opening Christmas presents, playing with them innocently, even as Mother smiles in the background; Josephine, Jo, and the children walking in Paris, the Place de la Concorde in the background; Jarry, sitting on his mother's lap, staring into her eyes; three of the children at church, perfect little French boys; five of the children and Josephine walking through the Village du Monde, all in white except for Akio, who is wearing a colorful set of pajamas and carrying an Asian-style umbrella. "Bienvenue aux Milandes," one Christmas photo (meant for magazines) read, with an image that included a splendid Christmas tree, a grand piano, an Oriental rug, and Josephine, Jo, and eight children, all dressed in white.[11] These are universal moments—not unlike *Life* magazine's 1947 spread on the Doss family—but with a rare, racially variegated quality, highlighting an explicit politics. In another such image, there are Josephine and Jo standing at the wooden doors of the Village du Monde with six of the children, with everyone dressed for winter. One of the children, held aloft in Bouillon's arms, is gesturing to a sign on the door announcing an antiracist conference at Les Milandes. What makes these images unique is the presence of Baker, whose fame guaranteed that they became ubiquitous.

Baker's public image here was radically revised. Gone were the ball gowns, the elaborate headdresses, and the feather boas. Instead, in many of these images, she seems to be wearing exactly the same clothing—the same sweater, the same smock, the same hair wrap, the same shirt with the Peter Pan collar—making it seem as if she, too, was wearing a costume. Of course, down at the cabaret at night, she might don a floor-length gown before a brief performance, but otherwise she seemed like a midcentury modern housewife. To be the mother of this apostolic Rainbow Tribe, she had needed a new image, one that emphasized her qualities as a mother, not her famous sex drive or her postwar glamour. So she invited the press into the kitchen at Les Milandes and donned an apron for the cameras. Strolling the grounds with visiting reporters, she carried herself with the regal poise of her friend Princess Grace. When she assembled the children for a photo opportunity or advertisement, everyone dressed perfectly and appropriately, including Baker, who had consigned her banana skirt to a museum. When she told the children the story of her life, she skipped over the 1920s. "She would say," Jarry recalled, "'I was poor and I came to France, and now here I am.'"[12]

You might also have read her book about the château. In 1957, she worked with the renowned children's illustrator Piet Worm on the children's book *La Tribu Arc-en-Ciel*. Baker was a master stylist, and Worm's remarkable artwork shows her influence. Eight children are arranged on the branches of a tree, with the boys clustered in an arc in the canopy and a single girl suspended where the trunk splits off into branches. Each child wears or carries some external marker of his or her ethnic or racial background—a bamboo hat, a Scandinavian patterned shirt, a three-string lute, a tropical bird, a fez—and there are slight variations in skin tone and hair color and texture to further indicate difference. The young girl, dressed as a little French maiden and carrying a small basket of flowers, is also wearing a crown. One child carries the French tricolor. The entire scene is staged under a broad rainbow that wraps around the crown of the tree and beneath two suns, with small, jaunty white flowers, replacing stars, scattered across the blue background. These children, appearing here at roughly the same age, height, and weight, are supernatural if not godlike, their relationship to each other a source of strength and unity. Baker herself is represented at the bottom corner as a wounded black hen, with the tips of her wings held aloft to signal orchestration, performance, and control. She is simultaneously diminished and authoritative.[13]

Revealingly, the plot of the book revolves around the bird, named Kott-Kott, the object of ridicule and shame, who searches the globe for her missing eye, her disfigurement hidden by a handkerchief. Instead of her eye, she finds acceptance at Les Milandes, where Baker's eight children offer her a faux consanguinity and their particular ethnic and racial histories, embodied by a set of archetypes, as evidence that she has found the one location in the world where she can be content, even whole. One by one, Baker's children invoke symbols of their particular racial and ethnic pasts, including the Buddha, a giant, the jungle, a French knight, the Old Testament prophet Moses, and various musical traditions, before Princess Marianne—who, as a blond, blue-eyed woman, the storied symbol of France, is herself an archetype—clutches Kott-Kott to her breast. When their embrace is ended, the children release Kott-Kott, smiling, as the sun sheds tears of joy and a white dove looks on. The dove, in turn, relates this story to other animals, who carry it to humanity. In the penultimate scene, the wide world heads to Les Milandes in shared contentment as a joyous sun looks on. The final page, no less saccharine, shows Kott-Kott, now happily without her handkerchief but still disfigured, leading eight different-colored chicks—orange and purple and brown and green—around a coop and toward a henhouse styled to look just like Les Milandes.

Beyond the near deification of her children as the vanguard of the wonderful future, Baker's rather practical hope was that people would read the book, get curious, and head south from Paris, literally investing in the dream, giving it power, allowing it to continue. Her children's book was a commercial fable, an attempt to establish Les Milandes as a kind of Shangri-la in Dordogne, where love and universal brotherhood could come together in uniquely powerful ways, and where all could be consumed for the price of admission.

It also pitched Baker as the fairy godmother of this assembled group *and* the main protagonist as well. It was the unseen Josephine Baker, the book proposed, who brought the children together. It was her genius that assembled the group, that established their relations in just the right way, that turned ordinary children into demigods. And it was the seen, symbolic Baker—represented by Kott-Kott— who was the focus of the book's energy. It is Kott-Kott who needs saving, whose body has been broken, whose ego has been bruised. And it is Kott-Kott who is passed from child to child before settling in Marianne's arms and receiving her cure. The double meaning here was appealing to readers, because it suggested that Baker had found comfort and healing in her children's arms even as they had found shelter and food and opportunity in her previously cold and empty castle.

It is interesting that Baker presents herself, in metaphor, as small, damaged, and black. She was so insistent elsewhere to portray herself as global, cosmopolitan, outsized. Since so many of her biographies have emphasized her deep-seated resentment of white supremacy and whiteness and her wounding at the hands of Jim Crow, one could read this enigmatic self-portrait as an illustration of a deeper truth, one usually hidden from the public eye. We could also see it as an illustration of the role of Baker's blackness at Les Milandes. Visitors to the Dordogne weren't just witnesses to the divine revelation of the Rainbow Tribe but also were privy to a particular sort of African Americana, with sister Margaret the baker and brother Richard the postal worker and Mama Carrie the wise elder looming over the production. Josephine and her St. Louis family, excavated from Jim Crow and reassembled in this strange French Disneyland, were representations of the old world and heralds of the new. Their production of blackness in the day-to-day of the Village du Monde was a reassuring, familiar thing, a reminder of the ubiquity of black faces in domestic roles in film and television and mass culture generally. At the same time, the great bulk of the work there was performed by white

French faces, local people from the region who were drawn to this
sprawling industry.

What makes Les Milandes so difficult to explain is that whatever
Josephine may have intended, and however it may have been received
by the busloads and carloads of tourists who arrived on the weekend,
it was also a collection of real people, with interests and psychologies
that couldn't be controlled. Sometimes these people were swept up in
Baker's creation, like cogs in a machine, purring and whirling to serve
their designer's will. And sometimes these people were there for other
reasons. "Margaret was fabulous," Jarry said. "She was the woman who
really took care of us." When Josephine was back on the road, Margaret provided caretaking stability, attention, and even love. She'd been
a fixture of the Village du Monde, and lived on a farm just down the
hill from the Château. And she had her daughter, Rama—a gift from
Josephine, a half-Hindu child brought back from Belgium after a performance there.

The industrial parentage of Les Milandes fascinated visitors. There
was a vast single room for the children, at least until they grew older.
A farm just down the road. A long kitchen table for family meals. And
a bevy of tutors and maids and servants, none of them staying long
enough to displace Baker as the primary caregiver. You weren't supposed to watch the servants, though. You were supposed to be dis-
tracted by the sight of the children.

Another visual representation, once again commissioned by Baker,
this time from the Scandinavian artist Leif Kristensen. A portrait of
Les Milandes as "Capital du Monde de la Fraternitè," it features seven
figures—representing the seven children who had been adopted by
1958, when the artwork was complete. They are connected by an arte-
rial flow, a blood connection that naturalizes the family but doesn't
destabilize race. As literary scholar Jonathan Eburne notes, the circulating flow doesn't "represent the mixed blood of miscegenation or,
for that matter, of colonial assimilation."[14] It merely links the children in a tribe, an unnatural affiliation forged by their mother. The

children's faces, however, are rendered simply, without any features except for skin tone, which is characterized in the most straightforward manner: yellow, brown, black, white. It is the visual back-and-forth here—the disconnection of the flow of blood linking the family and the striking dissimilarity of their color—that matters. Like Piet Worm's pinpointed illustrations, Kristensen's modernist rendering relied on bright, clearly defined racial borders between the children, on the utter absence of individuality for the children outside of stereotype and racial cliché.

If a family is a collection of individuals, Baker's assemblage routinely presented itself as something quite distinct. But it also worked differently. "I was one in the family," Jarry remembered. "There was no independence. It was everybody or nobody." In Monaco, years after Les Milandes, when the older boys wanted to see a movie, they had to choose a film that would also satisfy five-year-old Stellina. When Baker talked about the children, she would use the descriptive terms "brother" and "sister" and not merely the child's given name. "She would not say, 'Go to Marianne,'" Jarry recalled; she would say, "Go to your sister," emphasizing the familial bond, the artificiality of the construct.[15] The family was a unit, an ensemble; its identity was collective. "The children had developed a togetherness against the big one [Josephine]," Jean-Claude notes. "If someone broke a glass [and Baker asked who had done it], she would be confronted by silence, a cement wall."

She did nothing to hide her orchestration of their performance from the children. One morning, when the children were five years old, Baker brought them into the dorm for a family meeting. "I adopted you because I cannot have children," Josephine began. "I united all of you," Jarry remembers her saying, because "in the world they are always fighting between countries and races, colored white and black." Going around the room, she told each child the reason for their adoption, citing abandonment or, in Jarry's case, the impending divorce of his parents and their impoverishment. "That is why I want you to be a family," she continued, turning them into stakeholders in her project. "We knew that we were brothers from different countries," Jarry continued, "and had the sense that we had to be brothers to show the world that the union of races, religions, whatever, was possible."[16]

When Josephine marshaled the children out into the courtyard, she would ask them to play in front of their audience. Press photographers would be on hand, positioned inside the gates, to capture both the family inside the gates and the tourists outside. For Jarry, speaking to *Der Spiegel* in 2009, this meant that the children often felt like "pet monkeys."[17] Sometimes the children would be at the big metal gates of the château. Sometimes they would sneak away to a lower tier of the garden, though there was often a wall of faces above, watching and taking pictures. Sometimes they would be with their mother inside the brasserie, greeting their public through a glass door. Such work established great distance. At a greyhound race, a wire-and-wood fence was installed, more clearly delineating the gap between the unwitting performers and their audience. It was also draining, deleterious. "We grew in Les Milandes like a regular family," Jarry says. "We had fights. When you are kid, when you are obliged to do things, you go out with your mother and father, and suddenly you have all these people taking pictures, you get tired." Being a "family" was one thing, he said, but "show business" was different. At Les Milandes, he submitted, the family *was* show business. And it was endlessly tiring, a labor and not a love affair.[18]

The children of the Rainbow Tribe were both instruments of Baker's politics, conceived in a sketchbook and raised onstage, and individuals, struggling to understand their various relations, acting unpredictably, and engaging and undoing their mythic constructions. Baker's gambit, which provokes a lingering sensation of strangeness, was to provide official, racially clichéd biographies for each and to present

them as if they were a platoon, their particularities mattering less
than their shared effort. This depended on the near elimination of
the private sphere. It meant bringing the press everywhere. And it
meant carefully scripting the everyday experiences of the young men
and women in her family.

Baker assembled four large scrapbooks over the course of her life.
The first three are professionally assembled and chronicle her perfor-
mative and political accomplishments. But in the largest and final
book, Baker turned to her expanding family. Here, there is no evidence of a company hired to collect press clippings. There is only
Baker's handwriting, occasionally noting the source of an image or
an accolade, or encircling an intriguing passage with a pen. Her du-
tiful and professional archival impulse is gone, replaced by something more idiosyncratic. The rich green cover and light green pages
suggest the promise of growth and fertility, and their coloration surrounds the images of Baker with her many children, always in the
adoring spotlight. But the careful, documentary attention to presentation stops abruptly, with twenty or more pages to go. One could
see this scrapbook as a symbol of motherly intimacy, devoutly performed for a public. Or one could read it as sub rosa testimony about
Baker's preference for the abstract over the real, for in its pages the
children were not allowed to age. The only scrapbook that is incomplete
is the one linked to her creation of a new family, where the blank
pages stand as quiet proof of the Rainbow Tribe's inevitable future
tense and its impossible inconclusiveness.[19]

The utopian abstraction of the racially mixed, public family was,
for Baker and for many others, the benchmark against which the
material reality was measured. At Les Milandes, the myth would inevitably frame the reading of the tangible, no matter how dark or
troubled the children might look or act or how joyfully they played.
They had to get along and get along publicly, or the world was doomed.
Their moonstruck story is hard to understand, then, because their
everyday reality was always clouded by the fantastic, and because the

last chapter of their story was always unwritten, always off in the temporal distance, where yesterday's utopias become tomorrow's ordinary. Such stories, of course, do not end happily. Imagining the big, bold adoptive family as a future-tense thing, artificially constructed and preserved in the present, ensures that the potential for tragedy always looms on the horizon. The world can *never* be ready for such assemblages. They push the very conception of family to the edge of possibility and screw around with it so deeply, so profoundly, that they are always outliers of the real and the normal.

Baker's relentless habit of collecting newspaper clippings wasn't limited to the creation of scrapbooks documenting her celebrity. Her papers are filled with hundreds of stories, carefully cut out, their details circled in red, little scribbles running alongside in the margins: stories of racism, civil rights, human rights; a photo of a group of black college students in the Deep South; a brief piece on the snubbing of Nat "King" Cole. Her speeches and public commentary about rights were routinely peppered with bits about the United States, South Africa, Brazil, and elsewhere. Whenever and wherever she traveled, she surveyed the world and took notes. And when she got back to Les Milandes, with all of this in mind, she'd get the family dressed for their public, knowing full well the stakes of her venture. Disneyland was meant to make money; Les Milandes was meant to do far more than that.

Baker left us clues, easy to find and right out in the open, acknowledging all of this. In the late 1950s, just a few years after the US Supreme Court's decision in *Brown v. Board of Education* rendering segregation in primary and secondary education unconstitutional in the United States, Baker appeared on the cover of *Nå*, a Scandinavian monthly. She placed Jarry at the center of the cover, with his perfectly matched bow tie and sweater, his blond bangs, and his big smile. In his hand, she placed a black plastic doll, a doll not unlike those used in the famous Kenneth and Mamie Clark study used as evidence in the court case that led to the *Brown* decision. The Clarks had found that black children preferred white dolls, a phenomenon that heralded the internalization of racism, the general desire not to be black. But there, on the cover of *Nå*, is Jarry, a white child, smiling at a black doll. And there, behind Jarry, is Baker, laughing so hard that her eyes are squeezed tightly shut. It is impossible, looking at this cover, to miss the racial sight line. And it is just as impossible to miss the offbeat political point. Creating her own fairy tale, she was mocking white supremacy, doing in France exactly what was explicitly forbidden in the Jim Crow world. For African Americans, she was also providing an imaginative alternative to the rights-based struggles ongoing in the dangerous states of the American South.

7

Mother of a Wounded World

> I am Josephine, and if they do this to me, what do they do to the other people in America?
>
> —Josephine Baker (1963)

In the spring of 1964, sixty-year-old Josephine Baker arranged for several appearances at Henry Miller's Theatre in New York City, part of a larger American tour. "Josephine Baker—the Toast of Paris" featured a wardrobe from Dior, Balenciaga, Balmain, and the House of Lanvin worth a quarter of a million dollars, including one gown made of forty fox pelts—dyed pink, of course, and with pearls sewn into their skins, and worth roughly thirty thousand dollars. Singing into a bejeweled microphone in French, English, Italian, and Yiddish, and wearing an "astonishing array of splendrous raiment and towering headdresses," she was prone, one reviewer noted, to treat these semiprecious pieces of clothing as if they were "disposable," letting them fall to the floor and "kicking them into the wings in the course of a number."[1]

Whenever she was in the United States, on select Saturdays and Sundays, she would give a matinee performance, chiefly for parents who wished to bring their children to see the famous and dazzling costumes. Attending such a matinee was a big deal. Ruth Ann Stewart, who had just turned nine when she went, remembers attending one of these performances years earlier, in April of 1951. "I can see myself in a light color frilly dress with matching shoes and socks," she remembers. "My hair would have been in big fat curls down to my shoulders Shirley Temple style. I hated sitting still for this long process but my mother loved curling my hair with her long, elegant fingers using lots of water and a heavy brush." Stewart's mother had gotten her dressed up, and had labored so long over her hair, because she knew that Josephine would sometimes bring kids onstage. She'd made sure that Ruth Ann was seated right up front at the downtown Chicago theater so that she'd have a good chance to be caught up in the performance. And then it happened, like magic. And when it was over, when Baker returned Ruth Ann to her chair, she gave the young girl a precious Mars bar as a reward.[2] "I remember [her] as having a long pony tail," she recalls, "and wearing something satiny white with a wide flounce trailing off in a train and thinking how exotic and beautiful she was." Though she can't be sure, Stewart suspects this was a "birthday treat," that would likely have been followed by "glorious ice cream sundaes" in "the elegantly grown up Walnut Room at Marshall Fields."

In her press releases, Baker called these matinee shows a "family reunion," emphasized the need for "audience participation," and brought candy for the children. She had been using this reunion format since the early 1950s and returned to it during her tours in the 1960s, adding new features and details. Sometimes she would hold a dance contest for teenagers. At other times she would bring a collection of multihued dolls onstage, representing the various parts of the world and the children she had brought to her home in the Dordogne valley. At one of the major intermissions, the Caribbean-born dance impresario Geoffrey Holder would stage his remarkable, metaphoric interpretation of miscegenation, *Dougla*. One feature, though, was repeated throughout the 1960s. At some critical juncture, and after donning a new costume, Baker would step toward the audience, sit down on the stage, and call the children in the audience away from their parents, encouraging them to sit in a circle around her. And then, in a deep and serious voice, she would sing her childlike tribute to life at Les Milandes, "Dans Mon Village." As she implored this collection of other people's children to listen to her story of a world where race didn't matter so much, and where equality and harmony were not just trite concepts but also daily practices, she would gesture toward the faraway south of France, where her twelve adopted children lived in a castle.[3] "If our own village," she mused,

> Can serve all men,
> As bright witness
> As to what love can do,
> If everyone
> From everywhere
> Could see others
> As they are
> Without thought of race or color,
> We all would cease to fear.

"Dans Mon Village" wasn't a new song in Baker's repertoire, but the creation of the Rainbow Tribe gave it added significance. A soft, slow-moving ballad at the start, it evokes all of the classic Baker themes—love and universal brotherhood, peace and togetherness. But it is also an idyll to the rural French village as pure in a way that American—and perhaps French—cityscapes cannot be. Turning it into a staple of her new repertoire, Baker reminded her audience that France had made possible what America couldn't, a reminder that simultaneously enabled her continued criticism of Jim Crow and her enduring silence on racism in France.

Such a romantic, softhearted scene—a gesture to universal themes of love and brotherhood—also reflected Baker's enduring sense that bloody and angry nation-based efforts to secure rights were wrongheaded, that the idealistic, sincere human rights paradigms once ascendant and embodied in institutions such as the United Nations, or indeed Les Milandes, could continue to make a difference in the struggle for equality and dignity. Blessed with lifelong moral certitude, she never thought that such paradigms, which she imagined as bold, important, and dangerous, could be redefined as feminine, naive, or even old-fashioned. Yet this is precisely what happened to her over the course of the 1960s. What makes this interesting and important was her repeated focus on the United States, which stands in contrast to her silence about France—her unwillingness to comment on race, empire, and French politics, from the Algerian War through the political melodramas of 1968.

Offstage, though, "Dans Mon Village" seemed hopelessly idealistic. The steadfast white resistance to the civil rights movement left bodies broken and bleeding, churches and homes in ruins. It also hardened the hearts of those who sought to topple Jim Crow. Less than a month after the unprecedented March on Washington for Jobs and Freedom in August 1963—which Baker publicly described as the most important event of her life—the Sixteenth Street Baptist Church in Birmingham, Alabama, was bombed, resulting in the death of four girls. Two months later, John F. Kennedy was assassinated. "Our world is toppling," Baker bluntly telegraphed to Jo Bouillon after learning of Kennedy's assassination.[4] Baker would navigate this dynamic context—wherein her own sense of the global was increasingly estranged from the tactical importance of the nation—as deftly as she could, but the end result would be that by the end of the 1960s, she was as far from the center of things as she had ever been.

This, then, is the story of her navigation of the perilous, roiling political seas of the 1960s, when it seemed to many as if governments might crumble, race wars might erupt, and atomic ruin might be just seconds away. In the end, she could only make her way to safety for so long. Fate would catch up. And Les Milandes, a roaring attraction in 1960, would be gone by 1970.

Whatever we think of the Rainbow Tribe and Les Milandes, and however we measure Baker's efforts against, say, those of the Freedom Riders, it is clear that the great experiment in southwest France struck a chord with some unique demographics. One letter writer from Tehran, whose parents had been to Les Milandes the previous year, remembered a photo they had taken with Mama Carrie. "Although you know many elder men and women which admire you and your work," the letter said, "you might like to hear that also youngsters, like me, do not forget you and your aims."[5]

Her establishment of this family resounded globally in ways that clearly surprised her and should surprise us, too. Buried within the fan mail sent to Baker at Les Milandes were a range of petitions from single mothers looking for help, for refuge, or for friendship; often there were photos of small children, many of whom are presented as mixed-race, clipped to the corner. These letters of supplication to Baker were sometimes expressions of feminine solidarity and sometimes the pleas of an abandoned class of women. Rosalie from Austria had two children, both, she said, from the same runaway father. Now she wished to take up full-time employment and would have to deposit her children in an orphanage; not wanting to do that, she hoped to work for Josephine. Renée, the elderly adoptive mother of an unplanned child, chronicled the sorrowful tale of the birth mother's abandonment of her child and death on Martinique and the exodus of the daughter to France before asking for a subvention of 20,000 francs to pay for school clothes and books. "She isn't white," she wrote of her daughter, "but she is strong, and pretty, and intelligent." "Just a word," Baker dashed off to an English nurse and midwife named Mrs. James, "to tell you how pleased I was to meet you and your daughter and I think the baby is darling. Would you please have your daughter bring him here to my home [?] I have found a lady who will take him, and he will be well taken care of and loved."[6] James, in a reply that seems typical, happily agreed to forward the letter to her daughter, and then launched into a discussion of her own financial woes, a consequence of her daughter's unhappy circumstances, which would make it hard to get to Les Milandes with infant in tow.[7]

Baker's worldwide reputation as an impulsive rescuer of children and defender of the downtrodden and the voiceless, her undisputed and unusual status as head of household, and her on-the-ground efforts to publicize a very different sort of family promised to turn Les Milandes into a safe harbor, at least imaginatively, for a scattered band of single mothers with racially marked children, poor women with children who couldn't be well tended to, and broken families without resolution, all adrift in a protofeminist age. Such plaintive requests remind us that radicalism can't be limited to narrowly defined rights. Baker aimed to be the Mother of the World, not a Freedom Rider, and many people—more than we've previously supposed— saw this as the bigger, nobler, more important thing.

Of all of the people who appeared on the steps of the Lincoln Memorial in late August 1963, Josephine Baker was perhaps the most unexpected. But there she was, wearing stylish dark glasses and her deep blue Free French uniform, the bright, shining medals on her left breast—five of them—reminding everyone that her wartime service had been genuinely heroic.

It was something of a miracle that she was even there. The only woman among the main speakers, she had flown "all night from Paris."[8] A very late addition, she doesn't even appear on the program. Her presence on the dais was cleared by no less a personage than Martin Luther King Jr.; the visa restrictions that had kept her away had been lifted through the efforts of Robert Kennedy. Some may have felt that she was out of touch, not American enough, too foreign. The troublesome taint of her earlier collaboration with Juan

Perón—an outspoken critic of the United States—lingered, too. At least one newspaper suggested that she had been an uninvited guest, but she was not to be kept away. "I've been following this movement for 30 years," she told the *New York Times;* "now that the fruit is ripe, I want to be here."[9]

August 28 was "a scorching day," Bennetta Jules-Rosette—a high school student in 1963—remembers, with pavement "so hot that it burned through the marchers' shoes"; "many marchers passed out from heat exhaustion." Baker's words that day were offbeat and dissonant, less a call to "collective action," Jules-Rosette recalls, and more a matter of "individual agency against enormous obstacles."[10] "To be very frank and candid," John Lewis once told me, "I don't remember anything she said, but I remember her personality. I remember how good and well she looked in that uniform." Lewis had been preoccupied with his own speech, which he'd been asked to hastily revise, excising his criticism of the Kennedy administration. Still, he was struck that day by the surreal presence of this luminous figure, a piece of black folklore once archived in *Jet* and now suddenly and surprisingly brought to life, moving around the memorial, reminding everyone of her "brave" and "courageous" work on behalf of rights and revolution.[11]

Her unrehearsed speech went on for twenty minutes. "When I was a child," the legendary superstar began, "they burned me out of my home," and "I ran far away . . . to a place called France," a "fairyland place" where she "never feared" for her safety. Reminding the audience that she had "lived a long time and come a long way," she admitted that her initial interest in human rights issues was selfish—"what I did, I did originally for myself." Speaking to an audience all too familiar with images of bloodied civil rights workers, she suggested that her punishment for speaking up wasn't a physical beating but a psychological one: "They beat me with their pens, with their writings, which is much worse." Striving for a colloquial tone, she said, "I have walked into the palaces of kings and queens and into the houses of presidents . . . but I could not walk into a hotel in America and get a cup of coffee, and that made me mad." Summing it up coyly, she said, "All I wanted was a cup of coffee. But I wanted that cup of coffee where I wanted to drink it, and I had the money to pay for it, so why shouldn't I have it where I wanted it?"

Of course, Baker had wanted far more than a cup of coffee. On her tour in the early 1950s, she had demanded access to the finest hotels for herself and her accompanying band members. She had required a desegregated audience at every performance. And she maintained the right to dine in mixed company at the very best restaurants in the country without even the slightest hint of racism. Black college students in Greensboro, North Carolina, were just trying to get a cup of coffee; Baker had insisted on far, far more, and, by and large, had actually won more battles than she lost—at least until she was branded a Communist by the press and frog-marched out of the States. Still, she "screamed loud enough" to rattle the windows, so loud that "they started to open that door just a little bit, and we all started to be able to squeeze through it." ("Not just the colored people," she added ecumenically, "but the others as well, the other minorities too, the Orientals, and the Mexicans, and the Indians, both those here in the United States and those from India.")

"Now," she went on, "I am not going to stand in front of all of you today and take credit for what is happening now. I cannot do that. But I want to take credit for telling you how to do the same thing, and when you scream, friends, I know you will be heard. And you will be heard now." Wrapping up, she declared, "I have just been handed a little note. It is an invitation to visit the President of the United States in his home, the White House. I am greatly honored. But I must tell you that a colored woman—or, as you say it here in America, a black woman—is not going there. It is a woman. It is Josephine Baker. . . . Someday I want you children out there to have that great honor too. And we know that time is not someday. That time is now."[12]

Her friend and artistic collaborator Stephen Papich took note of the themes of bootstrapping that emerged from her unscripted remarks, and of the absence of any reference to her famous family. "She needed no Milandes," he wrote, "and she did not need to create emissaries, as she had tried to groom her children to be. She did it herself, and that is how it should have been."[13]

When she left the memorial, "she marched straight to her meeting with President Kennedy," who was, Papich recalls, "waiting on the steps of the White House for her arrival."[14] Kennedy had extended an invitation to most of the leaders of the march, not just to Josephine, and when the event concluded, they boarded a shuttle bus for the White House. Kennedy brought them all into the Cabinet Room and spoke to them at length about how he might strengthen the civil rights bill that was then winding its way through Congress. He broke down the vote for them and explained where they were in the process. Histories of this meeting mention King, of course, and Roy Wilkins, Dick Gregory, and others. They don't mention Baker, however, whose unusual role that August day—as a foreign interloper, and as a woman intruding on a male space—seems to have been systematically reduced over time until she barely warrants more than a line or two. It is possible that she didn't board the shuttle bus or didn't join the meeting in the Cabinet Room. It is also possible that she never actually got that note; she doesn't show up in the White House records as a guest that day.[15]

She'd given a stock speech, but a terribly effective one, because it heightened the contrast between Europe, where Baker dined with royalty, and America, where she could barely get in the door of a café. But this was all more folklore, an exaggerated portrait of what she'd done and what had been said at the March. Baker had phoned Papich twenty-four hours after her speech, and in the intervening time she'd invented a fuller, more important role for herself, and a longer transcript, too. The speech contained in Papich's memoir, published in 1976, bears little or no resemblance to firsthand accounts of her exhortations that day. Winzola McClendon's report in the *Washington Post,* for instance, noted that Baker began her considerably shorter speech by invoking a universalist tradition, one better matched to her great and ongoing experiment in France: "I am here because I believe in the rights of man . . . in the dignity of human beings." Describing the speech as "the happiest day" of her life, Baker remarked on the mixed audience, describing them as "together as salt and pepper, just as you should be," and "a united people, at last." Celebrating their accomplishment, she told the audience of 200,000 that she believed they were on "the eve of complete victory" and that "time will do the rest."[16] These words do not appear in Papich's account. Her autobiography, the source of many frustrations, is silent on the whole affair.

Despite her subsequent revision, the real version of her speech—much shorter, with none of the bootstrapping Papich adored—was well received, if completely overshadowed by King's extraordinary words at the close of the march. E. W. Kenworthy, reporting for the *New York Times,* noted that most of the ten speakers to follow Baker that day (all but King, he thought) were much less optimistic.[17] Indeed, whatever her reasons for altering the history of her participation in the march, one thing remains powerfully important: Baker had managed to muscle her way onto a stage dominated by men, in the midst of an extraordinary event planned by men, and into the middle of a conversation that seemed to be about men working things out. She may not have made it onto the program, but she got to have her say and, really, to do it on her terms.

Only a few days after the march, Langton Hughes informally nominated Baker for the NAACP's Spingarn Medal, given "to the man or woman of African descent and American citizenship who shall have made the highest achievement during the preceding year or years in any honorable endeavor." He worried, of course, that her French citizenship might exclude her on a technicality, but he didn't blame her for living abroad for a quarter century: "If I were a famous star and had made a great deal of money during my stardom, I would live abroad, too." Baker deserved to be recognized, he thought, because no other black person had ever accomplished anything so symbolically important. Hughes made his case simply and elegantly by narrating an evening in the 1920s when he'd been invited by the star of the Folies Bergère to a show. "I happened to arrive at the stage door just as Miss Baker's car drew up at the curb before a performance," he began.

A uniformed chauffeur opened the car door for her. A doorman was waiting to open the stage door. A maid just inside the corridor took Miss Baker's coat as she entered. Another maid at her dressing room door was waiting to begin to unbutton her. Since the overture had begun, still a third maid, or dresser, held in hand Miss Baker's first costume. By the time my greetings were over and I had gotten around to the front of the theatre and into my seat, Josephine Baker was coming on stage in a gorgeous gown created especially for her by one of France's great designers.[18]

Baker's servile assembly line in Paris, Hughes knew, didn't make it possible for poor black folks to vote, own a home, or send a child to college. It couldn't serve as useful evidence in a court case. It wasn't a useful model for progressive social reform. But it was an inspirational, exaggerated symbol of what was possible at the extreme end of wealth and fame, globally speaking, for anyone and everyone, no matter their skin tone or racial classification. But it also wasn't the end of her commitment to rights, to equality, to meaningful fellowship and a healthy civil society—there was a weekend's work at a soup kitchen, or a complicated negotiation over an antidiscrimination clause, or a scheduled conference on antiracism. She was as relentless in her human rights work as she was successful onstage, and it was that unusual combination of celebrity spectacle and political determination that brought her to the Lincoln Memorial that hot

August day. Josephine Baker loved her limousines, but she never once imagined that being seen in them was enough.

Even as she marched on Washington and toured the United States, she continued to downplay any critique of France, which she saw as the wellspring of her success. The French republic, the myth went, opened its heart to any of its colonial subjects, offering universal citizenship provided they gave up everything about themselves that was not French. Baker appears to have taken the French at their word.[19] In this, she was rather like Frantz Fanon, who famously rejected black nationalism in *Peau noire, masques blancs,* published in 1952. Fanon imagined his work, scholar Dennis McEnnerney reminds us, as a particularly French critique of France, as an effort to encourage the growing moral outrage of the "French black" and "to force white French people to recognize them as different—and French."[20]

Though it emerged from a different personal history and was expressed in different terms, this was Josephine Baker's project, too. Her creation of Les Milandes, deep in the idyllic and pastoral countryside, relocated and transformed the immigrant debate from the dystopian *banlieues* to the nostalgic country. She used concepts such as adoption, motherhood, and family, but she was also talking about immigration, universal citizenship, and France. She was her own nation-state, issuing her own faux postage stamps, developing her own self-celebratory museums and a university tradition, as most postcolonial nations would, extending her broadened social contract to the surrounding town, and ruling over the whole thing like an empress. This was a forceful intervention into the crumbling republic's racial politics, an attempt to bring the French ideal to life—and to simultaneously remove it from France—at exactly the moment when decolonization and revolution revealed the depths of Gallic racism.

In 1956, to make this point as clear as possible, she adopted two children from Algeria, six-month-old survivors of the Palestro massacre who, as the legend goes, had been found under a bush, "wrapped in swaddling clothes." Presenting the two infants to Jo Bouillon, she called his attention to the physical features she believed marked their racial and religious differences. "Look at them, Jo," she exclaimed, composing improbable backstories for them. "He's a Berber, probably the son of a wet nurse; she undoubtedly is a colonialist's daughter."[21] Renaming them Brahim and Marianne, Baker chose to raise one as a Muslim and the other as a Catholic, a perfect example of her use of hard-line means to secure utopian ends.

Still, despite increasingly sensational events in Paris—the 1961 massacre at the Saint-Michel Bridge, for example—Baker's habit was to soften the critique, to leave it unsaid or unwritten. In part, this silence on France was a matter of loyalty. A stalwart fan of de Gaulle dating back to her time in the Resistance, she would support him right through the 1968 protests, which nearly ended his tenure. She marched on his behalf, wrote letters of support to him, and generally enthused over him.

But it was also about Baker's conviction that France had made her a success. In the early 1970s Baker admitted that she had long felt "liberated" in France and had quickly become "more French than the French." "The French adopted me immediately," she remembered. "They all went to the beaches to get dark like Josephine Baker.... People didn't stare at me," she concluded.[22] No other African American could put it quite this way. There is a gap, I think, between the exile communities of Richard Wright, Paul Robeson, James Baldwin, and others and the world (or colony, or utopia) established by Baker within France. Becoming "more French than the French," even proclaiming "embarrassment" at the sound of an American accent, Baker was simply more comfortable in France, comfortable in a way that James Baldwin, her contemporary and friend, though emancipated by his escape from the United States, was not. Baker was something more than a transnational exile and something more than a "black American expatriate."[23] Put another way, she was "a lion abroad" and "a lamb at home"—an approach, one columnist concluded, that "made her a hit in Europe but left her a cipher" in the United States.[24]

This softer, more constructive approach to race and revolution in France worked to her advantage. She depended on a steady stream of French visitors to Les Milandes, which necessitated a more circumspect diplomacy at home than abroad. More than once when Les Milandes was in serious, short-term financial jeopardy Baker was able to draw on the support of her French audience as well as fellow celebrities such as Brigitte Bardot and leaders such as de Gaulle. She had been made a chevalier of the French Legion of Honor in 1961, a considerable distinction, and *Paris Match,* covering the ceremony, captured her lecturing her children while looming above them in her Free French uniform, a potent symbol of her commitment to France. Finally, she remained popular in her chosen homeland straight through one of the republic's most contentious political periods. In 1965—the same year that John Lewis and Hosea Williams tried to lead marchers from Selma to Montgomery, the same year that Malcolm X was assassinated, the same year that a race riot engulfed Watts—a "large cross section" of the French public seemed to support her nomination for the Nobel Peace Prize because of her assemblage of the Rainbow Tribe. Recognizing her broader accomplishment, and labeling the "great experiment" a success, longtime European correspondent Paul Ghali confirmed the wisdom of the French by noting, "The 11 children are so close to each other that they insist on going to the same school, studying with the same masters, learning the same things, and playing together."[25]

Baker wasn't quite so restrained when discussing Jim Crow. The black press, attuned to the racial dynamic in the French colonies, had noticed this disconnect between her rhetoric abroad and at home in the 1950s. Attending a political salon at the Sherman Hotel in 1951, the *Chicago Defender*'s correspondent wondered what it meant when Baker, who was presiding, indicated that she had come "to America to help the negroes." "The thought dawned on me," Willard Townsend mused, "that if Miss Baker, who claims to be a citizen of France, was interested in the affairs of darker peoples, why is it she has not begun this crusade in her native France? I wonder if Miss Baker is aware of the fact that only one out of forty-six children in French Colonial Africa have elementary education? I am wondering if, from her lofty position, she has not noticed that nearly all of the Negroes in Paris who receive jobs are those who can toot horns, dance, sing, and entertain? [And] how much of the social life of the upper classes can be enjoyed by unemployed blacks?"[26] The US State Department, concerned about her since the Stork Club, began once more taking note of her activities in the mid-1960s as she drifted slowly leftward into a parallel orbit with the nonaligned nations, which, though generally socialist, refused to choose sides in the Cold War.

She could say and do provocative things because fewer and fewer people were imagining her as dangerous, revolutionary, or radical. And also, of course, because she was French, a citizen of another country. Most of the time she was outside the gravity of American political culture, a familiar but foreign body just barely out of reach

She had performed, historian Kevin K. Gaines tells us, at the 1965 Organization of African Unity summit in Accra, her dancing and singing broadcast over Ghana Television "under the direction of Shirley Graham Du Bois," the widow of the legendary African American expatriate W. E. B. Du Bois.[27] When, in the winter of 1966, a military coup ousted Ghana's Kwame Nkrumah—a hero for many in the African diaspora—Baker wrote to Shirley to offer Les Milandes as a refuge. Writing as "your sister Josephine," she confessed her admiration for much of the work that had been done in the first independent African republic. "I want you, your son, and our Brother Nkrumah," she wrote, "to know that you are not without a home, for you can come *here when you want to,* now if you can, and stay as long as you wish . . . please don't give up—have the courage of your dear Husband." "Don't become discouraged, the struggle is hard but worthwhile,"[28] she advised a month later in a brief cover letter attached to a copy of a longer introductory letter (which she signed, "your big sister") to Guinean president Ahmed Sékou Touré.[29] These are extraordinary symbolic gestures—Les Milandes as a replacement for Accra, Baker as a performer at the OAU summit—reflective of a politically invested activist whose radicalism was shrouded in haute couture.

Of course, her visit was not without a little melodrama. Nkrumah's agent in Paris worried that, "in view of her extreme financial difficulties," Baker might plan "to use [the] Summit as a platform to campaign for funds to settle her debts and to avert the numerous court actions against her." Baker had asked for help from African leaders once before, but the response had been "poor." The emerging concern, then, was that Baker might once more "appeal directly to the individual African Heads of State present for financial assistance," and by doing so "detract (attention) from the magnificent and extraordinary importance of this African Summit."[30] Proactively, Nkrumah, referred to by the honorific "Osagyefo" in a series of cables and memos and telegrams, dictated in secret that Baker should only be present in Ghana for "her part of the program of entertainment." If she were to solicit funds, it would be "embarrassing." All of this was communicated to Baker—then in Conkarey, Guinea—through the Ghanaian ambassador.[31] Furthermore, her expanding entourage needed to be trimmed; "We can only," another cable stressed, "cater to herself and seven others."[32] Her visit to Accra, then, was hardly an unmitigated triumph. More importantly, this little melodrama reminds us that her narratives of diaspora—her appearance at the OAU summit or her gift of Les Milandes—were invariably more complicated or "articulated" than they might seem at first glance.[33]

In late December 1965 she flew to Havana for the tricontinental conference of solidarity against imperialism, sharing a plane with Cheddi Jagan, the onetime leader of British Guiana who had been deposed in a CIA coup, and "13 delegates from Red China."[34] The conference capped a half-century-long "quest," as historical and cultural critic Vijay Prashad puts it. While there, witnessing the birth of the nonaligned movement and sojourning with the avant-garde of the Third World, she attended the opening of Wifredo Lam's exhibition at the Museo Nacional de Bellas Artes.[35] She performed a few times for the distinguished guests. She surely witnessed and enjoyed the "oratorical inflation" of the affair, but she must also have been pleased at the way the conference failed to endorse armed struggle.[36] Even in this brief, relatively unnoticed radical groove, she was—and would always be—a very idiosyncratic radical, a leftward-leaning sympathizer who loved limousines and not war. In the official report on the gathering, prepared for the US Senate's Internal Security Subcommittee, Baker is listed as a delegate from France, elaborated as "American entertainer" in parentheses.[37] There is no other official record of her time there. The Student Nonviolent Coordinating Committee's Stokely Carmichael returned to the United States from the same conference and was for a long time afterward closely watched and hotly debated. Baker seemed like an innocuous hanger-on.

When she returned to Cuba in late July 1966 for the events commemorating the revolution, her visit was framed—inside of Cuba and out—as a family holiday in the tropics, not as an abrasive political statement. When the newspaper *Granma* interviewed the Tribe, Josephine presided over a well-rehearsed assembly line. Akio remembered meeting "vanguard boys and girls," seeing the gymnastic parade, and hearing "Uncle Fidel's" speech. Luis was taken with the "mountains of Oriente" and expressed his desire to be an "agricultural engineer." Like his brother, he was "glad to be able to hear [Fidel], because in Europe there's a great deal of interest in him." Jean-Claude waxed poetic about the coastline. Jarry, who came off as "serious," explained that he was going to attend hotel training school, before Josephine stepped in and translated this seemingly bourgeois professional interest into a language revolutionary Cubans could appreciate: "He takes care of all kinds of repairs in the house." Marianne, just ten, felt that Cuba was "clean like France." "I sure would like to live here," she exclaimed, "because this is a revolutionary country. . . . It's very warm here, too, and in France it's very cold," she continued, "but I like the change. I like to go back and forth from a cold climate to a warm one." Young Mara, eight at the time, got shy and simply repeated his oft-stated desire to return to Venezuela. Finally, Moïse, like the others genuflecting to the balmy climate, ended by talking about how "friendly" Cubans were and contrasting that with France. He noted that his brother "is a Negro" and revealed that "in school they made fun of him and I told Mama to take him out of that school."[38]

Cuba, like Les Milandes, appeared here as a postracial fantasy, a place where everyone was happy and openhearted, standing in contrast to the outside world, which was harsh and cold. To the press, the Tribe "expressed admiration" for Uncle Fidel and gestured toward lives that matched the socialist politics of the island; coming from the children, these same sentiments seemed somewhat more innocent than if Josephine had shared them herself. Jean-Claude Bouillon remembers Castro's arrival as a strange whirlwind, begun with "a sudden screeching of the brakes and the sound of car doors slamming," continued with the arrival of "two guards with machine guns," and concluded with "bearlike" hugs and gifts appearing "at the tips of his fingers."[39] On the last night at Castro's beach house, the children staged a fashion show for the leader of the revolution. In an accompanying image, Castro smiles broadly and claps while one of the young girls—Marianne, or her friend Jeannine, or their local compatriot Chavela—wears a makeshift gown.[40] Looking back on it, though, Jarry remembers that the Tribe was "petrified when Castro came to our villa in Cuba, because he had his armed bodyguards with him."[41]

Georgie Anne Geyer, returning from the conference, happened to share a Cubana Airlines plane with the Tribe out of Havana. Boarding the plane and seeing all the children, she was worried that the flight would be raucous and unrestful. However, she was "pleasantly surprised." "The children," she described, "of many races, ages, creeds, colors, cuddled under blankets with each other and slept, changed seats quietly, and helped each other. They were happy and orderly, for these were the children of Josephine Baker." When Baker walked down the aisle, Geyer grabbed her attention and peppered her with questions about the family and parenting. "I believe in discipline," Baker began, stressing that children shouldn't "run wild." When Geyer noted that Baker was traveling with only one person to help her, the entertainer shared that traveling was easy, because "they are very good children." Watching them for the rest of the flight, Geyer decided that the Tribe was "not self conscious about their experiment." "As I watched," she recounted, "Jarry, 11, from Finland, with hair and skin almost as white as the Finnish snow, first sat with one of the black-skinned African boys. Then he moved to sit with Moses, 12, the Israeli boy, a handsome child, who wants to be a lawyer to 'help the poor people.'"[42] If the children were unaware of their effect, of course, Geyer clearly was not.

By the late 1960s, then, Baker had moved to the left on a number of issues—even as she continued to support de Gaulle. She had come out against the Vietnam War, noting—as many others did—its impact on antipoverty programs and the civil rights movement in the United States. She had aligned herself, personally if not politically, with Fidel Castro's Cuba, and, more generally, with the nonaligned movement. And she wasn't generating any of the negative attention that she had in the early 1950s.

When she gave speeches in the United States, her tone became at once angrier and more egocentric. Appearing at an Operation Breadbasket fund-raiser with Reverend Ralph Abernathy in Chicago in February 1968, she insisted, "If I had remained here . . . there would no longer be a problem." Sounding rather different from her copanelist—a veteran of the Southern Christian Leadership Conference's civil rights efforts, who promised to bring the war on poverty to Washington in the coming summer—Baker expressed shock that African Americans "have accepted this kind of treatment over the years." "Why haven't you done something about it?" she continued incredulously (and sardonically), wondering how it was that "things are no better than they were 30 years ago." With that, she laid out her ongoing "project," involving "children from all corners of the globe." "Perhaps," she wondered, "it is too progressive for you."[43]

Elsewhere, she was even more caustically critical of the state of protest politics. "America is not the America you knew before," she argued to one US crowd in the late 1960s. "The black man has his right." This emerging truth, she continued autobiographically, has "given hope and satisfaction to those who are living away from America, and who cannot return to be on your side." This understandable optimism was rooted in a shallow soil, however, because the general sense of things perceived by those from far away was actually a "false conception of the real situation." Baker had believed that "the worst was already in the past," and that "future marches and the riots were the last existing troubles." Since her return, though, she had "read the black newspapers" and "heard people talk speeches" and "seen determination on faces." "I have found separation," she concluded. "Do you understand?" she railed, her words getting angrier and her tone more outraged. Did her audience merely hide from the truth "like an Ostrich," or "are you really blind and deaf"? If so, "there is no hope—you are a lost people." "Wake up to yourselves," she exhorted, "unite. Unite—that is the only way." Integration, Baker proposed, was the only true radicalism.[44]

In a parallel speech, she outlined her proposal for establishing a school—a version of the proposed university, or orphanage, or revised village she had been floating in the previous decade. In contrast to an increasingly divided world, Baker believed she had "united my children from all parts of the globe to be a symbol of True Brotherhood," a "complete unity" that should have shamed most adults. "They represent," she suggested, "what good can be done among all people if we want it to be." Now she hoped to build on the success of Les Milandes—the spiritual success, not its financial ruin. She wanted her school to foster "direct contact" between children from around

the world, "so as to create a better understanding later in their lives."
She insisted as well that she wanted to contest the classroom's reli-
ance on *crâniologie*, the practical assumption that racial difference
could be seen in the face and on the body. She did not "condemn the
explanation" or disagree with this ethnological sight line, but she
worried that a child in a mixed classroom might "automatically look
at the head of his neighbor, to see if there is a difference," and might
then share his or her findings at home, where racist parents could
enter the picture. She believed in the virtues of travel and cross-
national contact, in the "absolute respect for human dignity," and in
"mutual understanding if we want a better world tomorrow."

To our ears, these may sound like clichés of multicultural education, or perhaps like foundational, first-order concepts for a diverse
and equitable society, but Baker believed they were militant propo-
sitions, because they directly challenged what she saw as the ascendancy of racial separatism and black nationalism. She had "come
out of my shell," she told her listeners, "to defend my children—my
school—my ideal." "I am being made to fight back again," she announced, but the enemy this time wasn't merely Jim Crow: it was racial division more broadly.[45]

Visitors continued to come to Les Milandes, but they came in
smaller numbers now. And what they found was a version of the
same shiny, manicured spectacle that had greeted the eager tourists
who descended upon the Dordogne in the late 1950s, an endearing,
ritualistic performance. One set of guests was served champagne by
Josephine and then treated to a strange performance: when the children returned from school, Josephine lined them up by age, introduced each in turn, and had each child sing a song for the guests.
"They were all dressed beautifully," one guest remembered, and were
"perhaps too well trained."[46] After she returned from Les Milandes,
everyone in Paris wanted to know about the children, Poppy Cannon
White—widow of former NAACP head Walter White—told readers
of her column in the *Amsterdam News.* "Did you see them?" she

would be asked. "Are they happy? Are they being properly brought up?" Then, she continued, people would remark of Baker, "She is a great woman to do this," or "She must be quite mad." What Poppy actually found down in the Dordogne, though, was all of the children nestled in the courtyard of the nearby abbey "with their young professor from Dahomey," the boys all wearing the bright blue blouses that most French schoolboys wore, and Marianne "the picture of chic in a snow suit of nylon." Baker and the children communicated in "her characteristic mélange of French, Spanish, and St. Louis English." And then, after Baker introduced the children to the traveling journalist, "one by the one the boys came forward, greeted me, and kissed my hand," while Marianne "made a deep curtsy." She found the castle to be beautiful and impressive, but the private quarters to be plain, even "austere." And Josephine, instead of being an aloof queen, seemed to like to hang out in the kitchen with the gardeners and tell jokes. When Poppy, who had brought cookies for the Tribe, tried to give them her tiny gift, Marianne took on "quite naturally the role of the mother" and instructed their guest to give the cookies to "Maman," "because if you give them to us we will eat them all at once and we will become malades."[47] All in all, this was exactly the sort of portrait Poppy's friends in Paris—and her readers in Harlem— were hoping for.

There is so much attention paid in these and other accounts to the parenting of the children. And yet, without fail, the children appear to have played their assigned roles perfectly every time. A decade after their co-creation as the Rainbow Tribe, they regularly revealed to their publics a combination of charm and good manners. Deep into the 1960s, in the context of contemporary debates about the decaying black family and the rise of dysfunction in black domestic spaces, Baker's parenting of the Tribe was both a site of scrutiny and, by any measure, a public relations success. She was a saint. She was a heroine. She was mad for doing it. But she had apparently done it well.

Henry Hurford Janes, an old friend from North Africa, stopped by unannounced in the late summer of 1967, taking field notes for a book he'd planned on Josephine. With his acute eye for detail, he noticed "a small back staircase with a worn carpet and dirty walls," and was told that it was in constant use by the children. The salon in the château reminded him of the Victoria and Albert Museum, a collection of the obscure and the strange. Innumerable monkeys and nineteen peacocks waited by the kitchen door for scraps. The children played into the night and kept him awake, and then he woke to the sound of voices in French and Spanish. "There are so many children," he scribbled to himself, "that lunch is taken in two shifts." The telephones were always ringing, and Baker was "rushing from room to room speaking various languages." During his short stay, a new tutor and a new secretary arrived, hinting at the great and regular turnover of staff on-site. All of the guests had ideas about how to manage the children, and Josephine was eager to try out new approaches. When she orchestrated a massive children's pageant—with more than a hundred people, including fifty children, in the audience—her "actions and reactions" seemed beyond desperate. "From beginning to end," he chronicled, Baker was "giggling or roaring with laughter and kept falling about and on the verge of hysterics, falling forward, pushing her hair back, covering her mouth to stifle her laughter, slapping people on the shoulder."

What struck him most, though, was the decay of the dream, the entropy that seemed to be pulling apart the gleaming performance and replacing it with a maddening reality. At breakfast one morning, dining on bread and apricot jam and butter, Janes was greeted by a scene right out of *The Sound of Music*. "Jarry appeared at the door leading from the house," he recorded in his field notes, and greeted Janes with a formal "Bonjour M'sieur Harry." Passing through the kitchen and into the courtyard, the blond boy was "followed by eleven others, ten boys and one girl," one by one. Marianne, the only girl at this point, acknowledged him "with a curtsey instead of shaking hands like the others." Still, the cycle was quite simple, "all with the same routine, in and out," like the members of a military platoon presenting themselves individually for inspection. It was a perfectly scripted and well-rehearsed performance. But then Moïse, "the Jewish boy," snuck back in, hoping to grab some jam and butter. And then Brahim followed. Then "one or two more," all of them hoping for something to add to their plain bread. Suddenly they were scattered by one of the staff. "Butter and apricot is not for children," Janes wrote, "so many kilograms would go in no time." The children were given bread and ushered back out into the courtyard. The days of excess were over.

And then, he noted, there was the star performer's profound ambivalence about the presentation of the children to their publics. Attending to their posture, the former dancer and movie star obviously cared about how they carried themselves. Still, she also worried about overnight guests and touring visitors taking photographs. "She pointed," Janes recalled, "to the sight-seers who hovered outside the railings with their cameras and binoculars." All of the "main activities" in the house, he noted, were "exposed to public view." And she bemoaned the lack of privacy for her family, for whom she had created this fishbowl life. Then the very next morning, one day after calling everyone's attention to the tourist gallery outside and forbidding photographs from beyond the perimeter, she apologized to her guests and told them to take whatever photos they wanted.[48]

By 1968, Baker began to switch away from her civil rights work. After Baker arrived in New York in January, Robert Kennedy helped to mitigate yet another visa snafu. "I love my country," she said, but "this is the only country in the world where my visits are usually under suspicion." Still, she quickly reassured the press that she was in the United States for "nonpolitical reasons," and that she "planned no demonstrations with any civil rights organizations" (even if she would sneak in a few angry speeches here and there). Instead, she confessed that she had flown into New York—typically, with ten pieces of luggage for just a few days—to meet with a publishing firm that had expressed interest in her life story. Covering her arrival, the *Amsterdam News* couldn't help but attend to her wardrobe, her "navy blue St. Laurent tunic-style suit," her "white mink toque," and her "black suede boots." "She was Parisienne couture all the way," journalist Cathy Aldridge explained. Sharing pictures of the children, she pitched the school she was hoping to establish at Les Milandes in order to institutionalize what she had constructed with her family. The experiment was over, she implied; the Tribe was a success. Now it was time to make it a permanent feature of the world. Driven away from the hotel in a limousine by none other than Roosevelt Zanders— New York City's premier celebrity chauffeur—Baker chose to sit in the front seat. She proclaimed that she wanted to see *Hello, Dolly!* while in town. But more than anything, she wanted some "soul food and a glass of American beer."[49]

It was all an amazing performance, but she had a lot to worry about. Back in France, she owed nearly a million francs to creditors. She wasn't, in the end, a skillful businesswoman, and, every biography and memoir agrees, she'd been taken advantage of by many of the locals who'd been hired to fix this or restore that or remake this. Over the years she'd slipped deeper and deeper into the red side of the ledger. The modest income from her tours and performances couldn't erase her considerable debt. The tourists weren't coming in large enough numbers. And no miracles loomed on the horizon.

The Les Milandes complex was sold in February 1968, less than a month after she returned to Manhattan wearing her white mink toque. An injunction put the final sale off until early May, because French law prohibited eviction in the winter months. After noting that she had raised her "15 youngsters" there, the *Amsterdam News* revealed that she had hoped to turn Les Milandes into "an orphanage for children of all races." Such a dream—the latest of many for the site—was not to be. The initial sale of the château, the hotel, the night-club, and the farm, the paper reported, had "barely covered the singer's debts."[50]

Soon creditors swarmed the place, and Baker "locked herself in the kitchen and refused to come out."[51] The *Afro-American* reported in mid-March that while traveling through Austria, Baker had learned that her beloved château had been stripped of furniture and personal belongings. But her confidant Stephen Papich assures us that she secretly watched the whole sordid affair from her bedroom window. Her "unusual ivory figurine collection," the *Afro-American* reported, was auctioned off. So, too, were her "authentic Louis 13th buffets," her "Spanish Renaissance secretary," and her medieval "knight's wardrobes." Her "authentic corsair's chests" were, it seems, less interesting to bidders. Interest was revived, however, when her Louis Quinze desk was introduced for bidding. "The general atmosphere," it seemed, "though somewhat spirited, was sorrowful."[52] "There was a madness among the bidders," Papich writes, "but not the madness of outrageous bids."[53] The reckless auctioning off of everything she owned failed to cover her debts, ensuring that Les Milandes would be sold.

She still hoped, as always, for a divine intervention, for some deep-pocketed benefactor to appear out of the mist and wipe her debts away. Near the end of April Baker appeared at a department store in Paris, two of the Tribe in tow, and signed autographs for an hour. Rumors flew that she would be making a return to the Parisian stage for a "big engagement at the Olympia," ensuring her hold on Les Milandes. Later she announced that Empress Farah Diba, the wife of the shah of Iran, had generously offered $1,000 to stave off her creditors.[54] But then the May deadline came and went, and she became a squatter in somebody else's castle, someone else's idyll. She sent the children to Paris to stay with a friend, sleeping on an old army cot, biographer Lynn Haney narrates, and eating from tin cans. Eventually a gang of toughs hired by the new owner stormed the barricades, pushed her around, and threw her out in the rain. As Baker remembered the incident in 1973, confiding the details in a whisper to Stephen Papich, "They said words, and I can hardly repeat them to you, like 'motherfucker' and 'nigger' and 'a black bitch who fucks white men for money,' and they actually had me in the mud, and I could not believe it, but they were doing it to me. *To me, mind you!*"[55]

Cleverly, Baker arranged for photographers to arrive and capture her misery. In the final image of her at Les Milandes, taken just after her forced eviction, Baker sits in a crumpled heap at the side door of the château. There is nothing glamorous in her presentation. While she wears her ubiquitous black glasses, she is also clad in a frumpy wool sweater and a knit hat, and is wrapped in a flannel blanket. A bare foot sticks out from beneath the blanket. She looks old, weather-beaten. Her mouth is turned downward into a frown. There are no children present. They'd been sent ahead to Paris. Instead, a few cats—her willing ensemble—sit on a pile of blankets next to her.

Stuck in the rain overnight, she got a chill and was hospitalized. Or maybe it was that she was "roughed up" during the eviction. Or maybe, as Stephen Papich tells us, she had a heart attack as she left Les Milandes in a car, with a kitten on her lap. Help was coming, though, at least for the dream of the Tribe. A Spanish businessman had offered to "set up a new international children's village to house 500 orphans for Miss Baker." And Sidney Williams, former Urban League stalwart and head of Operation Breadbasket's African Affairs Section, was trying to plan a concert tour.[56] Les Milandes might be lost, but the humanitarian spirit of the place could live on elsewhere.

Baker would not be kept down for long. Only a few months later, she appeared at the Monaco Red Cross Gala, a well-heeled affair where a thousand guests consumed (one reporter estimated) 600 magnums of champagne, 850 lobsters, and 132 pounds of caviar. The "minor touches," Ollie Stewart recorded, included David Niven and Maria Callas dining with Princess Grace, and Gregory Peck serving "lobster sauce" to guests. Baker, not content to arrive like every other big star, came in "on a wave," emerging "out of the sea" like a fanciful creature. "Decked out in all her fabled plumes," she arrived on a barge, Stewart described, and was gently hoisted across the ballroom to the stage, an entrance that received a standing ovation. Then she settled into her song-and-dance-and-chatter routine, including a prayer and "J'ai Deux Amours." "Everything else," Stewart concluded, "was anti-climax."[57] She might be without her castle, and her family might be displaced, but she wasn't without panache.

Of course, unlike most of the homeless, Baker was rescued by royalty, namely Princess Grace and Prince Rainier, who swept in soon after the Red Cross Gala, scooped up the Tribe, and deposited them in a villa along the Mediterranean. The Tribe had been briefly scattered by the sale of Les Milandes, the eviction, and Baker's subsequent hospitalization. Now, just a short time after the Red Cross Ball, it would be reconstituted in Monte Carlo in a five-bedroom home on a large plot of land. In a perfect twist of fate, the Red Cross—the charitable beneficiary of Baker's most recent spectacular entrance— had offered to furnish it.[58] Baker "deserved it," the *Afro-American* concluded, and the children "deserve a home in which to romp and study and develop their talents." "It wouldn't surprise me," the paper's anonymous European correspondent editorialized, "if one or two of them didn't turn out to be somebody special. After all, they've got the culture of many lands behind them."[59]

8

Unraveling Plots

She liked little kids. Little, little, little!

—Jean-Claude Baker (2008)

Looking out over the Mediterranean from her new modernist flat, Baker seemed increasingly like an outlier. Les Milandes had been a perfect example of bootstrapping: a place bought on Josephine's terms, sited in a location of her choosing, and reimagined to her exacting specifications. Roquebrune, in contrast, was a place of refuge for the Tribe in unhappy exile, its very existence an emphatic skewering of the myth of the self-made Josephine Baker, an emptying of the fairy tale. "Some of the old elegance and murderous chic is gone," a reporter drolly commented, noting how far Baker had fallen from her most glamorous decades. Instead of wearing Dior, "she sits barefoot in a floppy pants suit on her terrace."

Baker's political positions, once at the cutting edge of the civil rights movement, now seemed to be drifting off in another direction. When the modest successes of the early 1960s proved to have made little structural difference for the great bulk of the poor and the powerless, the language of protest globally had become significantly more abrasive, more direct, and more forceful. She began to hear in the renewed, strident calls for revolution echoes not of the early words of Martin Luther King Jr. but of other, more dangerous ideas. The woman who "needled the bourgeois for a generation and hurled taunts of racial bias at U.S. authorities," the AP reported, was "worried now about the Black Power movement."

Philosophically, Baker was opposed to the word "Black," which she found "nasty" and "less accurate." She had just as much trouble with the word "Power," with its masculine connotations, its sense that fire must be fought with fire. "Don't talk to me about Black Power," she remarked. "All power is power." "I suppose," she mused, "they'd say I'm passé and an Uncle Tom. But I would ask the young boys and girls of color what they would do with the white boys and girls who believe in the right ideals." And she suggested that the "Black Power people would have discriminated against" the NAACP's Walter White, who had light skin and eyes and was "completely white in appearance." "The last time I was in Chicago," she mused, "a Negro boy told me he wanted to kill all the white people, he hated them so." The younger generation, she feared, had moved on, setting aside the idiom of open hearts and open minds, casting aside anyone with light skin (let alone white skin) and taking up the same language of race war that had produced Jim Crow in the first place.

"Miss Baker," the reporter noted, "feels that the world is still perfectable and that love will eventually smite hatred a terrible blow; racial antagonism will disappear too." Tellingly, though, Baker's antidote to the virus of race prejudice in Black Power wasn't the Rainbow Tribe, that powerful edifice that she'd started to build a generation earlier. Instead, drawing on her own life story, she professed, "I think they should mix blood. I think they must mix blood," she revised, switching to the imperative, "otherwise the human race is bound to degenerate." "Mixing blood is marvelous," she went on, evoking decades of commentary on mulatto chauvinism, and sounding rather like the Brazilian theorist of mixture, Gilberto Freyre. "It makes strong and intelligent men. It takes away tired spirits." Such sentiments, of course, can't be squared with her construction of the Tribe, with its hardened racial borders, strictly policed by Baker, and its emphasis on the forceful integration of unchanging racial archetypes. Realizing what she had just said, and amused by her endorsement of hybrid vigor, Baker laughed; "They'll never let me back in the States after that."

The Tribe seemed thoroughly diminished in her mind, a financial burden and not a human rights experiment. Worried that her shows might be "terrible or embarrassing," she confessed, "I feel I'm a bit of a clown, and I'm a little embarrassed when I think of a lady singing at 64." She was no longer doing it all—the singing and dancing, the epic wardrobe changes, the strenuous travel plans—to preach the gospel of the Tribe. Her work was purely mercenary. "I've got kids to take care of and I'm earning money to feed them the best way I know how."[1]

Her comments rubbed more than a few people the wrong way. Just one month later she was writing to her friend Robert Brady, the American expatriate and art collector in Mexico, with a defense. She began, of course, by explaining her outfit at length. "I admit that was not very attractive," she confessed, "but who does think about being attractive when one has to confront everyday worries and house tasks?" "Bare feet and slacks are not only comfortable but practical when one has to do so many things in a hot country like Monte Carlo in August." The focus on her wardrobe seemed excessive, she thought. Her children had been off to school, "my housework for the day was done," and so she had dressed comfortably, assuming that the interview was informal. She confessed, to continue, that when the reporter had used the term "Black," as in "Black Power," that she had been stung, alienated, even confused. She knew the word from its previous, negative context—as the negation of whiteness and civilization—and not from its new, redeemed contemporary meaning. Since the interview, she told Brady, she had picked up a copy of a book by noted historian Lerone Bennett Jr.—perhaps 1968's *Pioneers of Protest*—and had been recommending it to everyone. Moved to rethink her alienation from the term, she'd even written to Bennett Jr. for advice about what to say when next someone asked her about blackness. Bennett Jr., sadly, had not responded. "Do not forget," she lectured Brady, as if she needed to defend herself from the charge of racism, "that I adopted my children whom I called the rainbow tribe, who come from the five corners of the world, to prove that all people are equal, can live together, all religions can be respected, therefore they are a symbol of Universal Brotherhood."

There was more to be said, though. The world, Baker mused, was witnessing a generational revolt. "Our youth around the world," she began, "have been disillusioned, disappointed, and are trying to find the right road." And wherever she saw young people rising up in anger, Baker saw the evidence of poor parenting. Overpermissive parenting. Soft parenting. The catalog of mistakes was long. "Neglect, bad teaching at home, bad manners, the wrong influences, too much freedom, too much money, drugs, too many fine clothes, cars." Reading the agitations of Black Power as the signs of dissenting youth, Baker blamed the older generation in America for the undesirable excesses. "I deplore this kind of education," she wrote, confusing the signs of a dysfunctional home with the signals of a vaster broken social landscape, "I feel real sorry for those who are really heart-broken from insults coming from their children, threats to beat them, sometimes to kill them or others, the stealing, the looting, dope-habits, too much drinking and immorality." Baker admitted that the young represented "to-morrow" but stressed, as well, that they would never become "dignified human beings if they do not respect themselves and their educators."[2]

Roquebrune was an occasional backdrop for Josephine Baker's unraveling plots. The children had gotten older. "The little ones grow," Josephine wrote to Jo in 1965, noting the first changes. Of one of her sons she said, "He has a little down on his upper lip, and his voice has changed."[3] Baker had wanted a mixed platoon of youngsters, easily controlled, not a variegated and psychologically complex group of teens and preteens. She had scripted their performances, trained them to sing on cue, to arrive in a line, to curtsey and bow. She hadn't anticipated that all of them might be caught up in the general distrust of the older generation that seemed so infectious in the late 1960s and early 1970s. She hadn't counted on long hair and bell-bottoms. She hadn't augured the rise of Black Power, with its distrust of white institutions and its distaste for extravagant wealth. She hadn't thought she would ever lose Les Milandes. She hadn't believed she would ever be seen as the establishment. Most of all, she really hadn't considered that the children would shake off their costumes as they grew up, that they would try to break free of the script she had written for them.

Being relocated to the quaint Mediterranean town of Roquebrune seemed to accentuate the growing tensions between children who were now teenagers and who imagined themselves as representatives of a youthful radicalism. They were thirteen including Baker, packed into a modest (for her) apartment with two bathrooms, hardly the opulent surroundings they were used to. Baker micromanaged their rebellious fashions, worried that the boys were growing their hair too long (which made them look like homosexuals, she thought), and clashed repeatedly with the children as a group, staging melodramatic interventions before retreating to her room.[4] She dispatched them to Spain for the summer holiday, then drew them back to Roquebrune. She sent them away to boarding schools or to see old family friends, exporting the responsibilities for parenting. In short, as the children reached young adulthood, Baker's efforts to control their expression of identity or to fix them in her firmament became ever more severe— and ever more unsuccessful, given their own willful desire to be more independent.

But beneath the veneer of French Disney, there was an underground ethos of protest and resentment, especially as the children grew up. Even as young children, a few of them engaged in petty, opportunistic theft, stealing the belongings of visitors on occasion. They secreted themselves along the river to escape the public eye, building a fort where no one could see them. If the moment was right, they went back into the kitchen (as Moïse did when Henry Hurford Janes came to call) to furtively grab some butter and apricot jam, when all they were meant to have was bread. These tiny revolts grew in scale and intensity as they aged, until eventually they came to directly, openly challenge Baker's authority. With Les Milandes gone, all that was left was the Rainbow Tribe. Out of the spotlight, it had to be a family and not a construct. And when it began to fail, Baker grew weary and despondent, depressed by the reality of life after Les Milandes. Janes, writing to her, reminded his old friend of "the good that you have done by example." "How many people," he asked, "have visited Milandes over the years and left more wise and thoughtful of the needs of others?"[5]

Sentiment was not enough for Baker. There was always a plan to remake what she'd lost in the Dordogne. At one point she proposed to retrofit an old prison on an island near Naples into "a school where teen-age students from many countries would spend a free year and learn to live like brothers."[6] A year later, a proposal for the "College of Brotherhood"—now to be located on an island off Šibenik, a medieval port city on the Adriatic in Yugoslavia—was in the works. Meeting with the children, Baker assured them that their new "campus" would have a park even bigger than the one at Les Milandes, with a modernist "citadel," a statue out front to "glorify youth," a museum, sculpture, paintings. She described it as a work already in progress, with roads and telephones and water and electrical service all promised. All they needed was a boat to run back and forth between the school and the mainland. The children suggested that she contact the legendary shipping magnate Aristotle Onassis, who was then married to John F. Kennedy's widow, Jacqueline Kennedy. They needed a name for the boat, an international name, of course. "What about *Josephine?*," three of the children shouted, suggesting a name sure to please Maman; "that's international." And they wondered what would happen to their house in Roquebrune. "We'll sell it," replied

Josephine. She needed—and thought they all needed—that bigger, bolder, dazzling life again.[7] "And we began to dream of paradise again," Akio remembers.

Later, when the Šibenik dream fell apart, she wanted to raise the roof at Roquebrune, allowing for a set of small apartments for the children. "The top floor," Jarry remembered, "would be transformed into a cabaret so that she could do most of her entertaining at home." In a letter home, she asked the Tribe for volunteers to run the restaurant.[8]

Each revision of the plot was complicated, and seemed to require global diplomacy. Scheming to create a new school on a removed island off the coast of Italy, Baker cozied up to Princess Beatrice, the child of Italy's last king, Umberto II. The princess had settled in Mexico with her mother and an infant, and she was hoping for a second child. "Did the Princess finally get my letter and the documents on the school?," Baker asked Brady, serving as her liaison, "because she and her surroundings could help me a lot in Italy concerning our island and my school."[9] Once Beatrice was pregnant, Baker was even more solicitous, sending long missives—including, oddly, given her own family assemblage, a sort-of advice manual for expectant mothers.[10] Creating the illusion of friendship, though, was only a part of the charm offensive. Baker's Italian campaign also led her to a private audience with Pope Paul VI, which she assumed would be helpful in some unspecified way.[11] The most elaborate part of her scheme involved the creation of a massive performance in the Nevada desert ("Las Vegas is the only place to make fantastic sums of money and that is exactly what I need") where the princess would appear in the audience, *avec l'enfant.* "This baby is ours," Baker confided to Brady. She seemed terribly worried about money, and willing to do whatever it took to get more of it as quickly as possible. "Don't worry about the children," she wrote assuredly to Brady, who must have inquired about the impact of this Las Vegas plan on her family, "I can arrange to be away from them [for] the months that are necessary."[12] These elaborate plans—like all the others fizzled out. Beatrice lost her unborn child. "Please telephone Princess Beatrice," she ordered Brady, "and tell her that I think she has been a naughty girl in losing the second baby, but, on the other hand, she will certainly have a third one right away."[13]

Brady, a polished, globe-trotting American, was one of several confidants, but their relationship changed abruptly in 1973. Hearing that Baker was in a hospital in Copenhagen after a heart attack, Brady, a handsome man with an elegant mustache, telephoned and professed his love, promising to be a "good husband in spirit." And Baker, alone since Jo Bouillon left her, accepted the offer. "The idea suited Josephine," the elder Jean-Claude remembered, "[n]o sex and plenty of money at a time when she didn't want the one, and craved the other." She was quite taken with Brady's home in Cuernavaca, with every room jam-packed with painting and sculpture, and every morning beginning with fresh-squeezed orange juice delivered by a servant on a silver tray.[14]

At sixty-seven years old, Josephine Baker was, biographer Phyllis Rose concludes, "in love in the way a lonely person can be in love when someone turns up offering devotion: suddenly, totally, and gratefully."[15] They took their vows privately in a small Catholic church but shared the news with practically no one. "I think the combination is wonderful," Baker concluded with great self-satisfaction, "that is we are completely free and still so near each other without any ties what so ever—it would not work otherwise because I am a *nomade* from the *(désert)*. So are you. That is why it can work." "You are my husband, really," she added.[16] "I have a heart full of love," she admitted in another saccharine missive, "and so do you . . . and it is natural that we share it between us a little. It makes me feel so happy, Bob, and stupidly young like a girl in love for the first time." Baker signed the letter: "Your little crazy wife."[17] Their "marriage"—no less conventional than any of the others in her life, really—was, Baker felt, "like Romeo and Juliet, full of purity."[18] Elsewhere, she added, reassuringly, "Don't forget that you will never have any responsibility concerning me or the children."[19]

Rose interprets this marriage carefully, emphasizing Baker's sincerity. The chanteuse was traveling around the world and had no time for a fixed marriage set in a single location. A spiritual marriage, transcending time and space, seemed like a great idea. What mattered most, she concludes, was that it was emotionally meaningful. Just as importantly, "at a time when poverty was making her life so little gracious, [Brady's house] was a fairy-tale castle." Rose isn't quite so generous with Brady, though. An unmarried gadfly, Brady needed to surround himself with various partners to ensure that he was seen as straight and not gay. He also needed Baker to be seen, on his arm, in his pool, at his neighbor's house, if only to "shock the local gentry" and cement his status as a member of the radical avant garde.[20] But, behind closed doors, Baker was unwilling to be put on display.

Their "spiritual" marriage ended in January of 1974, after Baker's brief stay in Cuernavaca and a disagreement about going out in public. Asking Brady to send "pure thoughts" in her direction, she added, melodramatically, "I must not think of you as it hurts too much." She had felt watched in Mexico, and she hadn't enjoyed the experience. "I who love freedom," she explained, "it is torture to me to be here where all eyes are on me judging me every moment or more."[21] Despite her cheeky "Dear John" letter, they would remain friends until the end. As she worried about the filmic version of her life, or complained about those who sought to ruin her reputation, he would be a constant, comforting personality, a fellow traveler on the celebrity circuit, a kindred spirit in their public performances. Writing to Brady just a few weeks before her death, she told him that she thought her new show in Paris would be "a real triumph." "One thing was missing to complete my happiness," she suggested, after summarizing a successful dress rehearsal, and closing out their correspondence: "you did not come."[22]

Politically, Baker's approach to the widening human rights campaigns of the early 1970s defies easy summary, but she was clearly
still reading and thinking about the great struggles of the day. In the
late summer of 1970, as the occupation of Alcatraz by AIM activists
was ongoing, she likened the United States to a dying parent ("remember the fall of the Roman Empire, Greece, Egypt, Babylon, and the
great Arabic empire?") and made repeated references to the slaughter
and subjugation of Native Americans, linking that to Vietnam, Biafra,
and Cambodia. "Join hands with the American Indians," she advised
Brady . . . "Give them the chance to become president of the U.S.A. . . .
If this does not come to pass, disorder, crime, and injustices will continue and the end will follow soon after that." Noting that, like Native
Americans, black people "have been looted of our dignity and equal
rights," she concluded, damningly, "we have no more confidence in
our white brothers for we feel he has no word."[23] In South Africa in
the fall of 1974, she was sad to find the country's black population
dispirited, but their quiescence worried her. Brought there by an
"advanced liberal," she found it a "dead country, very rich but without
a soul." "This is a money factory," she noted, accurately. "The colored
people remind me of Harlem," she critiqued, "they have no personality, not like other black African countries we know."[24]

    She continued to believe in the power of her own voice, her own
celebrity, to change the world. In a children's story—written, a note
suggests, "in Beverly Hills, California, during the quiet peaceful hours
in the middle of the night on September 20, 1973"—Baker once again
offered herself up as the only person capable of speaking real truth to
power. In "The Fairy Tale of Wisdom," Josephine describes herself as
a "teeny, weeny little brown girl" named Molasses. She "often plays
with" the White Dragon, whose pure white exterior hides his deeper
sins and who "loved to eat little molasses-colored children because
he was greedy and loved sugar. He also loved to eat little snow
white children made of pure white sugar; also banana colored ones
and black candy ones, honey-colored ones and Indian red ones—

all because he was so very, very greedy." The "sweet people"—stand-ins, here, for the global South, for people of color, and for the white working class—decided to stand up to the White Dragon, so they "get together in a council." Their committee work now complete, and their goals and platform now established, they appoint Teeny Weeny Molasses to serve as their delegate, their "Representative of Politeness." Teeny Weeny reads their petition aloud, but also adds, in a classic Baker touch, a powerful bit of sentiment. She tells the White Dragon that he is no longer loved. In the swirling maelstrom that follows, it is her additional words, and not the committee-driven, jointly written bill of particulars, that vanquish the White Dragon. Teeny Weeny emerges, victorious, on the shoulders of her friends and allies. "Everyone rejoiced at her homecoming and felt renewed courage and strength," the story concludes. "Therefore they found peace, happiness, and faith forever and ever." There is much to see in this story: that Baker wished to be recognized as a spokes-person; that she believed, still, in the power of emotional appeals, and that she believed, in the end, that she would win. The Tribe, though, was absent.

One particular letter, written in early July of 1973, gives us a snap-shot of Baker's richly complicated, ever-changing private life. "I will never be like other women," she concluded, writing to Brady, "I can-not accept life without continuous free air." She slipped, inexorably, into business talk. *Ebony* magazine wanted to publish her work, so she assigned Brady a series of networking responsibilities. And then, without missing a beat, she asked him to hire a decorator for her house—the house she'd hoped to purchase in Cuernavaca—"because we have the same taste—we both like good taste and real elegance—not the taste *comme de nouveaux riches*." Brady had another lover (Eugenie Prendergast), but Josephine was not troubled by this at all. "I am so natural and African inside," she summed, "that I think it natural that a man has several wives—and he can love all of them in a different way."[25] Thankfully, Marianne and Stellina would, in just a few days, be dispatched back to England. She'd been having trouble with the children. "That is what is beating me down," she admitted.

Marianne was in trouble. In the winter of 1973 she had fallen in love with a local boy and had been sneaking out to meet with him at night. Her mother, catching her in the act of escape, had what was thought to be a heart attack, and needed to see a doctor to confirm her good health. Writing in the very early morning, "before the tribe wakes up," Baker confessed to Janes, her old army pal, that "everything is in order now," but she worried still about the temptations of sin. She had many children, but Marianne was special. "A really good convent might be the answer," her friend rejoined a few days later, "as Marianne, presumably, is Catholic?"[26]

The peace between mother and daughter was short-lived. Within a few months, her mother had decided to ship her off to Janes and his wife, Peggy, in the English countryside. The aging colonel, perhaps dubious that he could stamp out teenage misbehaviors, suggested an Ursuline convent near Brussels, but he still welcomed the young woman into his home in mid-July. Within a few days, though, he had made up his mind: Marianne needed to be cast out. "You must get rid of her somehow," he wrote urgently to Baker; "you have a duty to yourself." "No establishment in this country," he continued, "except what is called a reformatory for those 'beyond parental control' would accept such a child." Perhaps, he thought, Reverend Brian Matthews, previously a headmaster of a school in the navy, could help. In any case, "Peggy and I are old enough to be Marianne's grandparents—there is a generation between us and *that's* the gap! To them we are old and they are young." Writing a private note to one of Marianne's older brothers, who was scheduled to meet her back in France on her return, the colonel was blunter: "Believe nothing Marianne tells you," he stressed. "She is a liar and a thief."[27]

The story of Marianne's brief exile to the idyllic pasturelands of Britain is a challenging one, putting us at the crossroads of the histories of adoption and celebrity, and reminding us that children, unlike their parents, can't be archived in the same way. What we have is an unequal record, dominated by Baker's voice, shaped by Baker's interest—expressed, often, through her surrogates—in reversing the decline of the family. And of Marianne, most of what we have is the hidden transcript, the resistant actions of a child growing up, seeking control over her life, in an age marked by dramatic generational conflict. It would be easy to read Baker's determination to stamp out her daughter's imprudent sexuality as evidence of a generic 1960s rebellion against all forms of authority, but it is harder, and perhaps more important, to see it as a challenge to the very particular production of this very particular family. Caught up in the inevitable, entropic decline of a transnational icon, Marianne pushed back against the constraints of her own symbolism. And she was not alone. Other members of the family who pushed back were punished or sent off to some metaphorical Siberia. Their story, revealed in the fragmentary record, also suggests that the image of the innocent child, denuded of sexuality, sat at the center of Josephine's imaginary construct of the idyllic family.

This is a rich story, but the fragmentation of the historical record changes the kind of narrative that can be written. Instead of a fulsome record of voices, we have the subtle erasure of the child's voice, staged across a vast global terrain. Ironically, in the spotlighted family headed by Baker, the children are often as silent as the subaltern. That is, I submit, because their voices were significantly less important—less important to "Maman," and less important to their worldwide audience—than their racial visibility, their performance as an ensemble, their presentation as a part of a single object.

Asked about her childhood now, Marianne remembers it fondly. "Milandes will forever be my paradise lost," she writes, defining the site of her performance as a place of children's games and fairy tales,

as life in a "beautiful castle." Her story, she continues, was like that of
Snow White or Sleeping Beauty, and it often felt as if a "good fairy"
had been following her around. "I had a wonderful childhood."[28]
When questioned about her teenage years—the years of troubling
conflicts and forced exiles—she is more reticent and less revealing.
The conversation stops. And, to be frank, I'm not interested in pressing the point, because these are her memories, and not mine. And
because no one, really, can know what happened there, at Roquebrune, when it all came apart.

The man responsible for Marianne's supervision in England, Henry
Hurford Janes, was an old friend. In the midst of her troubled life
after Les Milandes, Baker appears to have rediscovered in him a certain kind of necessary confidant, the sort of loyal hanger-on that
enables the proper functioning of celebrity. Their regular correspondence in the 1940s ended, somewhat painfully, in 1948, a victim of
her return to celebrity, her marriage, and her work at Les Milandes.
Complaining in one letter about "the mystery of Josephine who begs
me to write but never replies," Janes told her in another that he "can't
go on writing and possibly boring someone who may not exist." Still,
they kept in touch, writing to each other over the years with a fondness and an innocence that is, in Baker's historical record, rather remarkable. "Peggy and I," he wrote in 1957, "often think and talk
about you and the little ones and Jo—all together in that old castle, a
strange assorted family, almost like a fairy story." He continued,
"One day I hope I will meet them all—before they are too old. They
looked so sweet in the picture you sent me." Having received his copy
of *La Tribu Arc-en-Ciel*, he told Baker that it "is a sweet and moving
tale and such a good idea—the toddlers of my family love it." "The
other difficulty," he confessed jokingly, referring to the final image in
the book, "is that they now want a little Dutch chicken themselves."

When, in 1967, Baker asked Janes if he would be willing to corre-
spond with Akio, Jean-Claude, Jarry, and Brahim, so that they might
learn "*English* and not *American*," Janes responded by encouraging

her to send the children directly to him on holidays. "Do you still have the courage to take some of my tribe?" she asked in 1970. "Be careful before you answer because they eat a lot." "We shall make it one of our first tasks," he wrote, anticipating a visit, "to make the little cottage in the garden suitable for an international family."[29]

In August of that summer, Baker dispatched Akio, Jean-Claude, Luis, and Mara—"all of whom have gotten good grades"—to the Janeses' country residence, where they arrived after what was termed an "epic journey." The brief stay that followed appears to have gone fairly well, considering that four famous teenagers arrived in rural England in the midst of summer vacation to be "parented" by a very old friend of their mother's, whom they barely knew. Janes tried to encourage them to write to their mother every day, but Akio—the spokesman for the children—insisted on just once every other day. Josephine worriedly wrote to Mara and begged him "not to do anything that Mother would be ashamed of." Janes, a steadfast loyalist, informed Josephine that he had turned down one interview request but was now concerned that a photographer had been stalking the youthful quartet and taking pictures of them as they hung out in the garden.[30]

The trip was a reward for good behavior, and when it was over a month later and they were back in France with their mother, ready for the start of school, Baker asked Janes for a full assessment of each child, which would help her determine their educational future. Janes had proved, Baker added, that "England [is] the best country for the children's education, naturally surrounded by the right people." At the bottom of her letter she hastily added a dramatic postscript, written just before she sent the letter on its way, to say, "Akio was absolutely impossible with me," she confided, "raising his voice, etc., threatening to beat me." Despite her request for a report, she decided not to wait for the full accounting, and instead sent the lot to boarding school. Janes, with great sadness, noted that Josephine had already sent Moïse away to a kibbutz in Israel for similar behavior. "I have puzzled all day trying to find an explanation for this ingratitude," he offered, before suggesting, "it could be that having ventured into another country in charge of three others this had gone to his head. Children here have the vote at 18. I deplore this but that has been decided." He suggested that she send all twelve away. "Whatever the outcome," Janes wrote reassuringly, "you have done a few fine things for these children— and whatever they do now—they will, later on, be grateful for the chances in life that you have given to them."[31]

This brief August stay—resulting, in a very abstract way, in the expulsion of several children to boarding school—brought Janes back into Josephine's closer confidence. Over the next few years the two corresponded regularly about the challenges of parenting and about how it felt to be unwanted, used up, and ignored by the young. When Baker, writing from Monte Carlo, asked Janes if he could take six of the children in the late summer of 1971, the elderly former soldier politely declined, citing age. After Baker confided in Janes about the latest adolescent uprising at home, Janes replied gently, "How cruel the young can be." And when Baker asked Janes for financial advice, he replied, with more than a little hand-wringing, that there wasn't much he could do or say, as the problems seemed endless and complex. "There seem to be so many loose ends and cul-de-sacs and some financial hardship," the small-town pensioner wrote, trying to make sense of the global scale of Baker's hardships. Confiding in Janes in the spring of 1972, Baker opened up about how badly she had been hurt by the brutal ending of Les Milandes. "The world," she spat out, "is *dirty, corrupted, and without respect.*"[32]

"Akio and Janot are leaving for Tokio . . . for their school there," she wrote one day, followed by "Koffie and Marianne are now in Abidjan." "Let them go when the time is ripe," Janes replied aphoristically, "as you're still there as their mother to 'pick them up and set them on their feet if they fall down.'" Baker's long-term plans for the children had always included a ceremonial return to their respective homelands, a task modestly complicated by her assignment of identi-

ties at the outset to meet the political needs at Les Milandes—for
example, Moïse, who was adopted in France, was sent to Israel. The
rather abstract necessity of return became psychologically important
as the children got older and began to rebel, each in his or her own
way, against "Maman." "You know perfectly well," Baker instructed
Moïse in an angry letter signed "J. Baker," "why you were sent to Israel: to soak up your people's history and to become a man worthy
of the name Moses." Meanwhile, Mara, brought from Venezuela,
was returned to meet his grandfather, his "Indian chief father," and
"other members of his tribe and family." "How wonderful for you
and for him," Janes acknowledged to Baker. "Everyone must belong,
have someone of their own flesh and blood and you are so wise not to
be possessive about your children which when they grow up will
bring them back to you with love and gratitude."[33]

Baker had unevenly maintained the racial and religious identities
she assigned to the children. Language tutors came and went. Identities shifted and changed, slightly or subtly. Baker traveled a lot, and it
wasn't easy to maintain a consistent education for each child in her
absence. More important, the children's common schooling—and
the need for each child to be first and foremost French—also miti-
gated her desire to define the children as costumed racial exemplars.
Despite her initial attempts to maintain traditional dress and style,
most of the photographs taken at Les Milandes, for instance, feature
the children in similar modern dress, and usually in some classic
white or blue schoolboys' and schoolgirls' outfits. Only a few of
the public relations photos show any of them—and usually only
Akio—in ethnic costume. Sending them back to their homelands, a
temporary repatriation, was a way to reinscribe them with race, to
provide them, she thought, with a richer sense of their own blood
inheritance.

Most of the children were sent to their homelands after Les Milandes. Koffi's return to Côte d'Ivoire was supposed to last for two
years. Coming from France, he was labeled a "faux noir," his only

connection to the cultures and peoples of his homeland coming from books. A local leader's child who had been educated in Europe was nicknamed, in a joking spirit, "Faux Blonde."[34] Mara, for his part, had not been back to Venezuela since he was two months old. On the plane bound to Caracas, Josephine explained soberly that if Mara wanted "to stay with them"—with his family—she would understand. Landing at the newly opened La Chinita airport, Mara found the runway mobbed with relatives and friends of relatives, "a swarm of people, all of whom seemed to be cousins." There was dancing—"right on the runway," he remembered, "to the beating of drums"—and drinking and celebrating. "I was a real *guajiro*," a roughneck of the backcountry. He realized, in a moment of racial reconnection, an acknowledgment that in this particular sight line he matched up with the carousers. "I could tell from the faces around me. I had their features, the same black hair." While Mara reconnected and met "almost every person of note in Caracas," Josephine proselytized for UNICEF, preached the gospel of her twelve apostles, and orchestrated a few "gala performances." "Wherever we went," he remembered, "we were followed by a flock of my tribal brothers."[35]

Like Koffi, Mara walked away from the experience with a profound sense of the vast distance between his life and that of his fellow *guajiros*. He noted the "obvious poverty" of his relatives and his shock at their repeated requests for money. "You can't blame them," Josephine explained, "they're desperate." Mara should be angry, she continued, at the social forces that made such desperation possible. She stressed that he should point the finger not at the poor farmer in the country but at a world "motivated by self-interest." This mad and selfish need for more, she concluded, was to be opposed by the Tribe. "That's why," she underlined for him, "our family's actions today and the way you behave after I'm gone is so important."[36]

Jarry's story was different. When he was discovered one afternoon in the bathtub with another boy, Josephine marched the teenager out in front of the Tribe. Raising the problem of "contamination," she asked for a family vote—including the votes of Margaret and her husband, Elmo—on whether he could stay, as queerness was a high crime for Baker. And then, the court-martial complete, she shipped him off to Buenos Aires, where he found a home, again, with Jo Bouillon.

Jarry's forced exile revealed that Josephine could move swiftly in a moment of crisis. The family's time in Roquebrune was marked by unraveling plots, as the fairy tale started to come apart. The tumultuous 1970s featured a rebelliousness of affect and aesthetic, slogans and symbols. Knowing this, Baker strictly policed her children's sexuality, homing in on the clothing, mustaches, and long hair of the boys. They pushed back, though, and refused to bend to her will. She imported male authority figures, without any luck. She declined to discuss her own youthful rebellions. She drew lines in the sand, fought for authority on every issue, and engaged in extreme parental brinksmanship. And eventually, after one too many arguments and fights, she just plain old "gave up."[37]

Jean-Claude Baker theorizes that the difficulty of dealing with youthful rebellion once the children were no longer small was why Josephine liked animals. Animals didn't become ungrateful as they grew older, didn't act out. Animals could be obedient, simple-minded. Over time, children become—whether we want them to or not—independent agents, with their own interests and concerns. For someone like Josephine, managing a dozen discrete personalities and psychologies as the children became older and wiser and self-interested was infinitely more complex, especially in the diminished surrounds of Roquebrune, than managing the display of smaller children. There is something to this argument, this sense that some of the melodrama after Les Milandes can be traced to the inevitable consequence of time, with all that it entails. Children are difficult to control; teenagers—as the world builds them today—can be even more so.

There is another way to see this, a complement to Jean-Claude's insight. What was being controlled here was not merely a psychological being but a political construct. Baker's presentation of Marianne as the "princess" at the heart of the family was a clever prophylaxis for her hidden critique of France. If the audience drawn to Les Milandes grew concerned about language instruction in Arabic or Yiddish, or about "white" children in a family with a "black" mother, there was Marianne, exquisitely, perfectly, pristinely French, providing direction for the whole family, drawing them into the nation-state and incorporating what had been thus far extrinsic. She was the child at the center of the symbol. The very internationalism of Les Milandes—lived by the children, but scripted by Baker—was enabled by Marianne's perfect provincialism, for she provided a soothing endpoint, the happy recognition of French superiority, for the necessarily mysterious and unusual assemblage offered up to visitors.

So when Marianne, named for—and raised as—the revolutionary icon of reason and liberty, got too wild, her mother shipped her off to an old British army man in the remote countryside of England, hoping that the stricter Victorian code of another, greater empire might provide rehabilitative moral certainty for her supposedly troubled daughter. This was a transnational solution for a transnational problem, and perfectly in keeping with Baker's global vision of the family. It also reflects, in the age of profound general generational upheaval, a near perfect match between the "trouble with Marianne" and the rapidly changing world.[38] And it reminds us, once again, that these were children, drafted into a celebrity's army, and not volunteers. "Marianne is giving me trouble," Josephine wrote to Robert Brady in the spring of 1974, before turning the great bulk of her letter to a description of two new dogs—Moustique and Fifi, one big and one small. Writing of the dogs, she told Brady, "I just must give my love to something or somebody."[39] Two months later, she added, "The dogs are well and the children are running me around like a top."[40]

In this telling, the transnational dimension of the Tribe's childhood matters a great deal. It is a central feature of their singular biographies and group presentation. It structured their education, their parenting, their experiences in France and abroad. In the end, though, their celebrity mattered just as much. It mattered precisely because it meant that their life stories were also given and constrained, not merely capriciously and arbitrarily made. It meant that their life was scripted and controlled, despite all the global movement, despite the cosmopolitanism that can be found at every step. In Marianne's case, it meant that once she began to "misbehave," her mother sent her away, and was then advised to "get rid of her." Costumed characters in a Disney theme park get sent back for retraining or fired when they veer off script; something rather like that happened to the children of the Rainbow Tribe, but a family can't be shaken loose.[41]

The plots may have unraveled, but they were never erased. Marianne's contributions to this patchwork "life" in Baker's autobiography were short and scarce. Recalling life after Les Milandes, she told the story of her mother's mad driving, her routine confrontations with other drivers, and her eagerness to manipulate the star-struck police officers who happened across the scene. "On a narrow inland road," she recalled, "we found ourselves nose to nose with an enormous truck. Maman got out of the car and shouted at the burly driver that it was up to him as a gentleman to back up. Just in case, she told me to find a policeman. When I returned with the officer, she was up in the cab, seated beside the trucker. They were exchanging snapshots of their children and swigging wine out of a bottle." Written only a few years after Marianne was dispatched to England and branded a liar and a reprobate, this simple souvenir seems, on the face of it, hardly critical. It is whimsical and respectful, winking at the reader, as if to share a laugh about Baker's all-around outrageousness. Marianne's place in the autobiography—like that of the children, generally—is uncertain. She functions here, on one hand, as an independent agent, recalling her mother's wild and crazy life. Her words are offered as testimony, honest and fair. And yet they are pressed into service once again as extensions of Josephine Baker's story. The very placement of her words has been determined by the gaps in her mother's life. And her role in the text is itself a reflection of the careful choreography of a surviving parent.

Stellina was the youngest member of the Tribe and the last best hope for Josephine to have a "good girl and an honorable little girl."[42] "I got very tired of being the only girl in the family," Marianne recalled. Visiting Italy with her mother, she had fallen in love with an orphan named Stellina, but the child was whisked away and given to another family. Back in France, pining for the lost child, Marianne pretended that she had a little sister and laid out clothes for her in the morning. When Josephine brought Marianne back to North Africa in the mid-1960s (Brahim and Koffi came along to be circumcised), they found another orphan, another child in need of salvage, and named the child—who was of Moroccan ancestry but born in France—Stellina, after the original orphan in Italy. A confusing genealogy, but a fitting one, perhaps, for a global family with a cosmopolitan mission. "I took care of her as if she were mine," writes Marianne.[43]

One morning Josephine phoned the Janes residence and spoke with Peggy at length. She shared her thoughts about "the difficulties with the children, particularly with Marianne who," Janes summarized in his research notes, "is sleeping with all and sundry and out all night, including unfortunately an Englishman." Three of the boys, Josephine continued, had "done all they can to be thrown out of the army" and had been threatening her, which led Peggy and Henry to encourage her to leave the villa to the Tribe and find a safe place to stay. Above all else, Janes noted, Baker was worried about the corruption of Stellina. "I must save her," she confessed, "just the one success. Otherwise she will be just like the rest."[44]

Fortunately, Janes and his wife had fallen in love with Stellina in 1973, when she'd accompanied Marianne on the elder girl's ill-fated sojourn to the English countryside. By 1974 Baker had essentially deeded the child to Janes, making her English agents responsible for the education of her youngest while she toured and traveled unencumbered. And Janes, a fan of the strict approach taken in religious schools toward the education of young women, promptly enrolled her in St. Mary's Convent school in Folkestone, a modest seaside town just across the English Channel from Calais, France. Baker, adding a postscript to a note of thanks, encouraged him to keep her there for "many years, so she will be a little girl well brought up."[45] Correspondence over the year that followed suggests a happy resolution, as the Janeses seemed quite taken with the young girl and she with them. "I received the report from the school concerning Stellina," Baker wrote in 1975, roughly a month before she died. "It is very good and I am so happy to have taken the decision of sending her to England. And many thanks to you if she is becoming a perfectly brought up young girl."[46]

Acting as a liaison between a nine-year-old girl and her globe-trotting, superstar mother wasn't easy. Marianne's influence over the girl, Henry guessed, was strong. Sagely, the older sister had encouraged Stellina to write to Josephine and complain if she wanted to leave the school, knowing that her mother would be moved by such concerns.[47] And occasionally the youngest of the Tribe showed a perfectly normal childlike capacity to stretch the truth. Josephine's gamboling around the world made it hard to figure out the truth sometimes. "Stellina is talking about leaving school three days early on 15th December," Henry wrote to Josephine, who was then touring in South Africa. "Perhaps I have misunderstood her or she you but she says you have plans for her to appear in your show with other little girls." "For myself," he continued, offering editorial comment, "I think it is unwise to confuse your professional life with Stellina's personal life."[48] Repeatedly Stellina would suggest that Maman wanted her somewhere at a given time, and Henry and his wife would have to get to the bottom of it. Sometimes Josephine wrote back, and sometimes she didn't. When Baker stopped writing or responding, Henry challenged her directly. "You have entrusted Stellina into our care while she is in this country," he reminded her, "and if we are to continue to watch over her, time must be found on your part for the usual courtesies—otherwise we give up!"[49] "Please don't listen to Stellina," Josephine implored via a hasty telegram, "I will naturally speak to you always about my plans."[50]

In truth, Baker had already moved on from her commitment to the Rainbow Tribe as the symbolic answer to the world's racial questions. Dispatching Stellina to England only confirmed that her interest in parenting had changed. She was well over sixty years old. Gone were the advertisements touting the children's love of this product or that. Absent were the lengthy paeans to domestic mixture and interracial play, the speeches about what the world could learn from Les Milandes, Roquebrune, or Šibenik. There were always plans for a future in some grand place, but those plans never left the drawing board. Josephine always seemed to be too busy touring, trying to cover her still considerable outlays. When Janes wrote to Baker in January 1975 suggesting that Marianne should become Baker's personal secretary and that Akio, Jarry, and Luis ought to help with the business side of things, he captured—unintentionally—the subtle reordering of priorities.[51] The entertainer came first; the family—the once glorified Rainbow Tribe—had become a temporary staffing solution.

The world had moved on, too. What had once seemed radical and revolutionary now seemed like pure camp, more Village People than United Nations. In June 1973, Baker began a sixteen-week tour of the United States. She started in New York and then went to Los Angeles. By early November she was in the Bay Area, moving between San Francisco and the Circle Star Theater in Oakland, California.

Backstage after one of her Bay Area performances, Baker and the author Alex Haley were discussing a prospective biography of the singer. Along came an older woman, a classic northern California type: blond, tanned, with a big smile. Introducing herself as an adoptive parent with many children, she took issue with Josephine's racial display of her children and with her commercialization of the Rain bow Tribe. Turning what was private into something public, pushing the children into the spotlight and on stage, trotting them out like stage props—it all seemed just too scandalous, too vulgar. Jean-Claude Baker, there with Baker and Haley, remembers that Josephine turned to him and said, "Take care of this, would you?" With that, Dorothy DeBolt, the locally famous mother of twenty children, many adopted from the war-torn regions of Southeast Asia and most of the adopted children physically disabled, was dismissed.

Baker envisioned the family as a United Nations, rich with lin guistic, religious, racial, and national diversity. Her emphasis was always on extraordinary variety, a diversity that went far beyond skin tone. For Dorothy DeBolt, however, whatever diversity existed in the family (and there was plenty in hers) was meant to be slowly, gradually, and permanently ground down. Skin tone, accent, and national background were surface reminders of a past that had been—or would be—replaced. If for Baker the family was a metaphor for the world, for DeBolt joining the family meant joining the nation, and becoming a member was akin to becoming American. For Baker color-consciousness was the point of the assemblage, while for De- Bolt color-blindness was the ultimate goal of adoption. Viewed this way, DeBolt's reaction to the Rainbow Tribe was predictable, even understandable. And her decision to confront Baker makes sense.

But all big adoptive families that are symbolically arranged like Baker's are public properties. They serve a political purpose, helping to script a better future and providing guidance on what the world might look like. Bob and Dorothy DeBolt were just ordinary Ameri- cans, not celebrities. He was an engineer and she was a homemaker. Despite this seemingly "average" pedigree, they knew how to act in front of the camera. Local newspapers and even *Ebony* had followed their creation for years. They had welcomed a documentary camera crew into their home and their lives for nearly two years. And they would write a book, too, the much celebrated *Nineteen Steps up the Mountain.*[52] The DeBolts—like Baker—completely collapsed the wall between private and public, giving the television viewing public a window into the industrial scale of the family-as-assimilation-factory. Whatever the race, origin, language group, or disability of any one child, they all had to work together to keep the system going. The De-Bolt family captured an American system of assimilation then in the ascendancy.

But the confrontation with Dorothy DeBolt is a lost fragment of history, a telling clash of ideologies that revealed the biggest unraveling plot of all: Josephine Baker's family was a political liability. Her parenting seemed to trivialize the children, to turn them into rich adornments for their mother, which seemed backward, even old-fashioned. To activists, it was no longer clear what problems were best addressed by the gaudy spectacle of the Tribe. The age of idealistic marches was over, and the age of riots, deteriorating cityscapes, and white flight had arrived. It wasn't just that the civil rights consensus had been fractured or that de Gaulle was gone; it was, instead, that the globe was drifting toward a future in which Josephine Baker and the Rainbow Tribe seemed like a rather quaint reminder of the past.

9

Rainbow's End

Special people who are soft touches come to the world and get creamed.

—Ishmael Reed (1976)

The story of Josephine Baker and the Rainbow Tribe ends, as one might expect, with a final burst of energy, an enthusiastic leap into the spotlight one last time, a last commercialization of the self for the good of all. She set out to create a fabulous review of her life, a monument to her enduring magnificence, all for her Parisian fans. And, of course, for her beloved Tribe. It would be a spectacle bigger than any other, more ambitious than any previous performance, with many more gowns and costumes than usual, many more songs and dances, and far more flash and glitter. They'd call it *Josephine*. This extraordinary choreographing and performance of her self-aggrandizement is classic Josephine Baker, the stuff of showbiz legend, the sort of plot point about egomaniacal superstars that gets recycled into movies and television shows. In Baker's case, though, the familiar melodrama was followed not by a sad, easy ending but by a desire on the part of those around her to continue the story. Not the story of the Tribe, really, but the story of *her,* the narrative of the commercialization of Josephine, and the sale of *her* to everyone. The end of Baker's life, then, was not an end at all, but a revenue-generating opportunity, a chance for someone else to make a buck, marked by crass competition and a deliberate reengineering of the cottage industry of *her* that she had so successfully pioneered. Through it all, the Tribe was an unwitting part of the scrum, an accent piece—for good or bad—in the repackaging of Josephine Baker.

Her last television interview takes place backstage at the Bobino, the ancient music hall in Montparnasse. "Le théâtre de la chanson et du rire," the massive sign outside reads, and right below that there is her name, blown up and oversized: "Josephine Baker." In her dressing room, a small bouquet of light pink roses sits in a vase on the dresser alongside rows of makeup brushes, face creams, and a compact mirror. Propped up at the edge of the dresser is a framed cover from the Dutch-language *ABC* magazine, featuring a younger Josephine with three of her children, then infants, playing on the floor with her. In the photo Baker wears a patterned scarf as a headdress, and the children, arranged from brown to black to white, are each dressed distinctively. Luis, in the middle, his dark brown skin in contrast with his brother's white jumper, wears only a necklace of conch shells. "Josephine Hervond Het Geluk," the headline reads: "Josephine regains happiness."[1] That background image of Josephine and the Tribe at Les Milandes contrasts with the image of the superstar positioned in front of the camera for a one-on-one, wearing her costume for the show's finale: a modern-looking military uniform, a khaki designer number, with a smart blue tie, simple gold epaulets, and a trim ribbon bar. There is glitter around her eyes. "The stripes you are wearing . . . ?" the interviewer asks, referring to the proudly displayed ribbon bar. "I earned them on the battlefield," she replies matter-of-factly.[2]

"C'est Si Bon," the finale, is a happy little number, a jaunty celebration of the quotidian. The song was sung by stage performers as different as Dean Martin, Brigitte Bardot, and Eartha Kitt. Baker's version begins with a slowed-down, whispery, casual tone. Gently sashaying onto the stage, illuminated only by a single spotlight, she sings in front of an army jeep full of young men, each swaying to the beat and smiling at her lyrics. It is a reminder at once of North Africa and of the reinvention that set her on a path toward Les Milandes, but also of her famous platoon of child soldiers, then scattered between Roquebrune, Paris, Britain, and elsewhere. Then, with a gesture of the hand, the beat shifts and the song changes, bringing the audience toward a rapid-fire, enthusiastic conclusion. As the music switches, the stage is swarmed by young men in uniform, all of them waving goodbye, smiling. "That's life," she concludes in French. "Always smile."

The interview continues. "How is your large family doing?," the journalist asks. "They are growing up and getting married," she answers with a smile, always with the smile. "One of my sons, Luis, is getting married on the thirty-first." "You have ten children?" he prompts. "Yes," she says, before realizing that he has gotten the number wrong. "No," she corrects emphatically, "I have *twelve* children. Ten boys, two girls." "Twelve!," he exclaims. "Yes, twelve," she admits, as if that is a lot. Then she chuckles, "It's a good thing the girls did not hear this." As if they might be upset to be left out of the Tribe.

"Are they coming to see you in the show?" the interviewer asks. "No," Baker answers, "they are studying." Asked if she regrets their absence—if she misses them—she phrases her response carefully. "Well, it is difficult to say. With all the rehearsals and work for the show," she admits, "it is a good thing they are not here, because when I'm with them I forget absolutely everything else. Only my children matter. But now I need calm and peace to focus entirely on my Parisian audience."

"Nostalgia is such a success," Eugenia Sheppard had written, "that Josephine Baker is planning to give the world a little more of it." Sheppard was referring to Baker's creation of a 1930s-style "Chez Josephine" in the basement of the Sherry-Netherland hotel in 1974, but she could have extended it to cover most of Baker's work in the decade of disco.[3] Like nearly everything she'd done since WWII, then, her final stage performance at the Bobino was a nostalgic survey and celebration of her life. It challenged her physically. She'd slimmed down in preparation for all the dancing, singing, and costume changes. There had been six weeks of choreography and rehearsals, six weeks apart from her Tribe. And, despite her history of heart trouble, she had decided on a comprehensive appreciation of her life rather than a selective look. She held a trial run, a performance for readers of *France Soir*, and made some changes to the work in progress. At the end of a rehearsal, she would fall asleep on someone's shoulder, "like a child." She cut an elaborate dance contest number involving the audience because "it burns up a lot of my energy without adding much." She celebrated Easter by reading a letter from the Tribe. "Luis had gotten married while Josephine was opening at the Bobino," journalist Jacqueline Cartier recalls, "but the fact that she couldn't attend the ceremony was unimportant." "What counted," she writes, giving voice to Josephine, "was that everyone was happy and each child contributed an affectionate word."[4] When "J-Day" finally arrived—the official opening of the show on April 8—a series of preview performances and test runs had already generated positive impressions and word-of-mouth. That final number brought her back to WWII, back to life before the Rainbow Tribe. And then when the stage lights dimmed, the response was the sort of music hall folklore that lives on forever in movies, with heartfelt standing ovations, lavish reviews, and hours of post-gala celebration.

Veteran *Afro-American* correspondent Ollie Stewart, who had been covering Josephine since her rumored death in North Africa, was thrilled to see her back on the stage. "Going back 50 years and stitching together the high points of her life," he advertised, "the Bobino extravaganza has something for everyone," from "costumes" to "pretty girls" to "lilting music." Even the bits that used her recorded voice—employed tactically, to give Josephine a break—seemed to Stewart "technically perfect." "Her voice is still sure," he marveled, "and her dancing still sparkles, but how long can she keep up the pace?" "She is well into her sixties," he continued, "she's been sick,

and she's had worries that would have floored most people." Propheti-
cally, he added, "It's still true what they say about the heart being
willing but the flesh being weak."[5]

Stewart was right to be worried. After two straight nights of *Josephine*
(the show ran two and a half hours), Baker was exhausted. Cartier
found her staring into the mirror at one point, assessing a face that
was no longer young. Determinedly, Baker worked out the kinks in
her hair, donned a simple black wig and sunglasses, and—"the picture of casual elegance"—walked across the street from the Bobino
to a little café, where she ordered a plate of spaghetti and a glass of
beer, a "favorite" meal. Then she adjourned to her hotel room, where
she donned a flowered robe, opened up the early reviews of *Josephine*,
and lay in bed, enjoying the universal adoration in black-and-white
print. At some point—lying there just like that, surrounded by the
voice of her public—she slipped into a coma. She'd had a massive cere-
bral hemorrhage. News of her hospitalization leaked slowly. The very
day the *Afro-American* ran Stewart's prescient piece, Baker passed
away at the Pitié-Salpêtrière hospital in Paris.[6] "Heard the news on
the radio at 6am," Margaret wrote to Robert Brady. "Got ready and
off to Paris I went. When I got there and saw her, knew rite away she
could not make it this time."[7]

The funeral in Paris was more like a parade, as the coffin wound its
way through the streets of Paris from the hospital to the Bobino and
then to the imposing Church of the Madeleine, the impressive neoclassical church built by Napoleon as a celebration of his army's great
prowess. The children were scattered, which meant that only Jarry
and Mara could join Jean-Claude the elder at the service in Paris. But
there were plenty of stars and just as many paparazzi. "It's not a funeral," Jean-Claude remembers thinking, "it's an opening." Thousands of ordinary people, present either for the sheer spectacle of the
public promenade or because of some genuine affection for Josephine,
lined the streets. Jo Bouillon arrived from Buenos Aires. "Baker always had a great appreciation for the grandeur, flair and style with

which the French do almost everything," Charles Sanders wrote for *Ebony,* "and she would have loved the way that Paris responded to this final curtain call."[8] Within the church, something rather like a state funeral took place, full of military honors and with an audience of ministers, celebrities, and cast members of *Josephine.*

The autobiography orchestrated by Jo Bouillon ends with this double triumph—the success at the Bobino and the miraculous "final curtain call." It closes with Mozart's Requiem, followed by the church's venerable pipe organ playing the notes to "J'ai Deux Amours." "The little song solemnly filled the vault," Jacqueline Cartier recalls, "then moved upward and beyond."[9] Equal parts parade, circus, and music hall performance, Josephine Baker's Parisian funeral was a coup of stagecraft and statecraft, a fitting end to a book that was always intended as an accounting of her great success. This language of triumphalism is replete across the press coverage of her death, too. "She knew that death hovered over her like a shroud," *Ebony* began. "Thus the old trouper had wanted *JOSEPHINE* . . . to be her show of shows, the most brilliant of her many triumphs. She was, she knew, the last of the grand stars of French music hall—Mistinguette, Edith Piaf, Maurice Chevalier, Josephine—and she would have to show Paris what being *une grande vedette* was all about."[10]

Just as soon as the ceremony was over, though, Josephine's body was "kidnapped" by Princess Grace and whisked off to Monte Carlo for a small, "more dignified funeral." This time nearly the entire Tribe was there. A large arrangement of white roses in the shape of a heart stood near the casket with a ribbon bearing the words "Papa et les enfants." Photos of the affair are striking, heart-wrenching, unnerving. Princess Grace, standing ramrod straight, is dressed in black from the tips of her toes to the ends of her fingernails. The Tribe, captured in color, looks shell-shocked, like they cannot believe that Maman is finally, truly gone. Below their collective portrait, *Ebony* helpfully provided parenthetical tags, so that the reader might know which child was from which nation—the sort of scrawl that might

appear under a photo of UN delegates. "It was for them," we are reminded, "that she decided, at age 69, to appear in what would be her
final show." Little Stellina, standing next to Jo, is dressed in a white
blouse and black skirt, her face warped by the struggle to contain
tears. Margaret Wallace, Josephine's sister and the longtime co-
parent of the Tribe, looks solemn, withdrawn. And there is Jo Bouillon, still the legal parent and guardian of the Tribe, most of whom
are too young to be on their own; some, in fact, barely remember
him. "Everything is now in Jo Bouillon's hands," Margaret admitted.[11] Jean-Claude remembers that a small blind girl, one of many
mourners that day, made her way to the casket and touched it "as
though she believed Josephine had special healing powers."[12]

The real princess—the former Grace Kelly, Baker's last, great
patron—had her mythic friend buried at the Cimetière de Monaco.
There Baker lies today, interred alongside Luis's child, who had passed
away, tragically, as an infant. Her gravesite, which is both easy to find
and often visited, is marked by an impressive dark brown granite edi
fice, including a tombstone with a large Christian cross and a brass
plaque in the shape of a feather, honoring her as a veteran of WWII
and a member of the French Legion of Honor. Blooming rosebushes
are nearby, climbing toward the sky, a reminder of the roses near the
kitchen entrance at Les Milandes. The polished stone is always covered with flowers left by touristic pilgrims who know Baker as a hero
and a trailblazer. The stone is beautiful. It took Princess Grace six
months to choose it, which meant that Josephine wasn't buried until
October. In the intervening months, Jean-Claude Baker tells us, her
body was stored in a gardener's shed.[13]

Baker had spent the last few years of her life engaged in the crafty
performance of aristocratic chic, directing attention away from her
increasing financial impoverishment, her hand-to-mouth dependency
on gifts and gate receipts. When she appeared in New York in April
1973 to see her old friend Bricktop onstage, she let it be known that
her hotel and airline tickets had "materialized" after she told Jack

Jordan, a film producer, that she'd wanted to see the show. Someone asked her whether she was "less than rich after so long and splendid a career." "Less than rich" is not the same thing as "poor"; rather, it is a sign that the woman who had lived in castles, and whose "shelter" after she'd lost Les Milandes had come in the form of a Mediterranean villa personally delivered by a princess, could never be truly poor. Baker, "her hair concealed under a tower of fox, her eyes behind Martian sized dark glasses," a "white scarf knotted at her throat," responded "silkily." Crossing her legs "in leisurely fashion," she professed, "I'm very rich, you know, but I don't have any money. I am very rich in my soul." "When people retire," she continued, pressing her point home, "they die. I don't have time to die right now. My youngest is only nine . . . I work a lot. I'd better work. I have to pay for all my children."[14] With her death, such performances ended. All the rhinestone sparkle, designer fashion, and extravagant chic were revealed as distractions. During the buildup to the Bobino, to "J-Day," the distraction had worked, because it was so compelling and well performed, and because the windfall from the show promised to keep her afloat, just "less than rich," to keep her children in school, in college, or merely clothed, fed, and housed. Then it all stopped.

Stellina, for one, was left in limbo. Henry Janes, her unofficial guardian, worried about the legal implications of his stewardship of the young woman's education. "Naturally," he wrote reassuringly to Jo Bouillon, "Peggy and I and family will fall in with whatever is decided as to Stellina and obviously you must have time to exchange views as to the future of the family with the older members of the family." "There are many things I should talk to you about," he added a few days later, "for the benefit of you and your family for in the course of this long time I have had many talks and hundreds of letters from Josephine." Days stretched on to weeks. Finally, Janes's nervousness—his repeated insistence that he'd been acting on Josephine's wishes, his worry that Bouillon might dislike much of what had been done in her name, and his concern for Stellina—led him to insist that Bouillon sign what was essentially a legal release, acknowledging that Janes's actions were in accordance with Josephine's wishes. "Arrangements since Josephine's death have been verbal or postal on a personal basis," he complained. He needed something in writing, something official. And he was concerned, too, that no one (at least from his point of view) had accepted legal guardianship of the youngest member of the Tribe. The form letter he insisted Bouillon sign included an admission of legal responsibility. And Bouillon, to his credit, quickly signed and returned it.[15] Soon Janes would write to Princess Grace to express concern about "the immediate future of this little girl," hoping that the princess would take her in.[16]

This would seem like a messy ending to a messy story, with a morass of hazy legal claims and half-articulated responsibilities, a scattered Tribe of children, and various relations involved. But it is a logical consequence of Baker's death. Socially provocative, managed properties such as the Tribe depend on powerful, nearly dictatorial leaders, iron-willed matriarchs or patriarchs with a certain glamour about them, to plot their course, propel them forward, and hold them together along the way. They require such irreplaceable, singular center points because they are unusually assembled, built as a symbol and not, at first, as a family. When these leaders pass away, chaos results. Baker left her heirs no scripture, no means of succession, and no charismatic substitute to fill her celebrity shoes. She left only a disorganized desk filled with incomplete files, idiosyncratic plans, and random letters to document her career as a righteous and certain family leader. It would take Bouillon some time—and he would need some help—to figure out what to do, to determine how best to incorporate her celebrity.

The practice of incorporation, Josephine knew, is central to the arc of celebrity. It isn't merely about a given superstar's self-commercialization—say, the course she plotted from Bakerfix to Cerveza Africana to Les Milandes. It is, instead, about the necessity of perpetuating the social life of the product well beyond the physical life of the superstar. It is about creating a market, a need, a culture of expectation in the general public, an anticipation of the magical work that only a specific celebrity can perform. Baker had been trying, for decades, to make it possible for the idea of "La Baker" to generate enough revenue and symbolism to enable her retirement, to do her "work" even in her absence, but it never came to pass. She'd hoped that the world would be drawn to Les Milandes, but that hadn't happened, either. She'd wanted to change everything, but to do any of that she needed to be successfully incorporated, so that the great system of meaning-making and salesmanship could sell *her* to an audience already desperate for what she offered. In death, Bouillon sensed there was one last chance to pull this off.[17]

Janes wanted to be a part of this incorporation. In the early 1970s, before Baker's death, he began to gather together some notes on Baker's life. He'd made his living as a freelance writer after WWII and had published a few fugitive pieces in little magazines and dailies. He'd written a few biographies and biographical sketches—most of them commissioned—and sent off a few scripts for television programming. In short, he made his living as a writer, and he had a nose for a decent story. He sensed in Baker's melodramatic life the potential for a great book. It is possible as well that she pitched the idea to him herself. After all, Baker had already asked Langston Hughes, James Baldwin, and Alex Haley, imagining that her arresting, epic biography required an experienced commercial touch.

Janes began taking notes on phone calls with Josephine, keeping a diary of the children's visits, and drafting sections of a memoir. In the section titled "I First Met Josephine Baker," he claimed that the very name of the family had come from him, tracing it to the postscript of a letter he'd written: "Love to the Rainbow Tribe." Still grinding the axe, he claimed that Marianne had been "a great disappointment." And he offered the first draft of what would become a powerful feature in Josephine's posthumous biographies: the narrative of the ungrateful Baker children. "There have been eleven heart-breaking attempts by Josephine," he wrote, excluding Stellina, "to give her orphans a good start in life."[18] Heartbreaking, he meant, because they had all failed miserably.

By August 1975, Janes began to get worried. He'd been planning to write the definitive book on Josephine, but rumors had reached him that Jo Bouillon was composing a book of his own. Even as Janes started his collaboration with Margaret, the two men engaged in a peculiar sort of chess match. In mid-August Janes wrote to Marianne and provided a catalog of items that were missing from his house, insisting on their return. A week later, writing to Jo, he tried to press a legal claim, asking for the return of any of his personal material—including letters— that Bouillon might find among Josephine's papers. Only a few days after that, he wrote to say that Stellina, still at school in England, had apparently taken a few things that belonged to Janes, including some signed photographs of Josephine. "When I asked Stellina in our home for them," he wrote, outraged, "she said she had given them to Marianne which she had no right to do. I telephoned Marianne yesterday and she denied ever having seen them. . . . I am sorry," he advised, "but one of your daughters is not telling the truth." As Baker's body lay in the gardener's shed in Monaco, Henry Janes and Jo Bouillon were gathering up their archives, each preparing to write the first and, presumably, authoritative book on Josephine.[19]

"The Book of Bouillon," as Margaret Wallace derisively called it, was *Josephine*, the autobiography that vexes anyone who studies Baker's life. Assembled from fragments of memoir and diary found after Josephine's death, the various holes in the plot are filled, as mentioned before, by the friends and family of Josephine: Jacqueline Cartier, Jo Bouillon, his brother Gabriel, the actor Jean-Claude Brialy, the older members of the Tribe, even Margaret. Listing "Jo et Jo" as coauthors, it dissembles, wanting readers to see it as an "unfinished" autobiography brought to conclusion by Bouillon after Josephine's untimely death, rather than an attempt to rush something—anything— to the marketplace, to take advantage of the public's sympathy for the children, a brief and temporary consequence of Josephine's show business death and pageant-like funeral. Bouillon's narrative closely matches the thematic and chronological arrangement of Baker's 1973 review, with its circular celebration of the superstar's celebrity, its notion that fame was reason enough for spectacle.

Janes went in a different direction. Reaching out to Margaret, he shared some of his material, including photocopies of the correspondence about Stellina. "It was the wish of your sister," he reminded Margaret, "that you should assist her with her own autobiography just as she asked me, in your presence in 1970, to assist in the same way."[20] With Janes's prodding, Margaret began writing her own memories of life with "Tumpy," starting all the way back in St. Louis. She had bills of her own to pay. "For the moment everything is fine," she wrote to Robert Brady, "only we [have] a little cash on hand. So if it is possible, you can send me a little. If you send me anything, please send it to my home address. For afraid, if I am not there, the kids will take it and have fun off of it. As they don't understand what it is all about. Because poor Josephine spoiled them."[21]

The collaborative intrigue of Margaret and Henry continued, even after it was known that Jo Bouillon was writing his own biography. Margaret routinely expressed her displeasure with what she saw as Bouillon's relentless bottom-line orientation. She'd held on to some personal papers, waiting to send them to Princess Grace until after Jo's book came out, not wanting to give over material that might be useful in their effort. When Bouillon left for Argentina, she joked with Janes that he'd given her the silent treatment, and reported that he planned to "rent out the villa and leave poor Jeannot [of the Tribe] out doors." "It has always been a matter of money to him," she concluded with bitterness. When Margaret wasn't invited to a gala planned for New York in 1976, she blamed it on greed. "Of course not," she explained, "because all the money will go to the kids. What a shame as they will never work if that keeps up." As the first biographies—written by professional biographers, agents of the star system—started to come out, Margaret got angry. "I just finished reading another book of Josephine's life story," she wrote to Janes. "Again lots of lies. I don't see how people can make up all these lies." At least, she thought, "the Book of Bouillon" hadn't made money. That was something. "Now he is crying broke," she added, with apparent glee.[22]

The rush to publish the first posthumous biography of Josephine resulted in some horrific prose, but it also established a template for rereading the arc of her life after WWII. Leo Guild, a veritable king of blaxploitation pulp, included a preface from a psychologist, who diagnosed the root of Baker's need for adoration as race hatred, and proclaimed that "whitey" was her enemy.[23] In Guild's rapid-fire, take-no-prisoners approach, Baker loved money and her fame more than her family. She was sincere in her desire for equality, but her Tribe was a crazy idea, evidence of her damaged psyche. A blur of mixed-up dates, names, and facts, Guild's biography is the kind of book that gets written only in Hollywood, over a long weekend, with a handful of obituaries as source material, by a writer with little more than a hazy memory of a recently deceased celebrity. It must have made Margaret quite angry.

More troubling was Stephen Papich's memoir, *Remembering Josephine*, published in 1976. Papich had been a longtime friend of Baker's and had directed her performances during her 1973 tour of the United States. By his account, Josephine had asked *him* to write a biography some years earlier, and the two had been having regular conversations about the subject for well over a decade. Papich's portrait is a sympathetic one and gives a great deal of space to Josephine's voice. The tone is quite distinct, and considerably more bitter than what Bouillon included in his own ensemble portrait. She was speaking to a friend who was also, like Janes, acting as a chronicler, as a journalist preparing her life for public consumption. She wanted to be sure to share her side of the split from Jo. And she was frank—too frank, perhaps, and perhaps too creative. It was to Papich that Baker relayed her version of the March on Washington speech, which now gets cited as authoritative. She told him as well about her suffering when she was physically removed from Les Milandes. And she confessed to him her version of the Tribe's permanent fracture in exile, offering it in confidence, though to a man she had appointed as a biographer. "When she revealed it to me," Papich wrote, justifying his indiscretion, "it ceased to be a secret." In his deft hands, her various self-fashionings—her innumerable confessions and complaints and reinterpretations, all shared by mail or phone, all offered as intimate communications—gained an extraordinary degree of verisimilitude. They became, in a word, authoritative.[24]

Papich singled out the Tribe for special condemnation. "'Bad blood,' Stephen, 'bad blood'": this was how Baker explained it to him, explained what she could never say publicly. "How could she tell the world," he asked, "that one of her children had stood in her bedroom screaming, 'You are nothing but a slut, a whore'"? She had invested decades of her life in promoting the Tribe as the harmonious proof of a better world, only to have it fall apart in Monaco: "She simply could not control them." In a string of cruel paragraphs, emphasizing the great betrayal and revealing its depths, Papich itemized the offenses of the group. The Tribe had been so badly behaved that the local police in Monaco had been ordered not to arrest them but to "deliver them to the Palace." "They pillaged her archive," he accused, and "pawned what they could, and sold or gave away the rest to American tourists." They stole money, became addicts, embarrassed her over and over again. "In their defense," Papich admitted, "not all were cut from the same cloth. But Josephine did not take them individually. They were a group—a fraternity." What one child did, his logic went, extended to all. This, he argued, was "what their mother thought of them in the late evening of her life." There was blame to be shared here. "These experiences," he diagnosed, "helped to kill her."[25]

This was not the story that Jo Bouillon wanted to tell. The Frenchman's *Josephine*, though, was only a part of his gambit. Working with Hank Kaufman and Gene Lerner, two talent agents who in 1971 had turned themselves into Broadway producers, he planned a tour of the States by the Tribe, a reversal of the State Department–arranged tours of Africa by black American artists and entertainers. "It was a wish of Josephine Baker," Lerner and Kaufman's somber letter began, that her children might "know something of the United States." "Friends and admirers of Miss Baker in American political, artistic, and minority circles," the letter continued, "have expressed their desire to receive the Baker-Bouillon family." The language of the planned trip evokes nothing less than a formal diplomatic tour. "The voyage to America has both an official purpose as well as its evident moral, good will, and humanitarian aspects, and also succeeds in fulfilling the wish of their American-born, French national mother," whose "vision and labors," they concluded, "stand as an illuminating symbol of the destruction of frontiers among the young of the world, regardless of their national, racial, or religious origins." Imaging this as a sort of royal tour, the producers went to great lengths to introduce each child in this decree, before confessing, somewhat shamefacedly, that "some assistance is needed to cover what will perhaps amount to twenty airline tickets," and that the additional costs might include the relocation of the younger children from Buenos Aires to Monte Carlo.[26] Casting a broad net, Bouillon wrote letters to the vice president of the United States and the secretary general of the United Nations. Senators Ted Kennedy of Massachusetts, Birch Bayh of Indiana, and Tom Eagleton of Missouri all indicated their willingness to meet with the Tribe.[27] But the missives reveal his deeper concerns, too: NBC, he informed Congressman James Symington (and others), was planning a two-hour documentary on Josephine, "wiping out the eventual compensation for the [Lerner and Kaufman] film which the children are counting on for their future."[28]

The tour was a part of a bigger roll-out planned by Lerner and Kaufman, to whom Bouillon had sold the "rights" to her story. Josephine, it turns out, had met with them in 1973, during her American tour, and had begun conversations about a film based on her life. The two men had been fans of Baker since the late 1940s, but they'd be formally introduced to Josephine in 1960 by the Italian actress Anna Magnani, in the context of one of "Josephine's numerous 'farewell engagements' to raise money for her children." Seeking investors, they presented themselves as serious dramatists with a personal connection, including a home in Grimaud, "a hilltop village not too distant from the Villa provided for Miss Baker by Prince Rainier and Princess Grace of Monaco." "Her sudden death," the two men wrote, in the midst of "negotiations which seemed endless," only whetted their appetite. Lerner, "recognizing the rare inspirational and entertainment values of her story" and sensing an opportunity, dropped everything to manage the project.

Josephine, ever fickle, had been negotiating the rights to this deal for four years. Jo Bouillon, suddenly responsible for a dozen children, took less than two months. By July 1975—the same fateful month in which Henry Janes angrily accused Marianne and Stellina of stealing his memorabilia—Bouillon had signed over to Kaufman and Lerner the exclusive worldwide rights to Josephine's life story. As executor of Josephine's estate, and as legal guardian for the members of the Tribe who were still minors, Bouillon signed on behalf of the entire family. Margaret signed the agreement, too. Kaufman and Lerner, Bouillon told the press, were ideally suited to craft a biographical film that was rooted in two continents. "I selected them from the many who came to me," he declared, "because they were Americans, [and] had twenty years of important background in European and international show business, with evident affection for France." The two men had agreed to pay Bouillon and the Tribe $300,000 for the rights to present her story as a Broadway musical (with $100,000 of that up front), in addition to a percentage of the profits from any production, a generous deal. Bouillon also agreed to serve as a consultant.[29] Lerner and Kaufman signed playwright Joe Masteroff to create a story line covering fifty years.[30]

The plan to tell Josephine Baker's story did not turn out to be the success everyone hoped it would be. The terms of the agreement between Bouillon and the producers kept changing, with Bouillon constantly trying to get the best advantage and Lerner and Kaufman trying to keep initial production costs low. Distant family members emerged from the past to offer themselves up as paid advisors,[31] even as they worked on their own smaller-scale versions of Josephine's life. Nephew Richard Martin Jr., for instance, orchestrator of St. Louis's Black American Folklore Society, traveled around the country, broadcasting through performance the idea that his aunt was a prophet of black dance.[32] When Bouillon's book was published, Martin wrote to Kaufman and Lerner and, conceding that "Uncle Jo" seemed like "a very nice man" with "quality and class," he presented himself as a better official advisor. He loved the book, he admitted. "However," he began, the book was all wrong. *Josephine* had presented Baker as "half-Spanish," which Martin knew wasn't true. And it fudged many of the St. Louis details, too. "Poor Aunt Tumpy," Martin concluded, offering up a biographical detail that Bouillon had left out, "she missed both of her parents' burials, but they would have understood because she had her own life and work." Dangling himself before the Broadway producers as a more accurate interlocutor, Martin added, as a teasing postscript, that he'd renamed his troupe of traveling children "The Rainbow Children." "They are all black," he assured them, "but all have beautiful colors." "My aunt would be so very proud," he suggested, attaching an image of Prince Charles of England receiving the troupe, "but jealous . . . [s]he was too impractical and would have spoiled the children by not making them work."[33] By January of 1978 Richard had his first check[34] and was hoping to be the official "American" advisor to the film. Learning of Bouillon's consulting fee, he scoffed: "Why does Uncle Jo need $150,000? Is he buying another castle?"[35]

In this swirling context, Kaufman and Lerner worked tirelessly to find investors and generate interest from major studios, but a deal with Paramount fell through, and months went by with little progress. Following the advice of Princess Grace, they settled on a Broadway-first policy, hoping that a movie deal would follow. But this caused them more trouble, because musical theater was increasingly saturated with African Americana. The rights issued dogged them as well because so much of Baker's life was public, and so many people felt empowered to speak for her—as did the agreement with the family, which Bouillon had revised in 1976 to generate (he hoped) more income for the family. The new agreement (the specifics were always changing) called for a temporary suspension of the remaining $200,000 in exchange for a continuation of the agreed-upon 1 percent of the revenues from any theatrical production. This, it was hoped, would pay dividends in the long run. But "La Baker" was a public commodity, and it wasn't clear what was "exclusive" about this story. From where veteran Hollywood producer Fred Brisson stood, then, it seemed as if Lerner and Kaufman had paid out a considerable sum for material that required no such outlay, and had bound themselves to the Tribe unnecessarily.

The story was great, but the legal knot was complex and perhaps not worth the time needed to unravel it. Writing to Brisson and pleading for a "practical" demonstration of his interest, Lerner admitted that the agreement with the family was unusual, but he cited "the particular nature of Josephine's family—the unique experiment with adopted children and the intense desire of Monsieur Bouillon to provide a heritage for them."[36] Brisson, in turn, encouraged a meeting with lawyers to discuss the ongoing concern about the family's rights, the terms of the agreement, and the impending Broadway show. "I presume you are aware that a 'Black Follies' show goes into rehearsal in October," he asked worriedly; "how many shows of this nature will

Broadway support?"[37] Lerner, in turn, pleaded for financial support, no matter how things looked. "The conditions with the Family and Heirs are what they are," he admitted, before insisting, "We are working intensely on getting better terms and have reason to believe there will be an improvement."[38] Brisson's lawyer, David Grossberg, worried that "a good part of her life is probably public domain and could be used by others," and encouraged the producer to "go slowly."[39]

Baker's own story line seems to have been killed off by polite disagreement. As Bouillon and Lerner and Brisson and Janes jockeyed for material, debated royalty percentages, and struggled to get the "real" story out, hoping to foreground Josephine's supposedly big-hearted contributions to the age of rights and revolution, other narratives were ascendant. Ishmael Reed, reviewing Stephen Papich's muckraking memoir for the *New York Times,* reduced all of *Remembering Josephine* to a single line: "Special people who are soft touches come to the world and get creamed. Are taken to the cleaners." Reed, pushing Papich's argument to its logical conclusion, described Baker as a dupe. "So good-hearted was she," he railed, "that she allowed herself to be taken by some 'Civil Rights' hustlers who made demands upon her to 'open Las Vegas to blacks.'" For this, he said, she was pilloried as an elitist, turned into a joke. "And then," Reed continued, building up steam, "there was the doomed multi-cultural experiment in which she brought together children of all races in hopes of building a community of brotherhood at Milandes. The children hated each other. One of the ungrateful wretches called her a 'slut' after which she suffered her first heart attack. The others became junkies, thieves, bleeders and cry-babies." In 1976 there was no room for Josephine's "experiment" to be seen as a clear-eyed tactic in the war for equality, as an instrument in her struggle to be famous, to be adored, to be relevant. "Poor Josephine," Reed remembered. "Sweetheart."[40]

The marketplace was suddenly saturated with stories of Josephine, all of them presented as "authentic" and "intimate." By 1980, Gene Lerner was appealing to Margaret Wallace for an endorsement, while

noting that "we are $150,000 in debt. We ruined our lives econom-
ically for this project. More than $500,000 and seven years of our
lives!!!!!!! All gone." "I am determined to get you some more money,"
he wrote, "but I can't promise when or how much."[41] Almost a decade later, pleading with Margaret and her daughter, Rama, to remain true to him, Lerner complained that the children were selling
him out. "I am going to Paris to consult my lawyer," he confided. The
children had "ignored their agreements," and Lerner was "determined
to not let them get away with their shenanigans." "They have to be put
in their place," he insisted. He enlisted Margaret and Rama as readers
of another script. But it was all for naught. Only a few years later HBO
would release a very different, more workmanlike television movie
about Baker's life with an entirely different production team, and
Lerner's letter-writing campaigns, legal wranglings, and transatlantic
sojourns would cease.

In death, Baker was a celebrity supernova. Family members sensed
a moment of opportunity, a sudden outpouring of sympathy and adoration, and the result was a mad scramble to profit from Josephine's
death. Books filled with salacious details were rushed to print. Most
relied on Baker's consistently revised and edited "story." On the US
side of the Atlantic, though, very few of them were concerned with
the material fate of the children, with the attempt to turn a celebrity
and her domestic ensemble into an industry. Indeed, most American
readings of her were not sympathetic to the children at all. Efforts to
incorporate her celebrity seemed to fail, and fail miserably. Scandal
and rumor ruled the day. Her stable of biographers, unwittingly competing with each other, couldn't agree on her legacy and dropped a
tricky and confused story into a context in which Josephine Baker
already seemed like an outlier, a baroque detail of a different age. It
would be easier just to call her crazy: "Poor Josephine. Sweetheart."
The life of the woman who routinely broke the rules, who challenged
nations, circled the globe, and hobnobbed with world leaders, was

bound to the earth by quotidian legal concerns, by worries over tiny margins of profit, by the "narcissism of small differences."

Perhaps this is what Baker intended. She had written the script of her life and passed it down. She'd written multiple scripts, in fact, all of them generally in agreement that she was a unique superstar, an unparalleled celebrity. She'd solicited a dozen biographers and scattered them, each with no knowledge of the others. She'd spent decades framing her life for her confidants, establishing chapters and breaks, highlighting the important moments, and stressing above everything else her own extraordinary singularity. Born into a world where there were no black geniuses and superstars, where every aspect of black culture was imagined as derivative, imitative, unoriginal, she had spent a life building up the idea that she was different. In the wake of her death, even those who ridiculed her Rainbow Tribe—even those who thought she was mad—did not dispute the bright aura of her fame.

Epilogue

I think of her as a combination of Michael Jackson and Angelina Jolie.

—Cush Jumbo (2013)

Jean-Claude Baker's Manhattan restaurant, Chez Josephine, sits on 42nd Street just west of the Port Authority bus terminal, on the edge of Hell's Kitchen. The building that houses the restaurant used to be a massage parlor—"a sign in this window right here," Jean-Claude tells me, "used to read, '$10 for Complete Satisfaction.'"[1] A perfect reflection of its amiable host, the narrow restaurant with red brick walls is chockablock with Josephine memorabilia. There are paintings and statues and figurines and menu decorations, hints of bananas and feathers in every sight line. At night someone famous might show up and play the piano. Sitting down for dinner, you might catch a glimpse of a Broadway star or two. The booze flows easily, the food is good, and the mood is light. When you enter, you are meant to think: if Josephine had a restaurant, this would be it. And then you remember that she actually had several restaurants, bistros, and nightclubs. Chez Josephine reminds you of those places.

Jean-Claude is, famously, the last Baker. The thirteenth, to be exact. A copy of his magnificent biography and memoir of Josephine is propped up behind the bar. As a young man working at a hotel in France, he was swept up into Josephine's entourage, and after a time he became her confidant, dear friend, and informally adopted son. In the 1960s, he organized fund-raisers to support the Tribe, which at the time was down on its luck. This important but small role grew into a big one, until for the last decade of her life he served as her occasional chargé d'affaires. When Josephine died, he arrived at Roquebrune along with Jo Bouillon, reassembled the Tribe, and helped to make immediate decisions about what came next for the youngest children. He became a television star, a minor celebrity in his own right, and a shepherd of the junior members of the flock.

At dinner, Jean-Claude is a perfect host, drifting effortlessly from table to table, always happy to share stories about Josephine. He is also a clever provocateur, much like his mother. Once, when his regular promotional postcard was banned by the post office in Manhattan because it featured an image of Josephine partially nude (and with a plume of green-colored ostrich feathers, too), he drummed up press coverage, splashed a satirical "censored" sign across her breasts, and eventually won the right to set her free to circulate around the world once more.[2] The walls of the restaurant are emblazoned with famous nudes of La Baker, an arresting visual for diners and visitors, and a deliberate challenge to prudish sensibilities. "Some people say, 'Oh my God. Have you no shame? It's your mother. Tits out, like that?' Why not?" Jean-Claude continues. "It is beautiful." His restaurant is a memorial to Josephine, an unabashed celebration of her majestic, extraordinary beauty and fame, with a heavy emphasis on her days as a siren in a banana skirt.[3]

It is also a way station for the children as they travel around the world. Koffi has worked at Chez Josephine. Jarry works there now, acting as co-host, switching among French and Spanish and English, stitching the restaurant's staff together.[4] It was Jean-Claude who introduced me to the children. After sharing lunch at the restaurant, he introduced me to Jarry and then to Koffi, and passed along contact information for some of the others. When approached, some declined to talk, while others sat patiently for hours. Given their shared history—the life in the public eye, their collective mixed feelings about Josephine—there is no surprise in any of this. For some, she is a durable model of humanitarianism, goodwill, and charity; for others, she was a whirlwind of cruel caprice.

"Go to Les Milandes," Jean-Claude encouraged me. "Figure it out for yourself." And so I did.

These days, much has changed in the Dordogne. Josephine Baker's fabled dressing room is reduced to a garbage dump. Soothing mint green still graces the walls, but only a single fluorescent bulb hangs from the ceiling. Every opened cabinet reveals a tattered banner from some lost and forgotten pageant, or a sodden pile of water-damaged posters. In the middle of the room sits a tangled pile of old mattresses atop a layer of folded chicken wire. And in this decaying aggregation— all of it carried from somewhere else to the top floor of the tower of a fifteenth-century castle—sits a torn-off mannequin's head with red lipstick and brown eyes. It rests on one mattress, a broken piece of the so-called Jorama, the wax museum documenting Baker's life. At the center of her unprocessed archive, Baker's faux head is gruesomely stylish even in artifice and decapitation.

I had been brought to this room by Madame Angélique, a Dordogne native who was, as she tells it, looking for a castle to own (preferably one with high-ticket revenues) and stumbled into a chance to buy Les Milandes. She has since devoted herself to its restoration as a museum and struggled to fix the place up, beginning slowly on the first floor. As we swept through the upper chambers, the chatelaine did not pause over the detached visage of Josephine Baker. Had she moved faster to restore that dressing room to its original grandeur, I would never have seen its squalid condition or dwelled on the meaning of its layered decrepitude.

Like the dressing room, the original grandeur of Les Milandes has been obscured by time. Shrubs and trees that were tiny when planted in 1955 have grown too large, changing sight lines. New hedges and fences, put in place by those who have bought smaller chunks of the land, mark the subdivision of Baker's estate and establish new internal borders. Additional walls have pinched off public spaces and turned them into private courtyards. The bakery once run by Josephine's sister is now a privately owned cottage for rent, with a small swimming pool of its own. The walkways and garden paths and picnic areas that once unified the vast complex are now overgrown. The riverside brasserie, pool, and nightclub are newly refurbished but are corporately distinct from the château atop the hill. An enclosure movement works against the history of this place, actively parsing the unity, collectivism, and weird majesty that were once foregrounded in Baker's enterprising, imaginative utopia. When one looks around today, noting how cleanly the politics of the place have been divorced from the restoration of basic commercial features, half of Josephine Baker's grand vision seems lost

The performance under close scrutiny here was the assembly, choreography, and display of a large multiracial adopted family, a collection of children from around the world that she called the Rainbow Tribe. Between 1953 and 1968—the span of her assemblage at Les Milandes—in the midst of global revolt and turmoil, Baker adopted a total of twelve children—they were from Côte d'Ivoire, Japan, Venezuela, Morocco, Finland, Colombia, and various parts of France—and settled them into an unusual new home in France. Across a familiar plotline that ran from the civil rights movement through the nonaligned movement, decolonization, and black power, Baker relentlessly pursued the establishment and expansion of this multiracial family, and set that family at the heart of her evolving politics and what she intended as an elaborate corporate venture. As the Rainbow Tribe, they were repeatedly offered up to the consuming public as a representation of the ideal, desegregated future—an ideal brought to life, she would repeatedly stress, by someone who was at once black and binational. The stage for all of this was an antique château, one of many in the Dordogne, which Baker renamed Les Milandes.

One could see Les Milandes as a minor failure amid a mass of midcentury modernization projects, with the third world brought into the first, or one could see it as a transgressive site that presages the present-day story of globalization, with its unpredictable jumblings and juxtapositionings of peoples, cultures, and histories. One could see Les Milandes as a house for twelve children, a stylized home fit for public consumption, an advertisement for the world of tomorrow, or a set piece for an idealized family. One could see it as a commercial venture collecting receipts or as a university with lectures and conferences. Finally, one could see it as a meeting ground for a radical antiracist politics or as the dreamlike seat of aristocratic glamour. While she lived, Josephine Baker presided over the entire enterprise like a CEO, skillfully managing these contradictory functions. Her most ambitious creation, Les Milandes, is at the center of her vision of the global histories of race and nation, the family, and international politics. And it is the keystone to the later life of Baker, who in her grand physicality traversed the nation-state, and who in her new, race-conscious motherhood anticipated a neoliberal approach to the reform of civil society's basic tenets.

For Baker, the scale of this enterprise was vast, and the stakes were high. She was keen to be a part of the great critique of racism and colonization, if only on her own spectacular personal terms. To make all of this possible, she'd almost single-handedly brought running water and electricity to a hilltop in one of the most rural regions in France, rebuilt a castle from the ground up, traveled the world in search of a suitable family, and presided over this complex mixing of Disneyland and the United Nations. She micromanaged the estate—hiring repair people, tutors, and service staff—even as she was forced back on the road when the estate failed to collect enough revenue to cover costs. She wasn't launching a movement, and she didn't expect that others would follow her lead. She wasn't the head of an organization, but she managed to be a part of many of the major civil and human rights actions of the era. In the end, she would be bankrupted, her reputation would be tarnished, and the children themselves, after rebelling against Maman's control, would be reviled by her fans and her allies as traitors.

Outside of Jean-Claude's memoir, this is not a story that has been well told before. Baker's case presents a subject that strays and eludes, and essential historical work has never been undertaken on her later life. She has a biography but no historical context. Or she is a "part of the décor" but not a central character of the story.[5] This makes her seem either mad or irrelevant, or perhaps both. We have no answers to some of the most fundamental questions about her life, and no way to chart her complex passage through the evolving civil and human rights movements. No single archive. No collection of speeches or letters. No consideration of her music. What we have instead is usually myth, rumor, guesswork, innuendo, and mistranslation, with interpretation driven not by careful scholarship but by the profit of celebrity. Thinly sourced celebrity biographies—heirs to the memoirs by Leo Guild and Stephen Papich—proliferate, and they usually skip over this period, while hard questions remain unasked. The archival shallowness of this literature has consequences for truly understanding what Baker proposed to do after WWII. It makes it easy to say, as British actress Cush Jumbo puts it, that Baker is reminiscent of both Michael Jackson and Angelina Jolie, and to think of her fame and presence as the best evidence of her heroism. In these surface-level portrayals Josephine Baker sits at the very heart of our cosmopolitan, internationalist age. There is little popular awareness of what she actually did. But then, we live in an age where fame itself is seen as a career, and where celebrity, once achieved, is imagined as victory. In the tabloid world we inhabit, all that matters is that Baker was famous, that she lived in a castle, and that she had a bathroom built to match the colors of an Arpège perfume bottle.

The lack of earnest scholarship on Baker is a partial consequence of her admittedly extravagant life. She had a penchant for spectacle that has been too easily marked as crazy—the monkeys and peacocks on the estate, the cheetah on the leash, the banana skirt, even the castle. In her flamboyant public kookiness and gaiety, she seems to be the very antipode of the grim, determined, and practical activist. The chief culprit here, perhaps not surprisingly, is the corps of celebrity biographers who have been repeatedly drawn to her habit of astonishing performances, and who sometimes seem to own Josephine Baker's life. This group has spent far more time discussing her mercenary promiscuity than the later years of her self-styled radical motherhood and the sense of global mission it contained. Most simply skip over her childhood as if she were born onstage, and they sprint through the last thirty years of her life as if she died there as well. Instead, they devote the lion's share of ink to the interwar period, when her fame was at its zenith, when she was the "créatrice du Charleston." Their fabrications continue to be repeated as truth. But that biographical tradition needs to end.

Of course, whether I like it or not, I am one more person tracking and telling this story, a part of the genealogy that dates back to the madness right after her passing, back to *Josephine,* to the Jorama.

"I am interested," I tell Georges Lansac, "in finding the grave of Carrie McDonald, Josephine's mother." Georges is the new owner of the Jardins des Milandes, the jazz club and bistro that sits along the riverbank. A few days earlier, Yvette Malaury, Baker's old housekeeper, had told me that "Madam's" burial was scandalous. Georges, equally aghast at the memory, sucks his teeth, darts his eyes, and confirms the story: that Mama Carrie, brought from St. Louis to help with the children, was buried like a pauper in an unmarked grave nearby. Josephine didn't see fit to place a stone where Mama Carrie lay.

In the years that followed, no member of the Rainbow Tribe had corrected the oversight. At least to some, the local scandal seems to be largely about this last generational elision of responsibility. Mama Carrie was essential to the care of those children—a factory worker in her daughter's domestic industry—in a way Josephine never would be. An old woman, she traveled halfway around the world and lived out the rest of her life in a country where she knew no one and spoke not a word of the language. The children, Yvette thinks, should have bought a simple gravestone to honor that grandmotherly attention. Georges and I got in the car, and within minutes we were standing over an unremarkable plot of land. The deteriorating remnants of a cheap plastic grave wreath lay on the ground, half covered by creeping vines.

Carrie McDonald, seventy-three years old, died on January 12, 1959. Notified of her mother's passing by the press while on tour, en route from Rome to Istanbul, Baker insisted, "This will take a lot out of me."[6] She would not make the funeral. Expressing his sadness in a letter to Baker, *Ebony* editor Allan Morrison remembered Carrie's "nobility of character, exceptional intelligence, and great dignity." "She played a very important role in making you what you are," he noted to Josephine. "The world, therefore, owes her a debt."[7]

"Poor Mama," Josephine's sister Margaret remembered, "so far from home." Materially comfortable for the first time in her life, thanks to her eldest child, the ever serious Mama Carrie—convinced that Josephine's world was "unsuitable for children"—would spend her last decade "wearing white or an occasional floral print," gifts from Josephine, who "never seemed to be around," always off visiting some famous person here or there. A dependable counterbalance to her whimsical daughter, and a reliable guardian of the children's interests, she was irreplaceable. "As I watched Mama's coffin being lowered into the vault," Margaret recalled thinking, "I wondered what else had died with her."[8]

Carrie McDonald, weighed down with the history of race riots and Jim Crow, yoked to her daughter's enterprising creation, lies buried as an exile from too many lands. She is in the small Catholic graveyard attached to the back end of the Château de Fayrac, just down the road from the Jardin des Milandes, and roughly half a mile from the old train station that once served as Baker's fantastic creation in the Dordogne. And while she may lie there without any gravestone, she is also buried, it seems, alongside the embalmed heart of Baker's former lover, Pepito Abatino, and the body of a favorite monkey that Baker routinely dressed as a child.

Baker had always been a lifelong believer in the power of an ensemble to communicate a profound point. As a performer, she enjoyed the support of a big band behind her. As a young woman, she accumulated a wealth of stray dogs and cats, tropical birds and jungle primates, a rich biopolitical backdrop. She also drew together a stable of lovers, which suggested that no one man could possibly satisfy her. As an older woman, she brought together her collection of children, inscribed in their bodies the ethos of racial diversity and multiculturalism, and set them to play in public. So when she buried her mother, it might not have surprised anyone that she wouldn't bury her alone, or that she'd include two additional—and meaningful—relics alongside her.

Still, this interesting triptych—her buried mother, her proto-child, and her ex-lover—is at the heart of the supposed outrage in Les Milandes. Proximity, the local thinking goes, establishes equality, and no one in their right mind would equate his or her mother with some simian companion or the heart of a faux count. Baker's odd tribute draws listeners away from thoughtful critique, perhaps even confirming Les Milandes as a precedent for the celebrity spectacle of Michael Jackson's Neverland, and linking her directly, in genealogical fashion, to the faddishness of celebrity adoption. It prompts the laughter of outrage or the dismayed rolling of the eyes, and establishes the sanity of the audience. And it enables, again, the great turning away from serious scrutiny.

Standing at the gravesite, I was reminded of the thoughts of Alice Walker on locating and then marking Zora Neale Hurston's burial site. There is a point, she wrote, "at which even grief seems absurd. And at this point, laughter gushes up to retrieve sanity."[9] Since that day, when I tell this story I have heard audiences laugh when deep down they mean to do otherwise. We should listen and look for the laughter, for the labeling of this story as "crazy," a response that sounds out the deep wells and dark swirls of Baker's enterprise, its cost for ordinary people—for Mama Carrie, for the children, for others—and attend to what is hard to imagine or understand or hear without amazement.

Looking for Josephine Baker reveals the hard limits of "race," "nation," and "family" in an age of global transformation. The search illuminates a woman who imagined herself as a prophet but who was defined as crazy. It includes within that illumination a dozen children, each raised as an instrument of worldwide salvation, but also framed as a set of troublesome racial and ethnic stereotypes. The story should be told as it was originally conceived: as a challenge to the most basic order of civil society, as a revolutionary social experiment and political transgression, and as a weapon in the holy war against racism. In that conflict, ordinary men and women such as Mama Carrie were caught up in the machinations of an ambitious celebrity questing at any cost for social justice, and were sometimes lost as collateral damage. This is what happens, in the end, when celebrity is mobilized for war.

Abbreviations

ELC	Eugene Lerner–Josephine Baker Collection, Stanford University
FBI	"Josephine Baker," FBI subject file #62-95834 (http://vault.fbi.gov/josephine-baker)
FBP	Frederick Brisson Papers, Billy Rose Theatre Collection, The New York Public Library for the Performing Arts
HHJ	Henry Hurford Janes–Josephine Baker Collection, James Weldon Johnson Collection in the Yale Collection of American Literature, Beinecke Rare Book and Manuscript Library
HL	Josephine Baker Papers (MS Thr 497), Harvard Theatre Collection, Houghton Library, Harvard University
JBPE	Josephine Baker Papers, Manuscript, Archives, and Rare Books Library, Emory University
JBPY	Josephine Baker Papers, James Weldon Johnson Collection in the Yale Collection of American Literature, Beinecke Rare Book and Manuscript Library
NAACP/JB	NAACP Papers, Library of Congress, folder "Annual Convention, 1951: Baker, Josephine"
SC	Josephine Baker Collection, Schomburg Center

Notes

Prologue

1. My reading of the banana skirt is informed by Anne Anlin Cheng, *Second Skin: Josephine Baker & the Modern Surface* (New York: Oxford University Press, 2011), 44–48.

2. On this longer, troubling history of spectacular performances, see Daphne Brooks, *Bodies in Dissent: Spectacular Performances of Race and Freedom, 1850–1910* (Durham, NC: Duke University Press, 2006).

3. Letter from Paris, *New Yorker*, October 9, 1926.

4. E. E. Cummings, "Vive La Folie!" (1926; reprinted in *Miscellany* [New York: Argophile Press, 1958], 65).

5. Three generally excellent biographies, each with a different take: Jean-Claude Baker, *Josephine: The Hungry Heart* (1993; reprint, New York: Cooper Square Press, 2001); Lynn Haney, *Naked at the Feast: The Biography of Josephine Baker* (London: Robson Books, 1981); Bennetta Jules-Rossette, *Josephine Baker in Art and in Life: The Icon and the Image* (Urbana: University of Illinois Press, 2007). More synthetically, see Phyllis Rose, *Jazz Cleopatra: Josephine Baker in Her Time* (New York: Vintage Books, 1989). Other biographies include Ean Wood, *The Josephine Baker Story* (London: Sanctuary, 2000) and Stephen Papich, *Remembering Josephine: A Biography of Josephine Baker* (Indianapolis: Bobbs-Merrill, 1976).

6. The doodle is reprinted in Josephine Baker and Jo Bouillon, *Josephine*, trans. Marianna Fitzpatrick (1977; reprint, New York: Marlowe & Co., 1995), 274.

7. Ishmael Reed, "Remembering Josephine Baker," in *Shrovetide in Old New Orleans* (New York: Athenaeum, 1989), 287.

8. My thanks to Leticia Alvarado for putting it just like this to me one day.

1. Too Busy to Die

1. "Josephine Baker's Glamour Recalled: Her Death in Charity Hospital in Africa Ended Great Career," *New York Amsterdam Star-News*, December 5, 1942; "Josephine Baker Reported Dead in Morocco Following Long Illness: Nazis Had Robbed Her of Her Fortune," *Baltimore Afro-American*, November 21, 1942.

2. Lynn Haney, *Naked at the Feast: The Biography of Josephine Baker* (London: Robson, 1981), 238.

3. "Arabs Deny Jo Baker Is Dead," *Baltimore Afro-American*, December 12, 1942.

4. "Jo Baker Is Alive, Well—Free French," *Chicago Defender,* February 6, 1943. See also "Remember Josephine Baker? She's Living in Morocco Now," newspaper clipping, FBP.

5. "Finding Josephine Baker, Reported Dead, Afro Scoop," *Baltimore Afro-American,* May 12, 1945. For a similar, unattributed report, see "Josephine Baker Is Safe," newspaper clipping, SC.

6. Langston Hughes, "Here to Yonder: Capt. Josephine Baker," *Chicago Defender,* August 5, 1944.

7. "Josephine Baker—Modern Cinderella," *Baltimore Afro-American,* October 25, 1947.

8. Hughes, "Here to Yonder."

9. Josephine Baker and Jo Bouillon, *Josephine,* trans. Mariana Fitzpatrick (1977; reprint, New York: Marlowe & Co., 1995), 128, 129.

10. Ibid., 157.

11. Ibid., xiii.

12. Haney, *Naked at the Feast,* 226–227.

13. Phyllis Rose, *Jazz Cleopatra: Josephine Baker in Her Times* (New York: Vintage, 1991), 196.

14. Jean-Claude Baker with Chris Chase, *Josephine: The Hungry Heart* (1993; reprint, New York: Cooper Square Press, 2001), 244.

15. Josephine Baker to Henry Janes, September 13, 1946, HHJ.

16. Baker, *Josephine: The Hungry Heart*, 244.

17. Ibid., 237.

18. HHJ to JB, February 13, 1946, HHJ. On the presumption of financial motive, see Janes to Baker, ca. 1946, HHJ.

19. Baker and Bouillon, *Josephine*, 144.

20. HHJ to JB, March 17, 1947, HHJ.

21. Baker and Bouillon, *Josephine*, 156.

22. "St. Louis Woman Takes Fourth Husband," *See*, January 1948, 21–23.

2. No More Bananas

1. Jayna Brown, *Bablyon Girls: Black Women Performances and the Shaping of the Modern* (Durham, NC: Duke University Press, 2006), 254.

2. "Keeping Busy," newspaper clipping, SC.

3. Jacques Abtey, *La guerre secrète de Joséphine Baker* (Paris: Editions Siboney, 1948).

4. "Misfortunes of the Ex-Broadway Ornament after She Insulted Frau Goering's Pet Cheetah and Lost Her Rabbit Foot," *Milwaukee Sentinel*, June 6, 1942. See also "Slump Set In When She Insulted Frau Goering's Pet Cheetah," *Mail* (Australia), October 3, 1942.

5. Phyllis Rose, *Jazz Cleopatra: Josephine Baker in Her Time* (New York: Random House, 1989), 121.

6. "Countess Josephine Baker Secretly Married to Conte Pepito Abatino of Italy," newspaper clipping, June 2, 1927, FBP.

7. Barbara Chase-Riboud, "The Life and Death of Josephine Baker," *Essence*, February 1976, 68.

8. Malek Alloula, *The Colonial Harem*, trans. Myrna Godzich and Wlad Godzich (Minneapolis: University of Minnesota Press, 1986), 106.

9. Ibid., 49.

10. Paul Colin, *Josephine Baker and La Revue Nègre: Paul Colin's Lithographs of* Le Tumulte Noir *in Paris, 1927* (New York: Harry Abrams, 1998).

11. I am playing here with Antonio Benítez-Rojo's notion of orderly disorder, expressed in *The Repeating Island: The Caribbean and the Postmodern Perspective* (Durham, NC: Duke University Press, 1997).

12. Elizabeth Ezra, *Colonial Unconscious: Race and Culture in Interwar France* (Ithaca, NY: Cornell University Press, 2000), 98.

13. Ibid., 99.

14. Rose, *Jazz Cleopatra*, 146.

15. Josephine Baker, *Une vie de toutes les couleurs: Souvenirs recueillis par André Rivollet* (Grenoble: B. Arthaud, 1935), 12.

16. Jean-Claude Baker with Chris Chase, *Josephine: The Hungry Heart* (1993; reprint, New York: Cooper Square Press, 2001), 32.

17. Josephine Baker, *Les mémoires de Joséphine Baker,* collected and edited by Marcel Sauvage (Paris: KRA, 1927), 47.

18. Rose, *Jazz Cleopatra*, 194.

19. For contrasting views, emphasizing the racist context of the imaginative possibilities, see Brett A. Berliner, *Ambivalent Desire: The Exotic Black Other in Jazz Age France* (Amherst: University of Massachusetts Press, 2002), and Petrine Archer-Straw, *Negrophilia: Avant-Garde Paris and Black Culture in the 1920s* (New York: Thames and Hudson, 2000).

20. Andréa D. Barnwell, "Like the Gypsy's Daughter, or Beyond the Potency of Josephine Baker's Eroticism," in Henry Louis Gates Jr., ed., *Rhapsodies in Black: Art of the Harlem Renaissance* (Berkeley: University of California Press, 1997), 85.

21. "Josephine Baker, No Bananas," *Time,* March 7, 1949.

22. "Jo Is Hailed by 6,000 in DC," *Atlanta Daily World,* July 14, 1951.

23. "To B'way, Bag and Baggage," *Baltimore Afro-American,* February 17, 1951.

24. "Josephine Baker Captivates First Audiences with Songs, Showmanship," *Los Angeles Times,* July 4, 1951.

25. "Josephine Baker Makes Her Video Debut on Kate Smith Show," November 2, 1951, newspaper clipping, FBP.

26. "Jo Is Hailed by 6,000 in DC," *Atlanta Daily World,* July 14, 1951.

3. Citizen of the World

1. "La Baker Is Back," *Life*, April 12, 1951.

2. "She Calls It Horse's Tail," *Baltimore Afro-American*, March 17, 1951.

3. Quoted in "New Jo Is French Maid with a Mission in U.S.," *Chicago Defender*, April 14, 1951.

4. "Anger over Stork Club Snubbing of Josephine Baker Grows," *Jet*, November 8, 1951.

5. Harvard Sitkoff, *A New Deal for Blacks* (New York: Oxford University Press, 1978); Nancy Weiss, *Farewell to the Party of Lincoln: Black Politics in the Age of FDR* (Princeton, NJ: Princeton University Press, 1983).

6. The full testimony is housed at "'You Are the Un-Americans, and You Ought to Be Ashamed of Yourselves': Paul Robeson Appears before HUAC," History Matters: The US Survey Course on the Web, http://historymatters.gmu.edu/d/6440 (accessed July 8, 2013).

7. Jackie Robinson with Alfred Duckett, *I Never Had It Made: An Autobiography of Jackie Robinson* (1972; reprint, New York: HarperCollins, 1995), 85.

8. Thomas Borstelmann, *The Cold War and the Color Line: American Race Relations in the Global Arena* (Cambridge, MA: Harvard University Press, 2003); Mary Dudziak, *Cold War Civil Rights: Race and the Image of American Democracy* (Princeton, NJ: Princeton University Press, 2000); Brenda Gayle Plummer, ed., *Window on Freedom: Race, Civil Rights, and Foreign Affairs, 1945-1988* (Chapel Hill: University of North Carolina Press, 2003); Penny Von Eschen, *Race against Empire: Black Americans and Anticolonialism* (Ithaca, NY: Cornell University Press, 1997); Penny Von Eschen, *Satchmo Blows Up the World: Jazz Ambassadors Play the Cold War* (Cambridge, MA: Harvard University Press, 2005).

9. "Josephine Baker to Return," newspaper clipping, FBP.

10. Mary L. Dudziak, "Josephine Baker, Racial Protest, and the Cold War," in Michael L. Krenn, ed., *The African American Voice in American Foreign Policy Since World War Two* (New York: Garland, 1998), 141.

11. "Josephine Baker, Songs, Dances," newspaper clipping, FBP.

12. Marshall Shepard, "The Christian Church," *Baltimore Afro-American*, April 14, 1951.

13. "Jo Baker Says That All Artists Should Insist on Fair Pay," *Baltimore Afro-American,* March 17, 1951.

14. "Jo Baker 'Stops' Case in Trenton, Cheers 6," *Baltimore Afro-American,* April 7, 1951.

15. *Chicago Defender,* April 14, 1951.

16. "Ike, Baker Plead for Trenton 6," *Amsterdam News,* April 21, 1951.

17. "Jo Baker Asks Nation to Pray for W. McGee," *Atlanta Daily World,* April 22, 1951.

18. "Jo Baker Fights to Save Willie McGee," *Atlanta Daily World,* April 5, 1951.

19. "Jo Baker Denies Saying CRC Swindled Funds of McGee," *Atlanta Daily World,* May 24, 1951.

20. "Jo Baker's Salary to Top 22G Mark," *Baltimore Afro-American,* March 24, 1951.

21. "Baker to Wear New Wardrobe on Her Harlem Day," *Amsterdam News,* May 12, 1951.

22. "Harlem Acclaims Josephine Baker, Blues Cinderella," *Washington Post,* May 22, 1951.

23. Walter White to Josephine Baker, May 3, 1951, NAACP/JB.

24. Unsigned letter to Madeline White, May 14, 1951, NAACP/JB.

25. Walter White to Dean Acheson, May 25, 1951, NAACP/JB.

26. Josephine Baker to Walter White, May 28, 1951, NAACP/JB.

27. "Josephine Baker Miffed," newspaper clipping, June 18, 1951, FBP.

28. Quoted in "DC Soda Foundation Refuses Service to Mlle Baker," *Atlanta Daily World,* July 11, 1951.

29. Walter White to Josephine Baker, May 31, 1951, NAACP/JB.

30. Walter White to Josephine Baker, June 6, 1951, NAACP/JB.

31. Walter White to Ralph Bunche and Eleanor Roosevelt, June 8, 1951, NAACP/JB.

32. Josephine Baker to Walter White, June 11, 1951, NAACP/JB.

33. "DC Soda Foundation Refuses Service to Mlle Baker," *Atlanta Daily World,* July 11, 1951.

34. "Gossip of the Movie Lots," *Atlanta Daily World,* July 17, 1951.

35. "Claims Justice Served in Coast Racial Incident," *Times-News* (Hendersonville, NC), July 18, 1951.

36. "Salesman Fined for Row over Singer's Race," *Los Angeles Times,* July 18, 1951; Harlan is quoted in "Singer Punishes Texan," *New York Times,* July 18, 1951; "A Negro Singer Goes Home: Los Angeles Hotel Affair," *Manchester Guardian,* July 18, 1951.

37. "Josephine Baker Gets Man Jailed for Abusive Remarks about Negroes," *Boston Globe,* July 18, 1951.

38. An example of international coverage: "Personalien," *Der Spiegel,* August 1951, 28.

39. All reprinted in "Press Hails Stand of Josephine Baker," *Atlanta Daily World,* July 20, 1951.

40. "La Baker's Tour Cut Short, to Leave U.S. August 11," *Atlanta Daily World,* July 28, 1951.

41. *France Dimanche,* August 26, 1951; "La Baker's Tour Cut Short, to Leave U.S. August 11," *Atlanta Daily World,* July 28, 1951.

42. Winchell, "On Broadway," *Washington Post,* October 26, 1952.

43. Unsigned letter to "Dear W.W.," October 29, 1951, FBI; cover memo, November 5, 1951, FBI.

44. Unsigned letter, December 19, 1951, FBI.

45. Unsigned letter to "Mr. Winchell," "Monday AM," FBI.

46. Letter from "A colored student" to Walter Winchell, October 28, 1951, FBI.

47. Winchell, "Notes of a Newspaperman," *Washington Post,* November 20, 1951; see also the letter from Jean Edienne to the Editor, *Amsterdam News,* December 1, 1951.

48. Memo to D. M. Ladd from A. H. Belmont, July 15, 1952, FBI.

49. "Exclusive Jo Baker Interview! Hits Some for Ducking Issue," *Amsterdam News,* November 3, 1951.

50. "The Letter of the Year," *Washington Post,* October 29, 1951.

51. "Jo Baker Slaps Suit for 400G on Winchell," newspaper clipping, FBP; "La Baker and 'Duke' Headline 1951 Events," *Amsterdam News,* December 29, 1951. The Mayor's Committee on Unity would later deem her complaint to be unsubstantiated. See "Josephine Baker's Bias Charge Not Proved, Mayor's Board Says," newspaper clipping, FBP.

52. "Jo Baker to Ask Legislature to Put Teeth in Bias Law," *Daily Compass,* December 11, 1951.

53. Neal Gabler, *Winchell: Gossip, Power, and the Culture of Celebrity* (New York: Vintage, 1995), 405.

4. Southern Muse

1. James Hicks, "Las Vegas Wide Open: Jim Crow Holds Sway," *Baltimore Afro-American,* May 17, 1952.

2. "Last Frontier, Las Vegas," *Variety,* April 23, 1952.

3. Jean-Claude Baker with Chris Chase, *Josephine: The Hungry Heart* (1993; reprint, New York: Cooper Square Press, 2001), 319.

4. "How Jo Baker Beat 'Jim Crow' Rap," newspaper clipping, May 13, 1952, FBP.

5. "Josie Baker Scores in Mex City Nitery," newspaper clipping, FBP.

6. "Josie Baker Heads Group Forming Anti-Bias Assn.," *Variety,* April 30, 1952.

7. Advertisement in *Variety,* March 26, 1952.

8. "Brasil, uma grande democracia racial," newspaper clipping, SC; "Brazil, simbolo democratico do mundo interio," *A gazeta,* July 18, 1952, SC.

9. "Speech Made at the Biblioteca Municipal in São Paulo, Brazil, on 30 of July, 1952," SC.

10. "Argentine Republic in Turmoil over 'Jo' Baker," *Baltimore Afro-American,* June 22, 1929.

11. "Josefina Baker visitará la Fundación Eva Perón," *Nación,* October 2, 1952; "Homenajes a la Sra. Eva Perón," *Nación,* October 4, 1952; Lynn Haney, *Naked at the Feast: The Biography of Josephine Baker* (London: Robson Books, 1981), 259–264.

12. "Inició J. Baker sus conferencias acerca de la discriminación," *La Prensa,* November 5, 1952.

13. "Sobre religion y cultura disertó esta tarde la eximía actriz, Josefina Baker," *Noticias Gráficas,* November 5, 1952.

14. These headlines are from *Critica,* November 6, 1952.

15. "La discriminación racial aniquila siempre a los inocentes," *Critica,* November 6, 1952.

16. "Josephine Baker Sorry for People in the U.S.," newspaper clipping, FBP.

17. "Josephine Baker Assailed by Powell on 'Distortion,'" newspaper clipping, FBP.

18. "Jo Baker Blast Tops Election in Peron Press," New York *Daily News*, November 6, 1952.

19. "U.S. Moves to Bar Josephine Baker," *New York Mirror*, November 7, 1952.

20. For instance, "Un cronista yanqui falsea en 'Daily News' nuestras notas," *Critica*, October 24, 1952.

21. "Pulse of the Public," *Amsterdam News*, November 22, 1952.

22. "Death Threats Told by Josephine Baker," newspaper clipping, October 16, 1952, FBP; "Josefina Baker sugirió una cruzada por la libertad de la humanidad," *La Prensa*, November 8, 1952.

23. Thomas Borstelmann, *The Cold War and the Color Line: American Race Relations in the Global Arena* (Cambridge, MA: Harvard University Press, 2003); Mary L. Dudziak, *Cold War Civil Rights: Race and the Image of American Democracy* (Princeton, NJ: Princeton University Press, 2000); Brenda Gayle Plummer, ed., *Window on Freedom: Race, Civil Rights, and Foreign Affairs, 1945–1988* (Chapel Hill: University of North Carolina Press, 2003); Penny Von Eschen, *Race against Empire: Black Americans and Anticolonialism* (Ithaca, NY: Cornell University Press, 1997); Penny Von Eschen, *Satchmo Blows Up the World: Jazz Ambassadors Play the Cold War* (Cambridge, MA: Harvard University Press, 2005).

24. "Powell Raps Jo Baker for Press Tirade in S.A.," *Baltimore Afro-American*, November 29, 1952; "Josephine Baker Assailed by Powell on 'Dis tortion,'" newspaper clipping, FBP.

25. Karen Chilton, *Hazel Scott: The Pioneering Journey of a Jazz Pianist from Café Society to Hollywood to HUAC* (Ann Arbor: University of Michigan Press, 2008).

26. "Dice Josefina Baker: En la Argentina no sólo se habla de democracia, también se la practica," newspaper clipping, marked "*Critica*," in SC.

27. For Baker ads, see, for example, *Nación*, October 29, 1952, and *Nación*, October 31, 1952; on the mammy image, see the ad for Harrods in *Nación*, October 29, 1952. Also, "Fué celebrada Josefina Baker," *Nación*, October 9, 1952.

28. The folktale appears across the Internet's wide terrain, including in Ruthie Ackerman, "Blacks in Argentina—Officially a Few, but Maybe a Million," *San Francisco Chronicle*, November 27, 2005.

29. George Reid Andrews, *The Afro-Argentines of Buenos Aires* (Madison: University of Wisconsin Press, 1980); Matthew Karush, "Blackness in Argentina: Jazz, Tango and Race before Peron," *Past and Present* 216, no. 1 (2012): 215–245.

30. "Josefina Baker sugirió una cruzada por la libertad de la humanidad."

31. Victoria Allison, "Devil with a Blue (Dior) Dress," unpublished manuscript in author's possession.

32. Cited in Joseph Page, *Perón: A Biography* (New York: Random House, 1983), 192.

33. "Little Eva," *Time,* July 14, 1947, 32 and cover.

34. Phyllis Rose, *Jazz Cleopatra: Josephine Baker in Her Times* (New York: Vintage, 1991), 230–231.

35. Ibid., 231.

36. Nicholas Fraser and Marysa Navarro, *Evita: The Real Life of Eva Perón* (1980; reprint, New York: W. W. Norton, 1996), 141, and, more generally, 122–125.

37. Mariano Ben Plotkin, *Mañana es San Perón: A Cultural History of Perón's Argentina* (New York: Rowman and Littlefield, 2007); Matthew Karush and Oscar Chamosa, eds., *A New Cultural History of Peronism* (Durham, NC: Duke University Press, 2006).

38. Baker, *Josephine: The Hungry Heart,* 296.

39. Rose, *Jazz Cleopatra,* 231.

40. Ibid., 322.

41. Haney, *Naked at the Feast,* 264.

42. From a fragment written in "Late Summer, 1953," in Josephine Baker and Jo Bouillon, *Josephine,* trans. Mariana Fitzpatrick (1977; reprint, New York: Marlowe & Co., 1995), 189.

43. Mary Dudziak, "Josephine Baker, Racial Protest, and the Cold War," *Journal of American History* 81, no. 2 (September 1994): 569–750.

44. Ibid., 543.

45. Baker, *Josephine: The Hungry Heart,* 314.

46. Ibid., 328.

47. Fragment, "Late Summer, 1953," 190.

48. Ibid., 189–190.

5. Ambitious Assemblages

1. "Joséphine Baker adopte une famille panachée," *Le Monde,* April 10, 1953.

2. Baker later suggested to Stephen Papich that she would have had a difficult time adopting as a single black woman. See Papich, *Remembering Josephine* (New York: Bobbs-Merrill, 1976).

3. Jean-Claude Baker with Chris Chase, *Josephine: The Hungry Heart* (1993, reprint; New York: Cooper Square Press, 2001), 336.

4. "Josephine Baker Adopts Children of Varied Races," *Washington Post,* September 7, 1957.

5. Baker to Sawada, May 7, 1953, SC.

6. Pearl Buck, *A Bridge for Passing* (New York: John Day Co., 1962), 62.

7. Ellen Herman, *Kinship by Design: A History of Adoption in the Modern United States* (Chicago. University of Chicago Press, 2008).

8. Baker to Sawada, December 16, 1953, SC.

9. Baker to unnamed recipient, May 7, 1953, SC.

10. Interview with Jean-Claude Baker and Jarry Baker, May 13, 2008; images in SC.

11. Baker and Bouillon, *Josephine,* 192.

12. Ibid., 194.

13. Ibid., 195.

14. Interview with Jean Claude Baker and Jarry Baker, May 13, 2008.

15. Baker and Bouillon, *Josephine,* 194

16. Sarah Seidman, "Tricontinental Routes of Solidarity: Stokely Carmichael in Cuba," *Journal of Transnational Studies* 4, no. 2 (2012), www.escholarship.org/uc/item/Owp587sj; interview with Jean-Claude Baker and Jarry Baker.

17. Interview with Jean-Claude Baker and Jarry Baker, May 13, 2008.

18. Jo Bouillon, "Introduction," in Josephine Baker and Jo Bouillon, *Josephine,* trans. Marianna Fitzpatrick (1977; reprint, New York: Marlowe & Co., 1995), ix–x.

19. The US press at one point reported that she'd adopted children from Israel, India, and South Africa, to go with her two Japanese children. "Josephine Baker Adopts Boy in Tokyo; Her Fifth," *Chicago Daily Tribune,* April 15, 1954.

20. "Josephine Baker Fails in Her Bid for Israeli Child," *Globe and Mail*, December 29, 1954, newspaper clipping, SC.

21. "Israel Bars Child to Josephine Baker," newspaper clipping, December 28, SC.

22. Baker and Bouillon, *Josephine*, 202, 203.

23. Phyllis Rose, *Jazz Cleopatra: Josephine Baker in Her Times* (New York: Vintage, 1991), 232.

24. Interview with Jean-Claude Baker and Jarry Baker, May 13, 2008.

25. Rose, *Jazz Cleopatra*, 232.

26. Interview with Jean-Claude Baker and Jarry Baker, May 13, 2008.

27. Essie Robeson to Josephine Baker, October 21, 1959, JBPE.

28. "*Life* Visits a One-Family U.N.," *Life*, November 12, 1951, 157; Herman, *Kinship by Design;* Barbara Melosh, *Strangers and Kin: The American Way of Adoption* (Cambridge, MA: Harvard University Press, 2002).

29. "*Life* Visits a One-Family U.N.," 159.

30. Helen Doss, *The Family Nobody Wanted* (1954; reprint, Boston: Northeastern University Press, 2001), 3.

31. "Japanese Youths Seek New Life," *Spokane Daily Chronicle*, July 22, 1965.

32. Baker and Bouillon, *Josephine*, 196–197.

6. French Disney

1. "Advertising: Fair 'Hits the Spot' with Pepsi," *New York Times*, August 21, 1964.

2. "Small World Salutes UNICEF," *Washington Post*, May 15, 1964; "125 Blind Children Have Fun at the Fair Despite Cameramen," *New York Times*, May 14, 1964.

3. Interview with Jarry Baker, September 18, 2008.

4. Jackson Lears, *Fables of Abundance: A Cultural History of Advertisement* (New York: Basic Books, 1995).

5. Josephine Baker and Jo Bouillon, *Josephine*, trans. Marianna Fitzpatrick (1977; reprint, New York: Marlowe & Co., 1995), 204; "Defender Visits Jo Baker Estate," *Chicago Defender*, September 29, 1956.

6. Jean-Claude Baker, with Chris Chase, *Josephine: The Hungry Heart* (1993; reprint, New York: Cooper Square, 2001), 329–330.

7. Shelia Fowler to Josephine Baker, May 16, 1958; Shelia Fowler to Josephine Baker, April 28, 1958; Shelia Fowler to Josephine Baker, January 20, 1958, JBPE.

8. Baker to Shelia Fowler, June 12, 1958, JBPE.

9. Bob Fowler to Josephine Baker and Jo Bouillon, March 5, 1959, JBPE.

10. Bruce Fowler to "Madame Josephine and Monsieur Jo," December 28, 1958, JBPE.

11. "Bienvenue aux Milandes," JBPE.

12. Interview with Jarry Baker, September 18, 2008.

13. Josephine Baker with Jo Bouillon, La Tribu Arc-en-Ciel, illustrated by Piet Worm (Amsterdam: Mulder and Zoon, 1957).

14 Jonathan P. Eburne, "Adoptive Affinities: Josephine Baker's Humanist International," The Scholar and Feminist Online 6, no. 1/6, no. 2 (Fall 2007/Spring 2008), http://sfonline.barnard.edu/baker/print_eburne.htm.

15. Interview with Jarry Baker, September 18, 2008

16. Ibid.

17. Merlind Theile, "Adopting the World: Josephine Baker's Rainbow Tribu," Der Spiegel, October 2, 2009

18. Interview with Jarry Baker, September 18, 2008.

19. The scrapbooks can be found in JBPE.

7. Mother of a Wounded World

1. "Josephine Still 'Toast' at 60, Gown of Fox Skins Cost 32G's," Baltimore Afro-American, March 7, 1964.

2. Ruth Ann Stewart, email exchange with the author, October 13, 2013.

3. Josephine Baker Clippings File, New York Public Library, Performing Arts Collection, Lincoln Center. A video of a later performance of this song at the Olympia in Paris can be found at www.youtube.com/watch?v=4unzkOi4-ns (accessed July 30, 2007).

4. Josephine Baker and Jo Bouillon, Josephine, trans. Marianna Fitzpatrick (1977; reprint, New York: Marlowe & Co., 1995), 238.

5. R. Dietrich to Josephine Baker, February 7, 1959, JBPE.

6. Baker to Mrs. James, May 20, 1959, JBPE.

7. James to Baker, May 29, 1959, JBPE.

8. "Celebrities Add Their 'I, Too,'" *New York Amsterdam News,* August 31, 1963.

9. "For 200,000 Who Were There It Was a Date to Live Forever," *New York Times,* August 29, 1963.

10. Bennetta Jules-Rosette, *Josephine Baker in Art and in Life: The Icon and the Image* (Urbana: University of Illinois Press, 2007), 235.

11. Interview with John Lewis, July 9, 2008.

12. Stephen Papich, *Remembering Josephine* (New York: Bobbs-Merrill, 1976), 210–213.

13. Ibid., 213.

14. Ibid.

15. My thanks to the Kennedy Library for checking on this for me.

16. "All Were Bit Players in a Drama World Watched," *Washington Post,* August 29, 1963; "Black and White Americans Joined Hands, Hearts," *Baltimore Afro-American,* September 7, 1963.

17. "200,000 March for Civil Rights in Orderly Washington Rally," *New York Times,* August 29, 1963.

18. Langston Hughes, "Medal for Dark Star," *Chicago Defender,* August 31, 1963.

19. Briefly appointed the "Queen of the Colonies" for the 1931 Exposition Coloniale Internationale, Baker never held the position because, in the end, she was not technically a colonial subject of France, but the nomination still reinforced her status as a "floating signifier for cultural difference." Baker became a French citizen by marriage, served heroically as a spy during WWII, and, in the process, became the continental version of Jackie Robinson— the play-by-the-rules racial exemplar, implicitly and sometimes explicitly held up for every other dark-skinned colonial or exile who wanted citizenship and not just a place to live, or who expressed the slightest bit of resentment at the glacial pace of acceptance. She would march in support of de Gaulle, whom she adored, during the Algerian crisis. At the March on Washington in 1963, she invoked "the rights of man," and praised the "salt and pepper" crowd as "a united people at last," as if the struggle had ended. When interviewed about the march by the American press corps, she wore her Free French uniform. Elizabeth Ezra, *The Colonial Unconscious: Race and Culture in Interwar France* (Ithaca, NY: Cornell University Press, 2000),

99; "All Were Bit Players in Drama World Watched," *Washington Post,* August 29, 1963.

20. Dennis McEnnerney, "Frantz Fanon, the Resistance, and the Emergence of Identity Politics," in Sue Peabody and Tyler Stovall, eds., *The Color of Liberty: Histories of Race in France* (Durham, NC: Duke University Press, 2003), 275.

21. Baker and Bouillon, *Josephine,* 210.

22. Henry Louis Gates Jr., "Interview with Josephine Baker and James Baldwin," *Southern Review* 21, no. 3 (1985): 597.

23. Ibid., 592–602.

24. "The Banana Girl," *National Observer,* April 6, 1964.

25. "A Nobel Prize for Josephine?," *Washington Post,* November 2, 1965; "Josephine Baker Named to the Legion of Honor," *New York Times,* August 19, 1961.

26. Josephine Baker, Great French Actress, Turns Advisor on Negro Life," *Chicago Defender,* April 28, 1951.

27. Gaines, *American Africans in Ghana: Black Expatriates in the Civil Rights Era* (Chapel Hill: University of North Carolina Press, 2007), 211.

28. Josephine Baker to Shirley Graham Du Bois, May 23, 1966, Shirley Graham Du Bois papers, Schlesinger Library, Radcliffe Institute, Harvard University.

29. Josephine Baker to Shirley Graham Du Bois, June 21, 1966, and enclosure, Shirley Graham Du Bois papers, Schlesinger Library, Radcliffe Institute, Harvard University. My thanks to Daphne Brooks for sharing this letter—and the previous one—with me.

30. Telegram, Ghanasamb Paris to Ministry of Foreign Affairs, September 22, 1965, in "Letters between Osagyefo & Individuals in Europe," SC/BAA/398, Ghana National Archives (GNA).

31. Cypher, M. F. Dei-Anang to Ghanasemb, Paris, marked "Secret," September 25, 1965, GNA.

32. Telegram, Bossman to M. F. Dei-Anang, September 27, 1965, GNA. My deep, deep thanks to Chris Johnson for calling this to my attention.

33. In the way that Brent Hayes Edwards means "articulation" as a point of separation and connection, in *The Practice of Diaspora: Literature, Translation, and the Rise of Black Internationalism* (Cambridge, MA: Harvard University Press, 2003), 12.

34. "Singer in Cuba for Conference," *Washington Post,* December 31, 1965.

35. Lowery Stokes Sims, *Wifredo Lam and the International Avant-Garde, 1923–1982* (Austin: University of Texas Press, 2002), 154.

36. Vijay Prashad, *The Darker Nations: A People's History of the Third World* (New York: New Press, 2008), 104.

37. United States Committee on the Judiciary, Subcommittee to Investigate the Administration of the Internal Security Act and Other Internal Security Laws, *The Tricontinental Conference of African, Asian, and Latin American Peoples: A Staff Study* (Washington, DC: U.S. Government Printing Office, 1966).

38. "Children of Mama Josephine," *Granma Weekly Review,* August 21, 1966. My thanks to Sarah Seidman for sharing this with me.

39. Baker and Bouillon, *Josephine,* 245.

40. "Baker Children Praise Castro," *Washington Post,* August 18, 1966; "Children of Mama Josephine."

41. Cited in Lynn Haney, *Naked at the Feast: A Biography of Josephine Baker* (London: Robson, 1981), 292.

42. "A Happy Surprise: Miss Baker's Kids," *Washington Post,* November 27, 1966.

43. "SCLC Aide Makes Spirited Capital March Call Here," *Chicago Defender,* February 5, 1968.

44. Draft, "Monday the 15th of January," JBPY.

45. "Les Milandes—Paris—New York," JBPY.

46. Quoted in Haney, *Naked at the Feast,* 294.

47. "Controversial Children," *Amsterdam News,* December 12, 1964.

48. "Research Notes—Visit to the Dordogne, S.W. France, and Monte Carlo, Monaco, 1967—August–September," HHJ.

49. "La Baker Returns, Looking Young and Chic," *Amsterdam News,* January 27, 1968.

50. "La Baker Loses Her Orphanage," *Amsterdam News,* February 24, 1968.

51. "Singer Locks Herself in Chateau Kitchen," *Los Angeles Times,* March 10, 1969.

52. "Baker's Furnishings Sold in Her Absence," *Baltimore Afro-American,* March 15, 1969.

53. Papich, *Remembering Josephine,* 224.

54. "Report from Europe," *Baltimore Afro-American,* May 11, 1968.

55. Papich, *Remembering Josephine*, 227.

56. "Backing for Josie Baker Reported after Eviction," *Baltimore Afro-American*, May 3, 1969.

57. "Josephine Baker Outshines Galaxy of Stars at Benefit in Monte Carlo," *Baltimore Afro-American*, August 30, 1969.

58. "Rainiers Befriend Josephine Baker," *Los Angeles Times*, September 17, 1969.

59. "Jo Baker Receives New Home Near Monaco Border," *Baltimore Afro-American*, October 4, 1969.

8. Unraveling Plots

1. "Josephine Baker Cites 'Black Power' Concern," *Reading Eagle*, September 9, 1970.

2. Josephine Baker to Robert Brady, October 6, 1970, HL.

3. Josephine Baker to Jo Bouillon, July 22, 1965, JBPE.

4. Bryan Hammond and Patrick O'Connor, *Josephine Baker* (New York: Bullfinch Press, 1988), 248–249; Ean Wood, *The Josephine Baker Story* (2000; reprint, London: Sanctuary Books, 2002), 382.

5. Henry Hurford Janes to Josephine Baker, October 8, 1968, HHJ.

6. "Prisoner of Love Idea Harmonious to Singer," *Los Angeles Times*, November 9, 1970.

7. Josephine Baker and Jo Bouillon, *Josephine*, trans. Marianna Fitzpatrick (1977; reprint, New York: Marlowe & Co., 1995), 273.

8. From a fragment by Jarry Baker, in Baker and Bouillon, *Josephine*, 277.

9. Baker to Brady, November 3, 1970, HL.

10. Baker to Princess Marie Beatrice, October 8, 1970, HL.

11. Baker to Brady, May 4, 1971, HL.

12. Baker to Brady, January 29, 1971, HL.

13. Baker to Brady, September 24, 1971, HL.

14. Jean-Claude Baker with Chris Chase, *Josephine: The Hungry Heart* (1993; reprint, New York: Cooper Square Press, 2001), 448.

15. Phyllis Rose, *Jazz Cleopatra: Josephine Baker in Her Times* (New York: Vintage, 1991), 255.

16. Baker to Brady, June 19, 1973, HL.

17. Baker to Brady, c. June 20, 1973, HL.

18. Baker to Brady, undated letter but probably written in 1973, HL.

19. Baker to Brady, undated letter, HL.

20. Rose, *Jazz Cleopatra,* 256.

21. Baker to Brady, January 15, 1974, HL.

22. Baker to Brady, March 25, 1975, HL.

23. Baker to Brady, September 23, 1970, HL.

24. Baker to Brady, October 18, 1974, HL.

25. Baker to Brady, July 2/3?, HL.

26. Baker to Janes, January 13, 1973; Janes to Baker, January 16, 1973, both in HHJ.

27. Janes to Baker, June 19, 1973; Janes to Baker, July 26, 1973; Janes to Baker, July 30, 1973; Janes to Akio Bouillon-Baker, July 26, 1973, all in HHJ.

28. E-mail communication with the author, March 25, 2013.

29. Baker to Janes, June 16, 1967; Janes to Baker, July 4, 1967; Janes to Baker, July 19, 1967; Baker to Janes, May 26, 1970, all in HHJ.

30. Janes to Baker, August 5, 1970; Janes to Baker, August 10, 1970; Baker to Mara, August 26, 1970; Janes to Baker, August 26, 1970, all in HHJ.

31. Baker to Janes, September 8, 1970; Janes to Baker, September 19, 1970; Janes to Baker, September 20, 1970, all in HHJ.

32. Baker to Janes, January 19, 1971; Janes to Baker, February 28, 1972; Baker to Janes, March 18, 1972, all in HHJ; Baker to Moïse, cited in a fragment by Moïse, in Baker and Bouillon, *Josephine,* 271.

33. Baker to Janes, September 16, 1971; Janes to Baker, October 1, 1971; Janes to Baker, February 27, 1973, all in HHJ.

34. Author interview with Koffi Baker-Bouillon, February 22, 2011.

35. Baker and Bouillon, *Josephine,* 277.

36. From a fragment by Mara, in Baker and Bouillon, *Josephine,* 277.

37. Baker, *Josephine: The Hungry Heart,* 417.

38. Thomas Borstelmann, *The Cold War and the Color Line: American Race Relations in the Global Arena* (Cambridge, MA: Harvard University Press, 2003); Mary Dudziak, *Cold War Civil Rights: Race and the Image of American Democracy* (Princeton, NJ: Princeton University Press, 2000); Brenda Gayle Plummer, ed., *Window on Freedom: Race, Civil Rights, and Foreign Affairs, 1945–1988* (Chapel Hill: University of North Carolina Press, 2003); Penny

Von Eschen, *Race against Empire: Black Americans and Anticolonialism* (Ithaca, NY: Cornell University Press, 1997); Penny Von Eschen, *Satchmo Blows Up the World: Jazz Ambassadors Play the Cold War* (Cambridge, MA: Harvard University Press, 2005).

39. Baker to Brady, March 7, 1974, HL.

40. Baker to Brady, May 8, 1974, HL.

41. The Project on Disney, *Inside the Mouse: Work and Play at Disneyworld* (Durham, NC: Duke University Press, 1995).

42. Baker to Janes, September 10, 1973, HHJ.

43. From a fragment by Marianne, in Baker and Bouillon, *Josephine*, 236.

44. Folder 181, Research Notes, "Josephine Baker," n.d., HHJ.

45. Baker to Janes, August 24, 1974, HHJ.

46. Baker to Janes, March 7, 1975, HHJ.

47. Janes to Baker, September 10, 1974, HHJ.

48. Janes to Baker, October 31, 1974, HHJ.

49. Janes to Baker, January 26, 1975, HHJ.

50. Baker to Janes, February 6, 1975, HHJ.

51. Janes to Baker, January 26, 1975, IIIIJ.

52. Dorothy and Bob DeBolt, *Nineteen Steps up the Mountain* (New York: Jove, 1975).

9. Rainbow's End

1. That issue of the magazine was published on June 21, 1958.

2. The interview is housed here: http://www.youtube.com/watch?v=K1Ok lfxCzO4 (accessed August 23, 2013).

3. "Inside Fashion," *New York Post,* January 24, 1974.

4. Cartier, in Josephine Baker and Jo Bouillon, *Josephine*, trans. Marianna Fitzpatrick (1977; reprint, New York: Marlowe & Co., 1995), 287.

5. "Report from Europe," *Baltimore Afro-American,* April 12, 1975.

6. Jean-Claude Baker with Chris Chase, *Josephine: The Hungry Heart* (1993; reprint, New York: Cooper Square Press, 2001), 289–290.

7. Margaret Wallace to Robert Brady, May 24, 1975, HL.

8. Charles Sanders, "A Farewell to Josephine," *Ebony,* July 1975.

9. Baker and Bouillon, *Josephine*, 293.

10. Sanders, "A Farewell to Josephine."

11. Ibid.

12. Baker, *Josephine: The Hungry Heart,* 488.

13. Ibid., 492.

14. "Jo Baker: Living Up to Legend," *New York Post,* April 4, 1973.

15. Henry Hurford Janes to Jo Bouillon, April 20, 1975; Janes to Bouillon, April 27, 1975; Janes to Bouillon, June 29, 1975; Janes to Bouillon, July 7, 1975, all in HHJ.

16. Henry Hurford Janes to Princess Grace, June 30, 1975, HHJ.

17. See, for example, Kathryn Lofton, *Oprah: The Gospel of an Icon* (Berkeley: University of California Press, 2011).

18. "I First Met Josephine Baker," n.d., HHJ.

19. Henry Hurford Janes to Jo Bouillon, August 25, 1975; Janes to Bouillon, August 27, 1975; Janes to Marianne, August 17, 1975, all in HHJ.

20. Henry Hurford Janes to Margaret and Elmo Wallace, April 14, 1975; Janes to Margaret Wallace, August 30, 1975, all in HHJ.

21. Margaret Wallace to Robert Brady, May 24, 1975, HL.

22. Margaret Wallace to Henry Hurford Janes, March 19, 1976; Wallace to Janes, October 17, 1976; Wallace to Janes, October 17, 1976, all in HHJ.

23. Laurence Schwab, "Preface," in Leo Guild, *Josephine Baker* (Los Angeles: Holloway House, 1976), 7.

24. Stephen Papich, *Remembering Josephine* (New York: Bobbs-Merrill, 1976), 161.

25. Ibid., 161–162.

26. Press release, "A Voyage to America," November 10, 1975, ELC.

27. These letters, all written in late 1975 or early 1976, are in ELC.

28. Bouillon to James Symington, January 20, 1976, ELC.

29. See the letter titled "The Producers," n.d., FBP.

30. "Broadway," *New York Times,* April 1, 1977.

31. Richard Martin Jr., to Jo Bouillon, October 20, 1975, ELC; Elmer C. Oberhellman to Gene Lerner, October 11, 1977, ELC.

32. Martin to Lerner, November 15, 1977, ELC.

33. Martin to Kaufman and Lerner, n.d., ELC.

34. Martin to Kaufman, January 11, 1978, ELC.

35. Martin to Kaufman, January 17, 1978, ELC.

36. Lerner to Frederick Brisson, July 5, 1977, FBP.

37. Brisson to Lerner, July 8, 1977; Robert Wachs to David Grossberg, July 26, 1977, FBP.

38. Lerner to Brisson, July 22, 1977, FBP.

39. Grossberg to Brisson, July 20, 1977; Robert Wachs to Irving Cohen, July 15, 1977, FBP.

40. Ishmael Reed, "Remembering Josephine," *New York Times*, December 12, 1976.

41. Lerner to Wallace, May 16, 1980, ELC.

Epilogue

1. Interview with Jean-Claude Baker, October 17, 2007.

2. Jim Dwyer, "Josephine Baker Unfit for the Mail? (It Wasn't Even a French Postcard)," *New York Times*, May 9, 2007.

3. Interview with Jean-Claude Baker, October 17, 2007.

4. Lia Petridis Maiello, "A New York Institution—Jean-Claude Baker Tells Stories from West-Berlin," *Huffington Post*, December 10, 2012.

5. Elizabeth Ezra, *Colonial Unconscious: Race and Culture in Interwar France* (Ithaca, NY: Cornell University Press, 2000), 98.

6. "Jo Baker's Mother Dead," *Baltimore Afro-American*, January 24, 1959.

7. Allan Morrison to Josephine Baker, February 3, 1959, JBPE.

8. Josephine Baker and Jo Bouillon, *Josephine*, trans. Marianna Fitzpatrick (1977; reprint, New York: Marlowe & Co., 1995), 217–218.

9. Alice Walker, *In Search of Our Mothers' Gardens: Womanist Prose* (New York: Harcourt, 1983), 115.

Acknowledgments

I owe a ton of people for this book: audiences at a dozen or so institutions, friends and family, cocktail party guests, fellow tourists, and even random strangers. I have talked about Josephine on three continents. I have spent years of my life underground in archives, in libraries, on airplanes, and in strange beds. And I have met some cool people and saw a lot of unusual things. At every step, in every little conversation or dusty folder, I learned something new. Thanks, good people of the world. When it is my turn to help, I'll do the same for others.

I owe a few specific people a lot. David Levering Lewis, the most talented historian of his generation, never tired of this project, and was a champion from the very start. After I briefly mentioned the idea during a phone call, David promptly took me to Chez Josephine for dinner, introduced me to Jean-Claude Baker, and started the conversation. Jean-Claude, in turn, was a host extraordinaire, sharing his voluminous memories, offering lunch and dinner at his restaurant, and introducing me to his sprawling, fascinating family. After years of faith, Kathleen McDermott, my indefatigable editor and friend, is the reason the book was finished. She gave me a deadline and kept me honest. Our dinner at Chez Josephine remains a highlight of my professional life. Finally, without Lydia Kelow-Bennett—budding scholar, doctoral student, and extraordinary archivist—this would still be on my laptop or in piles of boxes and computer files. Lydia brought order out of my chaos. She is going places, and I am very excited to be watching it all happen. Faith Childs, my agent, got me started, cheered me on when I needed it, and never bugged me over the interminable months of silence.

An inner core of friends and fellow travelers walked, talked, wined, and dined me through the details. That means you, Rosanne Currarino, Vivian Halloran, Hugh Hamilton, Caroline Levander, Kathryn Lofton, Marissa Moorman, Khalil Muhammad, and Todd Uhlman. There is no finer group of crack readers and listeners anywhere. Appreciative thanks also to Michael Adas, Leticia Alvarado, Anna Brickhouse, Stephanie Camp, Sarika Chandra, Jelani Cobb, Deborah Cohn, Denise Cruz, Finis Dunaway, Susan Gillman, William P. Jones, Jacques Khalip, Michael McGerr, Jason McGraw, Ralph Rodriguez, Tricia Rose, Julia Scheeres, Sara Seidman, Micol Seigel, Steve Selka, Christine Skwiot, Christina Snyder, Ruth Ann Stewart, Shane Vogel, Lora Wildenthal, and Ellen Wu. My Bloomington pals sustained me for years; more recently, the "Thursday Night" crowd, who loosened me up in the final days and weeks, deserves credit, too.

A personal hero, John Lewis invited me to the Capitol building and shared two hours of thoughts about Josephine. In France, Madame Angélique, Georges Lansac, Yvette Malaury, and many others were models of hospitality. Jarry Baker-Bouillon and Koffi Baker-Bouillon were both open-minded and openhearted, meeting with me multiple times to talk about what must seem like the distant past. Marianne Baker was kind enough to respond to my email, even when I asked questions in a manner that might have seemed rude. Rama Wallace took a long-distance phone call and graciously answered many, many detailed questions from a complete stranger. Taryn Tilton raced around Buenos Aires for me at the end, double-checking and triple-checking, and saving me a return trip. And the legendary Hermenegildo Sábat welcomed me into his B.A. studio and shared his thoughts about Evita, Baker, and celebrity.

I am fortunate to be alive at a moment when we still have libraries and universities. Thanks, then, to the librarians and archivists at Yale, Stanford, Emory, Harvard, Lincoln Center, and the Schomburg Center; and to the staff at Indiana University, Rice University, and Brown University. As a creature of the university, I owe a huge debt to some amazing colleagues. To all my folks at IU and Brown, thanks for asking about the book, for joking about the book, and for wondering when the book would be done. Paula Cotner, Carol Glaze, Sean Maguire, and Jeff Cabral kept the heat off and let me actually write. In short, they protected my time. There is no way this book could have been started without the generous institutional support of IU's College Arts and Humanities Institute, then directed by Andrea Ciccarelli, and the New Frontiers grant competition. Nor could it have been finished without Humanities research support here at Brown. Kevin McLaughlin, Robert Lee, and Corey Walker got me up and running, and never let me slow down. My research assistants were just awesome. Laila Amine spent a few weeks with me in France and made it easy and fun, and she continued to help right up to the end. Danille Christensen, Holly Mayne, and Liz Ericsson were just great at chasing down vague leads. And then again there was Lydia Kelow-Bennett.

This is, in a very weird way, a book about family. My mother celebrated this book from start to finish and wholeheartedly embraced the project when she had every right to raise an eyebrow and wonder what I was doing. Adoptive families "work" differently now, or at least we sometimes think they do, and I am eternally grateful to Jen Roth-Gordon and Derek Roth-Gordon, Deborah Cohn and Peter Sauer, and Kelly Compton and Frankie Presslaff for asking me about the circumstances of my parents' ambitious assemblage, and for talking to me about their own, even as we wondered about life in Josephine's Les Milandes.

I am very lucky to have Sandra Latcha in my life. Here and everywhere, she is my north star. She is perfectly willing to go gallivanting around France with two kids in diapers or to wander about a tropical rain forest with a baby in a sling, while insisting, as always, on a fair and equitable distribution of labor and responsibilities. Every word written here is time away from her. Our children, Robert and Maya, are too young to remember swimming in Josephine's J-shaped pool, or wading into the Dordogne, but we have the pictures to prove they were there. I am especially grateful to them for our conversations about "the fame thing" as the book's writing came to a close, because if you can explain it to a seven-year-old, you can explain it to anyone. Like everything I write and do, this book is for this wonderful trio.

One more thing: very few people know what a difficult book this was to write, and fewer still know why it was such a hard slog. To this tiny group—a beloved cadre of true intimates, loyalists, and, sometimes, rescuers, many of them mentioned above—I can only say, thanks, *mil gracias, merci bien,* forever and ever. I love you all.

Portions of Chapter 2 were originally published in Matthew Pratt Guterl, "Josephine Baker's Colonial Pastiche," *Black Camera* 1, no. 2 (2010): 25–37, and I am grateful to Indiana University Press for permission to reprint them here.

Index